FROM RIGS
TO RICHES

FROM RIGS TO RICHES:

The Story of
Bow Valley Industries Ltd.

PETER FOSTER

Bow Valley Industries Ltd.
Calgary

First published 1985
by Bow Valley Industries Ltd.
Box 6610, Postal Station "D"
1800, 321 Sixth Avenue S.W.
Calgary, Alberta, Canada T2P 3R2

Canadian Cataloguing in Publication Data

Foster, Peter, 1947–
 From rigs to riches : the story of Bow Valley Industries

Includes index.
ISBN 0-9692099-0-8

1. Bow Valley Industries Ltd. – History.
2. Petroleum industry and trade – Canada – History.
I. Bow Valley Industries Ltd. II. Title.

HD9574.C34B69 1985   338.2'7282'0971233   C85-098776-8

Produced by Collins Publishers for
Bow Valley Industries Ltd.

Printed and bound in Canada by John Deyell Company

For the Risk-Takers, Past, Present,
and — Most Important — Future

Contents

Preface

Many corporate histories are fictions written about the long and safely dead. To write one about a company where all the main characters are alive presents a rare opportunity of probing the human realities behind entrepreneurship and corporate growth. However, when I was first approached by Bow Valley to write this book, I was concerned that the objectivity of any commissioned work is inevitably open to question. In the end I decided to undertake this project because I was promised editorial freedom and because I saw it as a unique opportunity to gain access to the innards of a large corporation.

My written mandate from Bow Valley's chief executive, Gerry Maier, indicated that the company was prepared to fund a story "warts and all." It declared: "The Book ... should be more than just a corporate history. It should deal with failures as well as success, with errors in judgment as well as good decisions, with misfortunes as well as luck, and with human frailty as well as resoluteness. To keep events in perspective, the Book should include material on historical happenings and political and economic situations insofar as they are relevant to the story of BVI and would add to an understanding of the logic behind the key steps in its evolution.

"Above all, the book should have a positive tone, because we wish future readers of this piece of Canadian history to understand that despite hardships and adversity there have been corporate successes engineered by Western Canadians and that in this case the success transcends international borders."

I could obviously not have undertaken this task unless I had already possessed a "positive tone" towards free-enterprise. I had written three books previously about the Canadian oil business: *The Blue-Eyed Sheiks*, *The Sorcerer's Apprentices*, and *Other People's Money*. However, anybody familiar with these books — in particular the most recent, which dealt with Dome Petroleum and its disastrous involvement with the government and the banking community — would be aware that I am a far from uncritical observer of the business scene. *From Rigs to Riches* is about entrepreneurial adventures and corporate empire building, but it is not an unquestioning paean of praise.

Bow Valley was very open with me in allowing me access to minutes and files, but, as with my other works, the heart of this book lies in personal interviews, including at least a dozen with Bow Valley's founder and chairman, Doc Seaman. Among others who assisted me in my research, or in preparation of the manuscript, I have to thank, in alphabetical order: John Ashburner, Mac Baker, Dale Beischel, Don Binney, Jim Boyle, Jean Brown, Dr. Bill Chisolme, Al Cobb, Buzz Cotter, Cec Daly, Rod DeLuca, Stanley Ditty, Emil Dinkla, Jim Emmelkamp, Bob Engberg, Mike Everett, Charlie Fischer, Betty Fisher, Ted Fisher, Lloyd Flood, Sharon Fuller, John Gillard, Hal Godwin, Clyde Goins, John Gorsak, Pete Hamill, Dick Harris, Ned Hastings, Bill Hay, Harley Hotchkiss, Bill Howard, Major General Lord Michael Fitzalan Howard, KCVO, CB, CBE, MC, DL, Ken Hughes, Orest Humeniuk, George Hutton, Keith Lazelle, Trevor Legge, Angus Mackenzie, Ralph Mackenzie, Tony Mason, Stuart McColl, Rod McDaniel, Gerry Maier, Ron Mitchell, Ole Moller, Henri Moreault, Carol Hordholt, Jean Nutter, Peter Owens, Jim Palmer, Bob Phibbs, Henry Popoff, Larry Prather, Clive Randle, Gordon Rennie, Doreen Richards, Captain Terry Robinson, Stan Rokosh, Bob Russell, B.J. Seaman, Don Seaman, Dorothy Seaman, Mrs. Letha May Seaman, John Shepherd, Bill Siebens, Sandy Sinclair, Henry Smith, Lance Stanford, Ken Stiles, Bill Tait, Ron Thomson, Bill Tye, Harry Van Rensselaer, Len Walker, Mary Walker, Greg Warbanski, Bill Warnke, Bruce Watson, Fred Wellhauser, Patrick Wesley, Ralph Will, and Bud Willis.

In the editing and production of the book, I have once again to thank Grace Deutsch, Colleen Dimson, Jenny Falconer, and Linda Pellowe, not merely for their expertise, but also for their sense of humor.

1
The Mystery

There must be well over a thousand people here, thronging the Calgary Convention Centre for the $250-a-plate 1985 National Hockey League All-Star Dinner. The gigantic room is festooned with balloons and the pennants of all the teams in the NHL. In the middle of the ceiling hangs a larger flag, the "Flaming C" of the Calgary Flames. On each side-wall are two giant screens, set up to magnify the official proceedings and show videos. This, the thirty-seventh such dinner, is the first to be held in Calgary. It is one of hockey's great social occasions.

The two terraced head tables are filled with the All-Star teams, fresh-faced, fit young men sporting stetsons for the occasion. In the middle of the front table, where the Campbell Conference team is ranged, sits the slim — almost frail — figure of Wayne Gretzky, the "Great One," dressed in a tuxedo and Mississippi gambler's neck-tie.

Perhaps thirty feet from Gretzky, at one of the front tables, between Alberta Premier Peter Lougheed and well-known hockey lawyer Alan Eagleson, sits Doc Seaman. Other guests at the table include Calgary Mayor Ralph Klein and John Ziegler, president of the NHL. Everybody knows who Wayne Gretszky is; few outside this forum, his company, or the upper echelons of the business community are acquainted with Doc Seaman. But Wayne Gretszky and Doc Seaman have one thing in common: they are both, in their own way, mysteries.

Later in the evening, the audience, bedecked in their buckskins and string-ties and hand-tooled cowboy boots, will be shown videos on the charities towards which the funds from tonight's event will be donated; the Olympic Trust of Canada and the Canadian Special Olympics. Roger Jackson, the giant former rower and president of the Canada Olympic Association, mentions Doc Seaman in particular for his support of Canada's Olympic hockey team. It is an uneasy moment for Doc; he does not court praise. Doc is here as a part-owner of the Calgary Flames, a great personal supporter of hockey development in Canada, and a charter member of the Alberta establishment.

At two nearby tables are Doc's brothers, B.J., another part-owner of the Flames, and Don. This night seems somehow a fitting testimony to the status and success of the Seamans. In thirty-five years, Doc

Seaman — flanked by his two brothers — has developed his company, Bow Valley Industries, into an international oil, drilling, and manufacturing empire from a single truck-mounted seismic rig. In the process, he has established himself in the forefront of Canadian business. He is one of an elite group of less than a dozen oilmen in Alberta who have built both huge empires and personal fortunes in a remarkably short period of time. None, however, has built an empire of such diversity and geographical spread.

Bow Valley produces petroleum from the grey, storm-whipped North Sea, from the sparkling waters of the Arabian Gulf, and from the steaming jungles of South Sumatra — as well as from Canada and the U.S. It mines coal in the misty green hills of Kentucky. It runs the largest drilling operation in Canada, including three giant semi-submersible drilling vessels — together worth more than $400 million — off Canada's East Coast. It has manufacturing and supply operations from British Columbia to St. John's. It makes trucks, drill bits, heating and ventilating equipment, and machinery and parts for the forestry industry. It is even involved in some exciting developments in the unexciting field of waste disposal. In 1984, this empire produced revenues of $837 million, profits of $42 million and cash flow of $258 million. It invested more than $300 million in maintaining old ventures and starting new ones. It employed more than 3,000 people.

When examining the achievements of a Wayne Gretzky or a Doc Seaman, the same questions arise: How do they do it? What makes them so different? Wayne Gretzky isn't big, he isn't strong, he isn't spectacularly fast, and yet his mind and his body combine in a display of extraordinary talent that only becomes apparent when he is on the ice. Similarly, away from the business arena, Doc Seaman might impress you as a man with a quiet strength and the self-assurance of success; but there would be little to hint at the breadth of his corporate achievements.

Entrepreneurs may tell you what they've done, but they will have more trouble telling you *why* they've done it. Just as a Wayne Gretszky, or an O.J.Simpson, or a Bjorn Borg would be unable to explain the physiological and psychological peculiarities that make them exceptional athletes, so the successful risk-taker's essential gift is beyond analysis. We can say that the entrepreneurial pre-requisites are a bias for action and the willingness to take risks with one's own money, and (if one is persuasive or successful enough) with other people's. But that really tells us little more than that the pre-requisites for success in hockey are skating ability and a good slap shot.

Much of what is written about risk-takers concerns what they do with their money rather than how they create it. But just looking at the financial results of risk-taking skirts the essence and the mechanics of the act itself. The entrepreneur who doesn't indulge in 200 mph cars or exotic hobbies is somehow regarded as dull. The spending of wealth is something everybody can comprehend. Its creation is much less well understood.

Emerson said that an institution is the elongated shadow of one man. At Bow Valley, that shadow is Doc's. He has remained the germinator and inspiration for its growth throughout its history. He is perhaps most personally prominent in the early stages of this book. As the story progresses, it becomes one of an increasing number of people. This does not mean that Doc became less important as time went on. Rather, he became more so. B.J. or Don or other executives may well have been off engaged in exploratory missions, or corporate presentations, or complex and sometimes exotic negotiations. They and a number of characters who will appear in the following pages — and some who don't — undoubtedly made significant contributions to Bow Valley's growth and development. But the overall guiding force was always Doc. In board or executive committee meetings, it was the nod from Doc that was all-important.

As this book goes to press, Bow Valley is a company in transition. Although Doc is still chairman of both the board and its executive committee, and he and his brothers still own 16 per cent of the company's stock, a new management team, under chief executive Gerry Maier, has moved in to take Bow Valley through its next phase of development. Most of this book, nevertheless, is about the corporate creation of one man. It is a tale of what can be achieved starting, almost literally, from nothing.

2
The Road from Rouleau

Byron Luther Seaman came up from South Dakota to the rich farm-lands of Rouleau, Saskatchewan as part of the wave of immigrant homesteaders before the First World War. There, at a dance at Avonlea, he met Letha May Patton, the daughter of a farmer-turned-Pentecostal Minister from Nebraska. They were married shortly after he returned from a stint as a machine gunner in the American Expeditionary Force in Europe.

The young couple worked for a while on a farm, but then, in the early 1920s, Byron moved into road construction for local municipal-ities, and soon bought his own contracting company. The times were not auspicious. By the time they entered the Dirty Thirties, the Sea-mans had four small mouths to feed: a daughter, Dorothy, and three sons, Daryl, Byron Jr., and Donald.

Roadwork could only be carried out in summer, and for several years the entire family would take to the road during those hard-working months. The family and the road-gang would live out of old trailers. The Seamans slept in the front end of the cook car while the rest of the crew, which included relatives from the States, slept in the bunk car. The roadgang — and of course Mrs. Seaman, who had to cook for them — was up at 4:00 A.M., and didn't return until after six at night. When Mrs. Seaman wasn't cooking or baking on the old coal-oil stove, she was scrubbing away at the family's clothes on the cradle hand-washer, or stringing up a clothesline between two tele-graph poles while the old milk-cow that trailed behind the cook car looked on. As the crew sweated out another dusty mile or so of road with their straining tractors and graders, the kids would play in the haystacks.

Contracts dried up in the early 1930s. However, after a gap of a few years, Byron Seaman obtained some local roadwork from the municipality of Rouleau. The eldest boy, Daryl, by the time he was fifteen, was putting in a full day's work on the Caterpillar tractor.

The thirties were the toughest of years. Not only had the world recession caused widespread economic depression, but the Prairies were hit by drought and agricultural exhaustion. These were the blow-dirt years, when the ditches were filled with drifting topsoil, the farmers' disappearing livelihood. Once the family had acquired a home in Rouleau, young Daryl Seaman would watch the freight trains coming through with lean, hungry men hanging off them. Sometimes these drifters would stop off and make camp by the rail yard, and he'd talk to them. He even occasionally raided the pantry, or the garden, or the henhouse to provide a meal for them. It shocked him that these men — many of them from good families — were so keen to work and yet could find no jobs.

In Saskatchewan, public works programs were slashed and Byron Seaman felt that his conservative politics weren't too helpful in getting him a share of the contracts that were forthcoming from the Liberal government. Nevertheless, the family survived intact, perhaps becoming all the more tightly knit because of the hard times. They spurned the relief goods that came from Eastern Canada and took a fierce pride in their self-sufficiency.

The Seamans were not a bookish family, but their mother, in particular, stressed the importance of education. The children turned out to be excellent pupils. All four children were also fine athletes. The Seaman boys were renowned for their fierce competitiveness, a trait they would take into their later business lives. All the children studied Latin and at some stage started to call their parents "Mate" and "Pate," as corruptions of the Latin for mother and father, *Mater* and *Pater*. The designations stuck. Byron Seaman Sr. would be "Pate" to his children and all their friends and business associates until the day he died.

Pate taught his children by example rather than philosophy. His life stood for hard work. His every project was permeated with a respect for proper maintenance and economy of resources, a characteristic in which he was at least equalled by his wife. True economy is born out of an appreciation of scarcity and a respect for value. Their father's meticulous respect for his machinery and their mother's perfectly planted kitchen garden — which the children helped seed — would remain important images and valuable object-lessons even in the world of the biggest business. If you wanted things, or people, to work for you, you had to look after them.

Pate was also a zealous and highly competitive sportsman. He loved hunting and fishing, but in particular he loved curling, and was one of the top curlers in Saskatchewan. Although he reached the provincial finals several times, one of his great regrets was that he never made it to the Macdonald Brier.

Rouleau, meanwhile, with its churches, its skating rink, its golf course, and its schools, while not a pretty town, was a picture-perfect example of solid small-town prairie values, and the Seaman family were among its model citizens. Working hard and playing hard, they strived to excel at whatever they did. "You don't have to worry about

15

your family," Dr. Singleton, the local family doctor, would tell Mrs. Seaman, "because they're all too fond of things that are good for them." And when the Seaman boys weren't hurtling around the hockey arena, or the athletics track, or the baseball diamond, the good citizens of Rouleau would see them at Sunday school or at the United Church as ushers, taking up the collection.

Among the boys, Daryl, as the eldest, was obviously the leader. Athletically, he was very gifted, playing senior baseball when he was fifteen, and hockey for the famous Father Murray in Wilcox, the town next to Rouleau. When he was seventeen, he was invited to play for the Moosejaw Canucks, at the time one of the country's leading junior hockey teams. He was also asked to sign a "protection card" with the New York Americans of the NHL, committing himself to play for them if he turned professional. But he was also developing a reputation as a thinker, or, to put it somewhat less flatteringly, as a dreamer. Nevertheless, if he was prone to introspection, that tendency — like the roadwork — seemed to have little effect on his scholastic performance. Sometimes, when the class was meant to be writing an essay, his teacher would find him staring out of the window and request his attention, only to discover that he had already produced the best paper. It was young Daryl's visions that were to be the root of an international business empire.

War Takes a Hand

Pushed on by his high school teachers, in particular George Jones, the school principal, Daryl finished high school a year ahead of his peers. However, he had no firm idea of a career. For a while — about the time he was playing for the Moosejaw Canucks — he thought about becoming a pharmacist. Then he went out on the roads the following summer with his father, who was doing work under the Prairie Farm Rehabilitation Act program. Then one of the great formative influences of Daryl Seaman's life — and of his entire generation — came along: the war.

Daryl and his father had been sitting in the Chinese cafe down at Maple Creek, Saskatchewan — where they had a road-building contract — when they had heard the news of the declaration of war in September, 1939. Byron Seaman had lived through the First World War, and young Daryl noted the pained look on his face when he heard the news. The following summer, Daryl worked 12-hour night-shifts on an irrigation project at Maple Creek. Compared with those solitary nights, when he would have to hang onto the side of the "cat" as it traversed steep coulies in case it rolled over, even war couldn't have seemed so daunting. Daryl's sister, Dorothy, had by now entered the University of Saskatchewan and was enjoying academic success. Daryl wasn't sure if he really wanted to follow her. Nevertheless, in the fall of 1940, he signed up for a course in engineering. Shortly after the end of his first term at University, he enlisted.

Daryl's athletic coordination and cool nature enabled him to pass the demanding qualifications for acceptance into the Royal Canadian Air Force. For his mother, it seemed no more than a blink of an eye before he had put in his 200 hours of basic flight-time and was on his way to Halifax. There he embarked for Europe on the battered old troopship *Batory* — which the Germans would eventually claim to have sunk half a dozen times! Landing at Greenock on Scotland's Firth of Clyde, Daryl and the other young Canadians, many of whom would never return to their country, embarked by train for the long and uncomfortable journey to Bournemouth on England's South Coast. They passed close to Coventry as the city was being decimated by German bombs. In Bournemouth Daryl found himself with 1,200 other aircrew, many of them Canadians. On their third day in the little seaside town, eleven of these young men, most of them like Daryl still in their teens, were killed by German bombs.

The next few months were spent in intense training, in special flying and navigational courses where successful study was spurred by the simple fact that one's life, and the lives of one's colleagues, depended upon it. This was a time when many firm friendships were formed. Daryl found himself frequently billeted with another stocky young Canadian with a permanent grin and an impish sense of humor, Pete Hamill. They had first met on the *Batory*, drinking beer together on the top deck while their less seaworthy colleagues were violently sick in the bowels of the old ship. They had been bombed together in Bournemouth, did their advanced training and formation-flying practice in twin-engined Oxfords in Lincolnshire, and roomed together at the Majestic Hotel in Harrogate while studying astral navigation. They also both earned what Daryl termed the "Silloth Survival Medal" for coming through a particularly dangerous flying program in poorly maintained Lockheed Hudsons at Silloth in the North of England. Pete Hamill stayed posted in England. The young Seaman was sent to North Africa. By the time they were twenty years old, both had flown their first bombing missions.

Daryl was posted first to Algiers, then Tunis, and then — as the Italian army crumbled — into Sicily, Salerno, Corsica and finally to an airbase just north of Naples. Airmen were an understandably superstitious lot, and favored a variety of charms and talismans. Daryl sported a lady's silk stocking in his flying helmet. Its charm worked, for he was one of only a handful of those Canadians he trained with who survived the war. Even then, he had some pretty close shaves.

His squadron specialized in anti-submarine work and in shipping and harbor strikes. It was while out hunting for a crippled German sub that he had his mettle tested as it had never been before. His Hudson — armed with eight rockets to sink the U-boat — was jumped by a Messerschmitt sent to provide air cover for the submarine. Strafing the bomber, the German fighter immediately mortally wounded Bill Fletcher, the wireless-airgunner sitting just feet behind Daryl, and blasted machine-gun shells through his own left calf and right thigh. With these crippling injuries he managed to find cloud-cover and lose the Messerschmitt as his crew laid the dying airgunner above the bomb-bays. He had his badly damaged left leg strapped to the rudder pedal for additional leverage, and piloted the plane back to the mainland in bad weather. The aircraft's receiver had been knocked out in the fighter attack, and there was some concern over whether the bomber's distress message had reached headquarters. Nevertheless, as the bomber crossed the coast, it was greeted by the welcome sight of a flight of Spitfires, which escorted the damaged plane to a safe landing. Doc spent six weeks in the American field hospital. He left hospital on his twenty-first birthday, and within thirty days he was flying again. On another occasion, Doc's crew was cited for devotion to duty by the French airforce for helping to locate two French fighter pilots lost at sea in bad weather and for saving one of them.

For young Daryl Seaman, as for so many of his colleagues, the war was of enormous importance. It had broadened his horizons greatly. He had been tested and he had passed. Just as life out on the road with Pate in the bunk cars and cook cars had helped prepare him for the hardships of billets in North Africa, so the responsibilities and dangers of war helped temper his belief in his own powers and prepare him for his first entrepreneurial leap. However, that leap was several years away. First came the business of finishing his interrupted education.

Back to University

During the war, the Seaman family had moved to Saskatoon, and the two younger brothers were now well into their mechanical engineering courses at the University of Saskatchewan. Daryl came home on leave at Christmas, 1944, and was told that he would not be returning to active service. He and his close friend and navigator,

Tom McGlade, were told that if they did not want to continue to serve in Canada, they could go to university under the war veterans' program. So Daryl started back to the University of Saskatchewan in January, 1945, ahead of most of the veterans. Byron Jr., who had now acquired the nickname B.J., would graduate that same year. Don would graduate in the spring of 1947, and Daryl himself in the spring of 1948.

Soon the Saskatoon campus was chaotic with men in their early twenties, fresh back from war and keen to take advantage of the educational opportunity the war had given them. Military mess-halls were transported to the university to accommodate lectures. Some of those lectures had 300 students present. The air was so thick with pipe and cigarette smoke that the lecturer could hardly see the less enthusiastic attendees playing bridge at the back of the hall!

Daryl had some trouble getting back into the academic side of engineering and into the concept of regular weekdays and weekends. To earn money, he put his sporting ability back to use and played for Saskatoon's senior baseball team. They would be North Saskatchewan champions in 1945 and 1946 when Doc was playing for them. It was during this period that he earned the nickname that would stick with him for the rest of his life. He carried his baseball clothes in a little black satchel like a doctor's bag, so his friends started to call him "Doc."

Brother B.J., meanwhile, was the first of the boys to graduate and the first to get into the oil business. He had gone to the University of Saskatchewan in the fall of 1941 and, during the summer of 1943, had worked as a seismic engineer for an affiliate of Imperial Oil, Canada's largest oil company. He was given that job by Cam Sproule, the geologist who would go on to play such an important part in promoting the exploration of Canada's Arctic Islands. B.J. worked for the same company in the summer of 1944 and joined them full-time when he graduated in 1945. In 1946, Imperial wanted him to go on a long-term contract to South America. He got as far as Miami before deciding that he wanted to stay in Western Canada, so he quit the company and went to work once more with his father.

Pate had sold his construction business during the war and had bought two combine harvesters. In the spring of '46, Pate and B.J. and a small crew went south to get contract harvest work. From May until the fall, as they followed the harvest season north, B.J. hauled and shovelled grain, sometimes in 110 degree heat. When they came back to Saskatoon, he became an instructor in mechanical drawing and surveying at the University of Saskatchewan before moving east to work at British American's refinery at Clarkson, Ontario.

In 1947 it appeared that all the Seaman children would wind up in

Central Canada. The country's economic future, after all, seemed firmly rooted in the industrial heartland of Ontario and Quebec. Dorothy had married Hugh Hamilton, an engineer from Regina, and moved to Burlington, Ontario; Don had graduated and gone to work for C.I.L., first in Shawinigan, Quebec and then in Kingston, Ontario. In the summer of 1947, Doc came down to take a vacation job at the Stelco steel works in Hamilton. Mate and Pate, meanwhile, were thinking about moving to the West Coast. But then, in 1947, an event of seminal importance for the West — and for the Seaman family — took place. After drilling 133 consecutive dry holes in Western Canada, Imperial Oil struck an oil gusher at Leduc, south of Edmonton.

The Road to Oil

Alberta's involvement with the oil business dated from before the turn of the century, when engineers of the Canadian Pacific Railway had struck gas while drilling for water. Periodic bouts of oil fever had hit the streets of Calgary as a number of finds had been made south of the city in the Turner Valley. However, these finds were more remarkable for the psychological frenzy they produced than for the impact they had on Canadian domestic oil supplies. In 1947, Canada produced only 10 per cent of its petroleum needs, mostly from Alberta. Leduc — coming after a decade without a major find — changed all that. Leduc was the geological key that unlocked very significant oil reserves. In 1947, only 19,500 barrels a day of Canadian oil were used in domestic refineries. Ten years later, that figure had leaped to 347,500 barrels.

Of course, the significance of the Leduc find was far from obvious at the time. Doc had been offered a permanent job by Stelco when he graduated. However, he had a restless urge to do something "on his own." He wrote a number of letters to municipalities with a view to reviving the family contracting business. It was with construction in mind that Doc, B.J., and Pate decided to take a trip by car from Saskatoon to Fort St. John in B.C., where Doc saw potential for buying heavy equipment and securing some earth-moving work. However, on their way to Fort St.John they had to pass through Edmonton. Although the activity related to Leduc was still relatively small-scale, Doc sensed the excitement and became convinced that this was where the action was going to be.

Doc and B.J. returned to Saskatchewan with Pate, packed their bags and moved straight back to Edmonton. B.J.'s experience as a seismic engineer meant that his job skills were in great demand, and soon both he and Doc had been hired by a company called Western Geophysical to work on the same seismic crew. Seismic work is a key element of petroleum exploration. Shallow holes, called shot-holes, are drilled at regular intervals, dynamite is exploded within them, and then the sound waves that bounced from various layers of subterranean rock strata are recorded with sensitive instrumentation. Through the patterns revealed, a picture of rock formations is given which help geologists plot likely oil and gas-bearing structures.

B.J. signed up as an instrument operator, running the sensitive recording equipment in the seismic truck, while Doc signed on as a surveyor, with responsibility for laying out the "lines" that would be bulldozed and along which the dynamite holes would be drilled and the charges laid. The pay was $250 for a 240-hour month.

Accommodation was a good deal more scarce in Edmonton than work, and the brothers found themselves sharing a basement room at the home of a young English couple. In August, 1948, the brothers were both moved north and assigned to separate crews. Doc worked on seismic party 50 at Athabasca, while B.J. was assigned to party 34 working at Colinton a little further south. As befitted brothers who always had — and always would — do so much together, Doc and B.J. married their sweethearts — B.J. on the Saturday, Doc on the Monday — on the 1949 Labor Day weekend. They drove back to Athabasca with Doc at the wheel beside his wife Lois and B.J.'s wife Evelyn, while B.J. sat cramped in the back under all the presents. Their honeymoons consisted of arriving back at work a day late — and having their pay docked!

It was at Athabasca that Doc decided to make the critical jump from being an employee to being an employer, from being a job-taker to being a job-maker. He made that decision that separates the risk-takers; he decided to go out on his own.

Taking the Plunge

As with so many other parts of the oil business, seismic companies subcontracted part of their work. In particular, they subcontracted the job of drilling the shot-holes into which the dynamite was put. These shot-holes were drilled by special, truck-mounted rigs. Each day, Doc had to take the ferry across the Athabasca River to get to the site where his crew was working. On the ferry he used to chat with a man called George Bennett, who owned a shot-hole rig that was being used on another job in the area. Bennett told Doc how he'd decided to get into the business, and then Doc started to ask him about operations and costs and about the process and the prospects of shot-hole drilling. Rapidly, a plan began to form in Doc's mind. His experience with his father had taught him a good deal about sub-contracting with specialized equipment. The oil industry was booming and opportunities were obviously growing for work in the seismic field. Shot-hole drilling was attractive because it would be relatively easy to enter. Nevertheless, Doc realized that he needed a partner, partially to share the financial burden of the rig purchase, but also to provide the experience he lacked in the operation of a rig.

A truck-mounted shot-hole rig requires two men to operate it, a driller, who is responsible for the operation and maintenance of the machinery, and a "water-jack," who's job is primarily that of fetching and carrying the water used in the drilling process. Doc needed a driller so he approached one of the men working on the Athabasca job, Bill Warnke, and laid out his plan to him.

Warnke had been born and raised in Alberta, the son of Russian parents who had come to the province at the turn of the century from Brazil. After war service, he had been working in a lumber camp when the Leduc boom hit the province. He had moved into the industry as a water-jack on a seismic crew, and by the beginning of 1949 had become a driller. When Doc approached him, Warnke had thus been a driller for only a few months. Nevertheless, in that fledgling Alberta industry, such experience made him a veteran. At first, Bill Warnke had doubts about going into business for himself. Although Doc, who had more money saved, would own 75 per cent of the partnership, Warnke's share would still require him to put up all his savings of $1,500, and go into debt as well. After work, Doc would sit him down with a piece of paper and a pencil and take him through the economics of the deal, but in the end it was faith in Doc that persuaded Bill Warnke to risk his savings on the venture. "After all," he persuaded himself,"what have I got to lose but $1,500?"

In April of 1949, during spring break-up, Doc hitched a ride into Edmonton and talked to representatives of Seismic Service Supply, the company that held the Canadian agency for the U.S.-built Mayhew truck-mounted rig used for shot-hole drilling. After "road-ban" — the period in spring when rigs were prohibited from moving so as not to damage the muddy highways — Doc returned to Athabasca to hand in his notice. At the beginning of June, Doc called in at Western Geophysical's office to bid his colleagues farewell. Then he headed south to Calgary to put in his order for a rig.

With Doc's savings thrown in, he and Bill Warnke came up with a total of $7,500. However, that still left them several thousand dollars short and with the perennial problem of business: where to find external finance. Percy Smith, the affectionately remembered "big old cowboy" who ran Seismic Service Supply in Calgary and who was renowned for the quality of service he gave his customers, suggested that Doc approach a company called Tait, Lowes & Mirtle.

Clarence Tait, Art Lowes and Frank Mirtle primarily ran an insurance business. However, over the years they had expanded into financing the equipment they insured. They loaned seed money to a lot of fledgling companies in the post-Leduc boom and, when young Doc Seaman turned up at their office on the corner of Seventh Avenue and Third Street, it didn't take them very long to accept him as a worthwhile risk. They were being asked to put up just half the cost of the equipment, which would provide the collateral for the loan. As soon as he had secured the money, Doc set about getting the rig.

3
Expansion and Diversification

Included in the price of Seaman & Warnke's shothole rig was a one-way ticket to Dallas. In June, 1949, Doc boarded a Western Airlines DC3 for a flight that hopped down through Montana, Wyoming, and Colorado on the way to Texas. When he arrived the rig wasn't finished and he had to kick around for a few days. Then at last he was able to climb behind the wheel of the brand spanking new truck with the rig mounted on the rear, all primed and painted "aluminum with red trim," for the long drive north.

To avoid the sweltering summer heat, Doc drove by night, and slept during the day in the shade of the truck on an old army cot he'd purchased for a couple of dollars. He arrived at Coutts on the Canadian border on July 4, a date that would stick in his mind for the simple reason that the checkpoint was closed for the Independence Day holiday!

Don eventually arrived back in Calgary with the partnership's rig, but they still had to find a contract. Doc knew Ralph Wales, the head of geophysical work at Texaco Canada, who had told him that work would be coming up. However, the job did not materialize at once, so Bill Warnke carried on working at Athabasca for a while. In the meantime, Doc followed any lead in Calgary that might get the new partnership work. While he was searching, and to conserve scarce cash, Doc stayed at the Calgary YMCA. B.J. helped out by loaning Doc part of his salary.

Finally, one Friday afternoon, when Doc was at the Seismic Service Supply yard, a man called Andy Lees approached him and asked: "Is that your rig?" Within a few minutes, Seaman & Warnke had their first contract. Doc, both delighted and a little relieved, said: "Fine, we'll start on Monday."

"The hell you will," said Lees, "you'll start at once!"

Doc contacted Bill Warnke and they met up for the job, which was at Hughenden, east of Edmonton. The contract required a certain number of drilling hours per month — which usually meant that the two men had to work six days a week. When the hours had been put in, or when there was a lull in the work, Doc would take a bus or hitch-hike down to Calgary both to take care of the administrative side of the partnership and also to look for further work. Seaman & Warnke Drilling Contractors Ltd. was incorporated in August, 1949. For Bill Warnke, moving into business for himself was a quite big enough step for the moment; but Doc already had a restless — and much bigger — vision of business opportunities. In Calgary, he would use the office of a young accountant, Harold Livergant, whom the brothers had known from the University of Saskatchewan. There he began to feel his way around the strange new world of being an independent businessman, dealing with accounting and legal requirements for the first time and preparing his first profit and loss statements for the taxman.

Soon, Ralph Wales came up with the Texaco job on which Doc had originally counted. But of course Seaman & Warnke's single rig was tied up. Doc contacted B.J. and explained to him that there was an opportunity for a second rig if he was prepared to find the money. They were still short of the amount they would need for their equity stake, so Doc wrote to their father, not exactly asking for the money but just pointing out that the business opportunity was there. Pate sent back a draft for enough money to make the downpayment on the second rig.

B.J. and Bill Warnke went off with the second rig to the Texaco job at Grimshaw, while Doc stayed at Hughenden. Doc was joined briefly by Bill Warnke's brother, Dick, but Dick quit at Christmas, 1949, and Doc found himself suddenly elevated, of necessity, to the role of driller. Doc had picked up the principles of shot-hole drilling from Bill Warnke, and he hired a truck driver to be his water-jack, but his task was made the harder because the winter of 1949-50 was one of the toughest on record. Doc and Lois moved for the winter into a house at Rimbey, but were forced by the cold to close down all but one room. Out with the seismic party, it was a full-time job merely to keep the equipment operating in the minus-40-degree temperatures.

Things were scarcely any better in Grimshaw, where B.J. and Bill Warnke also struggled to drill their contracted number of feet in the bitter temperatures. Nevertheless, although they found the weather a considerable obstacle, they never had any trouble keeping up with the opposition. And despite the hardships, the two still found plenty to laugh about. That winter saw the great Grimshaw fire, when a considerable number of the town's wooden buildings burned down. The previous fall, B.J. had done a lot of shooting and had stored his bag of ducks and geese and prairie chickens in a locker at the local butchers. Thanks to the great Grimshaw fire, the birds were well cooked but never eaten!

After continuing to operate through the summer of 1950, Doc and B.J. brought their youngest brother, Don, into the business that fall. Don had undertaken an industrial training program with C.I.L., and then had moved into design engineering. However, Don also entered the business via the shothole drilling side, and put down money that he borrowed from Pate and his Uncle Don — who lived in Wisconsin — towards the brothers' third seismic rig. Then he, too, rolled up his sleeves to do his stint as water-jack. His driller on the third rig was Jim Thompson, who would become part owner of the Seamans' drilling interests. Thompson eventually took some equipment to Australia and wound up buying the equipment but selling his shares in the company.

The opportunity for the third rig came about because B.J. had been approached by Wes Rabey — who had started his own seismic business, Accurate Geophysical — to run the crew's recording truck. The Seamans agreed that B.J. would go on the condition that they were given the shothole drilling contract. Rabey agreed and the brothers' third rig — with Don serving his water-jack apprenticeship — wound up working for him. B.J. found that the personal price he had to pay for gaining the shot-hole contract was being stuck inside an old and mechanically cranky instrument truck, whose machinery was likely to seize up at the slightest provocation! Don, meanwhile, had been thrown in at the deep end. On the first occasion he was dispatched to fill the water-truck, he had to travel there and back in second gear because nobody had bothered to explain the intricacies of the truck's gearbox to him!

Fraternal affection was to be strained the same year when Accurate Geophysical demanded that the Seamans drill on Christmas Day. The equipment seemed itself to be demanding a holiday and it was only after a good deal of arguing that six holes were drilled. However, at lunchtime the party manager showed up and said the crew could stop work. Brotherly love returned and the arguments were soon forgotten.

A Broader Vision

Bill Warnke in the meantime had become a little concerned about the pace of the partnership's expansion. He thought that perhaps they should pay off the funds borrowed on the first couple of rigs before expanding further. He was bought out of the business, and the company's name was changed to Seaman Engineering and Drilling Company Limited, Sedco, which survives to this day as the shallow drilling division of Bow Valley's resource service arm.

Bill Warnke recognized Doc's drive, and got on well with B.J., but he was essentially happy with a level of business that Doc Seaman soon ceased to see as a challenge. Bill Warnke was, and would remain for many more years, a skillful shot-hole driller, content with the practice of his expertise, but Doc was always looking for new horizons, new opportunities. He could find no contentment in the practice of a single skill. Men like Bill Warnke — the men in the field — form the backbone of the Albertan oil business. They, after all, do the work. But Doc Seaman felt a higher calling; he wanted to be one of the people who *made* the work. Looking up from the partnership's books after work one evening, he had confided to Bill Warnke that he believed he could get to the top. He had tested himself in the market and he liked the feel of success. Having gained a toehold within the seismic business, the next logical steps were to expand within it and to diversify into other types of drilling.

Mac Baker, who came from Ontario and had attended the University of Toronto, had been the chief of the seismic crew that B.J. and Bill Warnke had provided shot-holes for at Grimshaw. Doc and B.J. approached him with a view to forming a company to provide complete seismic services. Baker agreed and a company called Seismotech was formed with Baker as president and the Seamans as partners.

Soon, Seismotech would become Don's speciality. Having graduated from water-jack to driller, he moved into the field office and became a supervisor. In 1952, he moved to Regina, where Seismotech's operations were based and where he would live for the next four years.

Seismotech provided shot-hole rigs, survey crews, instrument trucks and base interpretation as part of a comprehensive seismic package. It ran what it called "hotshot" crews, where a small group would go out into the field and do a complete seismic job of surveying, recording, computing, and interpreting data. Because of the desire to be competitive, crews were kept small and each member of the crew learned *all* the skills required of the team. The hotshot crews developed the reputation of being fast — and good.

The other branch of the Seamans' diversification was into "slim-hole" or "core-hole" drilling, which involved larger rigs and deeper holes than the shot-hole business . Slim-hole drilling was essentially another geological mapping technique. Rigs would drill to a predetermined geological horizon and then run electro-logs as a means of determining the likely presence of hydrocarbons. The Seamans entered partnerships on two slim-hole rigs and within a few years would be running eight of their own.

Doc was now beginning to gain a closer understanding of the route to business success. He had an eye for opportunity, a way of handling people and — perhaps most important of all — once he had worked through a prospect in his mind, he *acted*. Nevertheless, he was still a neophyte in the requirements of accounting and the law. Doc, forever on the lookout for ways to cut costs, tried to save $50 by incorporating the business himself, but the registrar of companies kept writing back to him pointing out that he wasn't doing it properly. The problem — which Doc didn't realize until afterwards — was that there was a legal distinction between the word "Limited" and its abbreviation "Ltd." Jack Sasseville, who had now taken over as the Seaman's accountant, persuaded Doc that it was about time he got himself some professional legal advice. Sasseville recommended Bill Howard, a struggling young lawyer who would not only continue his association with the Seaman business until the present, but would go on to head one of the most prestigious law firms in Canada (and, as a sidelight, become a major-general in the Canadian Army Reserve).

First Diversifications

One of Doc's key corporate strategies quickly evolved as diversification into related business areas through acquisitions. For the oil business, which put heavy demands on the machinery it used, machine shops — where repairs were made and specialty equipment was put together — were of critical importance. The Seamans had met Ernie Rice when he was doing work for Percy Smith at Seismic Service Supply, the company through which they had bought their truck-mounted Mayhew rigs. Setting up a machine shop would not only mean they would save money on metal fabrication on their own growing fleet of equipment, but also that they would earn profits through third-party work. But there was an additional rationale for the move: Doc Seaman had visions of developing a new kind of service vehicle that could move over and operate on muskeg, the gooey bog that covered much of Alberta's prospective oil-bearing lands in summer and made exploration activity difficult or impossible. The machine shop would give them the opportunity to put their ideas into reality. So, with Rice as a minority partner, they set up Rice Machine Services.

Leaving Ernie Rice with 25 per cent of the company was a key part of Doc's fledgling corporate strategy. Doc believed that an essential element of any new venture or acquisition was the management expertise either installed in or that came with the acquired company. In order to retain and motivate that expertise, Doc believed managers should be left with equity or with some profit incentive scheme. There were no greater motivators than pride of ownership and the prospect of a share in success. There were also tax advantages to the arrangement. These, however, disappeared with changes to the tax laws in the mid-1960s.

Another diversification, which was also a link to the old family business, came through a joint venture in the road-construction and earth-moving business with Stan Rokosh, an old colleague of Doc's from the University of Saskatchewan. One of eleven children, Rokosh had grown up on a farm just north of Regina. He had served in the army during the Second World War and had gone to the U. of S. on a veteran's scholarship. He met Doc through the Engineering Society, of which he was president and of which Doc had been Treasurer the previous year. After graduation as a civil engineer, Rokosh had moved to Calgary as a consultant. In 1953, Doc, whose business was now showing healthy signs of growth, approached him and said: "Pick a business field that appeals to you and we'll go into it together." Like many of Doc's diversifications and later acquisitions, the move was based on an assessment of personality.

Rokosh picked road construction — a tough, competitive business — and the operation was financed two-thirds by the Seamans and one-third by Rokosh, who bought a tractor and went to work. His early ventures included clearing the ground for the Calgary Power Reservoir at Bearspaw. In 1957, he received a major sub-contract for part of the Banff-Windermere highway. At the height of the summer, Rokosh Engineering employed more than fifty people.

By the mid-1950s, the Seaman business was booming. The corporate head office was a less-than-palatial old steel building at 320, 39th Avenue South East, near to the Stampeder Hotel. Just to the north, Ernie Rice's machine shop was set up. However, the company's main business was out in the field, where the shot-hole and slim-hole rigs, and the seismic crews, were serving the fast-growing Western oil business.

Doc was prepared to look outside the oil business for work. Drilling rigs didn't drill only for oil, and the brothers hit on the idea of using the rigs to drill water-wells for farmers. Doc was prepared to stretch his philosophy of taking a piece of the action to this activity too, and, with a view to acquiring livestock in part payment for wells, the company bought a spread of land at Priddis, south of Calgary. In fact, the scheme led the Seamans to acquire some pretty scrawny cattle — and develop a healthy respect for the trading abilities of Alberta farmers! — and the farm was eventually bought by Doc and B.J. for themselves.

Although Doc now had one hundred or more people working for him, his business ambitions were far from sated. Indeed, they were only just being whetted. It was almost inevitable that the Seamans would move into larger, oilwell drilling rigs. From there, it would be another logical, if at the time somewhat controversial, jump into exploration itself. The problem, as ever, was funds

Funding the Move into Big Rigs

The Seamans started oilwell drilling by using their slim-hole rigs to drill shallow natural gas wells at Medicine Hat. Then they rented some old specialist drilling rigs and started to drill wells in Saskatchewan. However, the Saskatchewan business died off temporarily in 1955, as did most other business in the Western oilpatch.

For the Seamans and for almost everybody else in the exploration business, 1955 was a tough year. Doc still had enormous faith in the ultimate fruits of expansion, but the circumstances made it tougher than ever to borrow from the banks. Doc had mortgaged almost everything he had in his bid to acquire additional hardware.

Doc saw that if he was to get his hands on the magnitude of funds his ambitions demanded, he was going to have to go further afield. Like so many oilmen before him and after him, he trekked east. Doc drew on his slim list of Eastern contacts, and in particular visited his old friend and navigator from air force days, Tom McGlade, who was now in the investment business on Wall Street. McGlade in turn introduced him to his own contacts in Toronto, but they all told Doc that they would only be prepared to lend him money to buy rigs if he could show them a drilling contract. A drilling contract was good collateral since it meant the rig would be capable of paying down its loan out of its own assured earnings. But Doc could gain no contracts because he had no rigs!

Doc trekked the inhospitable streets of Toronto's financial district, following any lead that might result in financing. Eventually, he found himself in the offices of the Canadian subsidiary of a small British merchant bank, Charterhouse. There he was interviewed by the company's shrewd but sometimes irascible Canadian representative, Bill Hulton.

Doc's failure to raise further cash was hardly a case of perversity on the part of the banks or the lending institutions. The oil business

30

was notoriously cyclical. Nevertheless, Bill Hulton liked what he saw in — and what he heard from — the cool young westerner. He was prepared to recommend that his head office in London put up some cash. But there was a price. Charterhouse was a venture capital organization. It provided money for promising young organizations, but it also demanded a piece of the action — an equity stake. Hulton and his young assistant, D'Alton "Sandy" Sinclair, wrote a report and submitted it to London. London, however, saw few attractions in upstart colonial drilling companies. The request was turned down.

Doc was, of course, disappointed but undeterred. He returned to Calgary and, after another six months of steadily improving results, returned to Hulton once more. This time, Hulton was not to be denied. He sent a telegram on a Friday afternoon urging head office to reconsider its earlier decision and saying that, if he did not hear from them by Monday, he would assume that they had reconsidered. It somehow slipped Hulton's mind that the following Monday was a British public holiday!

In April, 1956, Charterhouse Canada Limited acquired 25 per cent of the common shares of Seaman Engineering and Drilling Company Limited for what, in retrospect, seemed the bargain basement price of $35,000. The main injection of cash into the company came through Charterhouse's purchase of $150,000 of preferred shares. Bill Hulton, despite a parting of the ways with Charterhouse, stayed on the Seaman board until his death. Sandy Sinclair, who also ultimately left Charterhouse, remains on it until this day.

The injection of funds from Charterhouse helped with the expansion into big rigs that the Seamans had already begun. The small drilling division — which Don would inherit — became known as Sedco, while the big rigs came under Seaman Engineering and Drilling. Cec Daly, an affable and meticulous young drilling specialist whose skills included being a part-time professional pianist, was hired to help organize the big rigs, and Seaman Engineering and Drilling gradually acquired a full-scale drilling staff. Some of these men, like the tall, rangy John Gillard, one of the company's first toolpushers (the men responsible on site for drilling a well), would stay with the Seaman organization for more than thirty years.

An Innovative Approach

The Seamans made their reputations in exploration drilling through a number of innovations and through simply working harder, faster, and more cheaply than the opposition. They outbid other drilling

31

companies first, by offering to take a piece of the exploration action in lieu of cash — always attractive to explorers hungry for funds — and second, by offering "turnkey" contracts. Under this system, instead of bidding so many dollars and cents per foot, as was the normal practice, the Seamans would offer to drill a well — and provide all related services, such as cementation and casing — for a fixed price. Doc would get the contracts, while B.J. — who was renowned for his tremendous memory — would look after all the costs.

The Seamans' other great skill was their utilization of the Cardwell trailer rig, which had been developed by Bill Cardwell, who was based in Wichita, Kansas. The rig, with its manoeuvrability and its capability of drilling to a depth of 5,000 feet, was ideal for operating in southeast Saskatchewan, where there was a great deal of drilling activity in the latter part of the 1950s.

In the drilling business perhaps more than anywhere else in the oil industry, time means money. However, to drill merely as fast as possible inevitably invites problems. The essence of speedy operation thus lies in the expertise of the staff. By handpicking its crews, and through B.J.'s skill at scheduling rig-use so as to assure minimum "downtime," Seaman Engineering and Drilling acquired an enviable reputation. Between Doc's sharp contracting, in particular the concept of the turnkey operation and of "taking a piece of the action," and B.J.'s scheduling, knowledge of the market, and almost photographic memory, the Seamans believed that there was always money to be made. And they made it. Opposing drilling companies would marvel that a Seaman rig would have come onto location, drilled, and departed while they were still rigging up.

The 39th Avenue offices were less than grandiose, although Doc now allowed himself the luxury of a carpet. The long building had a hallway down its centre, and anyone entering through the main door at the south end would quite likely find himself facing B.J., who used to pace up and down the building while he carried out business calculations in his head. The general office was on the left as one entered. That office was run by Bob Dunbar, but in 1957, a fresh-faced young chartered accountant, Keith Lazelle, was hired with a view to succeeding Dunbar. Lazelle would remain a key member of Bow Valley's management team for the remainder of his career. The Seismotech office, where Mac Baker, Hal Godwin, and the other seismic specialists were based, was on the right. Up from the general office were the offices of Doc and then Jim Thompson, and facing them were the offices of B.J. and Don, split by the office where Stan Rokosh and Cec Daly worked.

B.J. and Don concentrated largely on the operating side of things, while Doc dreamed his dreams of expansion, assessed markets and prospects, and made decisions. Sometimes he would wander into Cec Daly's office, where Cec would be making his meticulous records of every foot of well drilled by a Seaman rig, along with the drill bit used to drill it, and stare out of the window for a long time. Then he would leave without a word. Most Friday nights, everybody would chip in and Hal Godwin would be sent off to buy some beer. Then, for a couple of hours, Doc would open up a little and reveal some of his plans and ideas. Nevertheless, to most of his staff, Doc remained something of a mystery.

But if he was a mystery, he was also an inspiration. For Doc, business was a twenty-four-hour-a-day proposition. He'd go home thinking of a problem, carry it to bed with him and sometimes come up with the solution in the middle of a sleepless night. Then he couldn't wait to get to the office in the morning to implement it. He once admitted to one of his colleagues that although he'd start out for work in the morning driving at normal speed, he'd soon find himself accelerating to get to the office as fast as possible. And everybody else was expected to display the same attitude. Hal Godwin — who had met Doc Seaman on the Athabasca seismic crew and who had been hired by him at the beginning of 1953 — remembers being dispatched by B.J. to trek often thirty miles a day into the wilds of Alberta looking for work for the rigs. Stan Rokosh, who on payday would find himself still at the office at 2:00 A.M. in the morning, recalls working "like a dog;" and Cec Daly, with typical humor summed it all up by saying: "Life was simple then. You just worked your ass off!"

The whole team worked together and played together. The Seamans retained their keen interest in sports, and remained enormously competitive, whether it was on the golf course or the handball court or the curling rink. Stan Rokosh once invited Doc and B.J. and their wives over for a social evening, mentioning casually that there was a skating rink closeby. Doc and B.J. turned up with their hockey sticks and Stan and his wife began to fear after a couple of hours that they would never get them back into the house! The relationship between Doc and B.J. on the ice was a little like their relationship in business. B.J. would hustle and bustle, dashing up and down the rink or ferreting away in the corner to bring out the puck, while Doc would float effortlessly around, unerringly pick his spot, and score.

Pate would be a frequent visitor to the office. He loved to do odd jobs and just chew the fat with the staff. During the winters, meanwhile, the Seaman boys and their father would take their competitiveness out onto the curling rink. And they just hated to lose a match almost as much as they hated to lose a drilling contract.

4
Hi-Tower: A Quantum Leap

By 1959, Seaman Engineering and Drilling was ready for a quantum leap in its operations. Doc would make this leap — encouraged and advised by Charterhouse's Hulton — through a bold acquisition, swallowing a company more than twice the size of Seaman Engineering and Drilling, and financing the acquisition largely with the acquired company's own money. The company was called Hi-Tower Drilling Co. Ltd., and its origins could be traced to one of the almost mythical figures of the Canadian drilling business, Ralph Will.

Will ranked as a giant, both metaphorically and literally, in the Canadian drilling business between the time he came to Canada in 1937 and the time he effectively gave his business to his employees in 1950 to form the company that would become Hi-Tower.

Ralph Will was born in Colorado in 1902 into a farming family that traced its history back to German mercenaries who fought the colonists during the Revolutionary War. He had a typically hard upbringing. However, he was driven in his youth by the fervent desire for an education. At the age of fifteen he had run away from home because of his father's opposition to his going to high school. After a couple of years, he was reconciled with his father, but his quest for education continued until he had succeeded in putting himself through the University of Oklahoma, where he was an athletics, football, and wrestling star. Only once during his wrestling career were his shoulders ever pinned, and that was by a wrestler forty-seven pounds heavier than Will and who had represented the U.S. in the Olympics!

Despite the athletic prowess of the 210-pound six-footer, education came first. As well as spending 8:00 A.M. to 5:00 P.M. in the classroom and laboratory, Will worked an average of five hours a day to support himself. In 1929, he emerged from OU with his Bachelor of Science degree in geology. Ironically but not untypically, the young graduate found the best-paying jobs in the oilfields were not for geologists but for roughnecks — the tough men who dealt with the bone-crushing lengths of pipe and spinning chain on the rig floor.

During the following five years, Will worked the oilfields from Oklahoma down to Texas and up through Montana and Wyoming. In 1934, he was given his first job as a driller, and by August of 1935 he was General Superintendent of the Rocky Mountain Drilling Company. The company's operations — eighteen rigs spread throughout Wyoming, Montana, North Dakota, and Utah — involved Will routinely travelling over 2,500 miles every two weeks, quite apart from the occasional 1,000 mile dash across dusty roads to supervise a "fishing" job — where equipment had become stuck in the drill-hole — or fight a blow-out. At the best of times, the work was a twelve-hours-a-day, seven-days-a-week commitment; at its worst, it kept Will awake for nights on end, as well as occasionally threatening his life.

Will once lost 50 pounds while fighting a blow-out. During his rig floor days, he was up on the derrick twice when wells blew out of control. On one occasion, when 3,000 feet of drill pipe blew out of the hole and passed him in a matter of seconds, he had jumped 30 feet to the ground to cut off the well. On another occasion, his life had been saved by a 40-mile-per-hour wind that had prevented him from being burned alive when the well blew out and caught fire within seconds. On that occasion he had wound up with scorched ears and wrists after escaping over the red-hot tin roof of the engine house. Most of the crew on the rig floor had finished up in hospital with permanent injuries. In another accident, Will had not been so lucky. He had had his hand badly mangled. He was left with a fleshy claw, that, because of its appearance, earned him the nickname "The Alligator."

In 1937, Will was lured to Canada to work for the Anglo-Canadian Oil Company as general field superintendent. The big American shook up the company in short order, firing nine of the company's fifteen drillers (all of whom happened to be fellow Americans for whose skill Will had very little regard) and putting all his employees on the higher U.S. wage scale. That made his workers happy although it didn't entirely endear him to the rest of the Canadian industry.

Will drilled many of the wells in the Turner Valley in the latter 1930s and his value to Anglo-Canadian was clearly shown by the fact that when he wanted to resign in 1939, they offered him a share of the net profits in addition to his $10,000 salary. This brought him in bonuses of up to $60,000 annually in the following five years, a very large amount of money for the time.

In 1945, Will made a bold move. Anglo-Canadian believed that Alberta oil activity was winding down, so Will offered to buy five of the company's rigs, with an option on the other four, for $1.48 million. With financial help from the Royal Bank, he formed Drilling Contractors Ltd. The move paid off. Within two years, Imperial's find at Leduc had sparked a fresh boom in drilling. Will not only exercised his options on the remaining four Anglo-Canadian rigs, but also bought three others. Will was the first outside drilling contractor employed by Imperial at Leduc. During the five years he owned Drilling Contractors, Will drilled or supervised about 600 wells. He also made a well-deserved fortune.

Ralph Will was revered by all those who worked for him. He expected his employees to work no harder than he worked himself, and there were very few capable of that. Betty Fisher, who came in daily from Okotoks to work as a secretary for Will (and would come in from Okotoks to work for Doc Seaman for twenty years) recalled that Will always seemed to pick the worst weather to visit "the boys" on the rigs. And the boys loved him for it. It was not just that he was fair as well as being tough, it was also that he was *expert*. He had a feel for the workings of oil rigs, for the quirkiness of the machinery, and for the stresses and tolerances of drilling that amounted to more than just experience.

Giving the Company Away

By 1950, Drilling Contractors was a very rich company. Indeed, as far as Ottawa's Department of Internal Revenue was concerned, it was too rich. Will was told that since the company had a considerable cash surplus in the bank, it would have to declare a dividend to its shareholders. Of course the only shareholder was Will, who would have had to pay a very hefty portion of any dividend in taxes. The solution Will hit upon was to sell the company to a number of his key employees, who formed McIvor Drilling Company Ltd. in 1950. In 1951, McIvor went public, which not only gave the key employees enough money to pay Will for his company, but also made for a bonus of some $275,000 each. Within five years, public shareholders who had bought the company at $10 a share had received their investment back in dividends alone, while the shares traded at over $20.

Will continued to play an important behind-the-scenes role at McIvor, which changed its name to Hi-Tower in 1954, and also went on to work for two years (as a $1-a-year man) for Ottawa's "Minister of Everything," C.D. Howe, importing tubular goods (the pipe that was so important to the oil business both for drilling the wells and transporting the oil). Alberta Premier Ernest Manning then appointed him the first president of Alberta Gas Trunk Line (since renamed Nova Corporation) — the utility set up to gather all the natural gas in the province. He became a director of well over a dozen companies.

McIvor/Hi-Tower meanwhile rode the cycles of the 1950s, as did the much smaller operation of the Seaman brothers. By the fall of the slump year of 1955, following a modernization and rationalization program, Hi-Tower had eight rigs with depth ratings of between 4,500 and 10,000 feet, "a range of modern rigs as good if not better than any company of comparable size in Canada." The following year was a boom year for the company. The directors' report for the year ended February 28, 1957, noted: "The past year has been a very successful one for the Company. We have drilled more wells and made more footage than in any year since the Company's inception."

The next couple of years were not as profitable. Nevertheless, Hi-Tower was conservative in its investments, avoided debts, and built up a considerable amount of cash in the bank. In some ways, it was the company's fiscal conservatism that was to lead to its takeover. By the end of 1959 the company had almost $1 million in current assets, including more than $300,000 in cash. Those assets made it a very attractive takeover target.

For the Seaman brothers, and for Charterhouse, the brothers' financial backer, Hi-Tower held corporate charms beyond its brimming balance sheet. Not only would such an acquisition mean a quantum leap into the "big rig" field into which the company had been moving, but it would also take the Seamans "public," via the back-door route. Although Doc had misgivings about the step into the limelight involved in going public, Charterhouse was enthusiastic about transforming its holding in the Seamans business into that of a public company, and thus clearly showing the value of its investment in Doc and his brothers.

Under the terms of the deal effectively masterminded by Charterhouse's Hulton, 70 per cent of Hi-Tower's shares were acquired by Charterhouse and the Seamans for $1.2 million. The brothers borrowed their share of the acquisition cost from the bank. By the middle of 1960, they would be able to pay the money off when Hi-Tower bought out all the shares of Seaman Engineering and Drilling for $924,000 and 55,000 shares of Hi-Tower, worth $660,000. Although they were scrupulously careful to gain independent assessments of the value of their shares, and did not vote when the issue came before the Hi-Tower board, the Seamans had effectively used Hi-Tower's own money to pay for their acquisition of the company.

New Corporate Horizons

The deal not only took Doc and his brothers into a different level of business activity, it opened Doc's eyes to new corporate horizons. When Stan Rokosh had gone into Doc's office on 39th Avenue to discuss some bill for $10,000 related to his earth-moving business,

Doc would explain that their problems were the same, it was just that his own had yet another zero on the end. It was all relative. Now the Hi-Tower deal added another zero on the size of the deals Doc felt within his grasp. Buying a company turned out to be just like buying a rig; you did it because you figured that you could make more money on the deal than you invested. Buying companies required a little more financial sophistication, but for Doc it was really just a matter of "more zeros." And the zeros now reached to the magic number of six. Suddenly Doc was dealing with millions. The acquisition had cost over a million dollars and had brought the Seamans a company with $1.7 million in assets. In the year they acquired it, Hi-Tower had a net income of $128,636.18 and a cash flow of almost $300,000.

Doc became president of Hi-Tower, B.J. became vice-president and general manager and Don took the title of vice-president of geophysical operations. The young Seaman Engineering accountant, Keith Lazelle, who had knowledge of Hi-Tower because he had been one of the company's auditors some years before, became secretary-treasurer. From the Hi-Tower side, the key men were Joe Wark, who was now appointed executive vice-president, and Don Binney, who assumed the title of vice-president of drilling operations. The Hi-Tower acquisition also brought with it some rock-solid drilling men who would remain for many years the backbone of the company's rig operations, in some cases until the present day. These included men like Buzz Cotter, Norm Vetters, Bob Engberg, Red Bryden, Al Garries, and Elmer "Pistol" Snyder.

Joe Wark was renowned and respected as a tough and capable drilling man. Bob Engberg, one of Hi-Tower's toolpushers who would go on to become operations manager for all Hi-Tower operations some twenty years later, recalls being stuck in the deep bush six hours out of Peace River for two months while drilling a well. Finally, desperate for a glimpse of civilization, he drove into Peace River and called Wark. "Where the hell are you?" demanded Wark. "I'm in Peace River," said Engberg. "There is no goddamn drilling rig at Peace River," Wark bellowed down the phone. "Get back to the rig!"

Don Binney had worked with Ralph Will briefly before the war in Turner Valley, and, following war service in the navy, had returned to work for Will's company, Drilling Contractors, in 1946. Binney would go on to become a key figure in the Seaman's operations, earning a reputation as one of the most knowledgeable drilling experts in Western Canada. He would eventually become a senior vice-president and director.

Understandably, there were some misgivings among both management and staff at Hi-Tower about the Seaman acquisition. After all, who were these upstarts with their little operation who had never even *worked* on a proper drilling rig?

Early in 1960, at Don Binney's suggestion, the company organized a joint business-cum-social get-together at the Stampeder Hotel for the management and toolpushers of Hi-Tower and their wives. There, Joe Wark and Don Binney said a few words, while B.J. did the talking for the Seamans. Then everybody had a few drinks and things loosened up a bit. Soon things really loosened up and some of the boys began to engage in some competitive events, such as "squaw wrestling" — lying on their backs, linking legs and trying to pull their opponents over. The big muscular guys from the rigs soon discovered that although the Seamans were far from bulky, they were wiry and strong — and they played to win. One of the Hi-Tower toolpushers would carry around his snuff tin between his knuckles and challenge anybody else to grasp it and take it away from him. Both Doc and Don did. Nevertheless, Doc could never beat Joe Wark — whose legs, Doc remembers, were "about a foot longer" than his own — at squaw-wrestling.

The year 1959, which saw the plotting of the Hi-Tower acquisition, was undoubtedly a turning point for the company. There was a parting of the ways with Mac Baker, who bought out the Seamans' share of Seismotech under an arrangement in which he also sold to them his stake in the overall Seaman operation. Stan Rokosh also bought out the Seamans' stake in Rokosh Engineering.

One of Stan Rokosh's last major projects under the partnership was the flattening of a chunk of land that Doc had picked up cheaply around 42nd Avenue and 9th Street SE at Highfield. The land had been cheap because of the natural hill on it, but Doc had immediately seen its potential. Not only did he have new headquarters built on the site, but sales of parcels of the land would make a good deal of money for the company in the years to come as industry moved southeast from the city's growing downtown core. The Highfield industrial development would be just one of a number of highly profitable real estate ventures into which the company would enter.

When the Seaman "big rigs" had in fact consisted of not very big rigs operating in southeast Saskatchewan, Doc had told one of his best drilling men, John Gillard, that one day they would be part of the biggest drilling company in Canada. Gillard hadn't meant to be impolite, but he had kind of laughed at the notion. Could Doc be serious? But Doc hadn't been joking. With the Hi-Tower acquisition, the company gained control of nine deep rigs to add to its own shallower drilling units. Moreover, within little more than a year, another six rigs would be acquired — three from the takeover of Dale Simmons'

Pennant Drilling, and three bought from "Goat" Ryland — to bring Hi-Tower's rig count to twenty-one. By 1964, the company would be the second largest drilling contractor in Canada.

Hi-Tower also moved into the international field through the acquisition of a 25 per cent interest in a consortium called Worldwide Drilling Company Limited, which had been formed to take advantage of drilling opportunities outside Canada. The other partners in the consortium were the drilling companies of Norm Gustavson, Jack Storey, and John Scrymgeour. Soon Worldwide was drilling in both Mexico and Australia.

Doc also continued his thrust towards the acquisition of other ventures that would aid integration of the company. First he was the key figure in pulling together a group of companies to form Western Rockbit, which was designed to cut out the middlemen who distributed drilling bits to the industry. This step led in 1962 to a much more significant move, the acquisition of the Canadian interests of Cardwell Manufacturing Company, Ltd., the equipment supply house that sold the trailer-mounted Cardwell rigs that had been such an important element in the Seamans' early exploration drilling success. To run the newly acquired company, Doc hired a friend, Bob Phibbs, who was working for a company called Jones & Laughlin in the steel distribution business.

Phibbs had come to Calgary from his native Ontario after captaining the Canadian Olympic basketball team at the Helsinki games of 1952, and had come to know the Seamans through curling and other social activities. One day in 1962, Doc had surprised Phibbs by throwing the financial statements of Cardwell to him and saying: "Do you want to run it?" Phibbs did, and would remain with the Seaman empire for over twenty years. With the Cardwell acquisition came another figure who would bring a lot of financial accounting expertise to the growing Seaman interests, a young Trinidadian-born accountant, Trevor Legge. Over the years, Legge would develop a reputation for being a hard-nosed and cost-conscious controller.

Bow Valley Is Born

Soon it was decided to change the name of the company from Hi-Tower to something that would better reflect both the broader range of activities and the aspirations of the organization. Don Seaman and Keith Lazelle kicked some names around one night and out of that session came the name Bow Valley. On June 1, 1962, the company

40

changed its name to Bow Valley Industries Ltd., although the Hi-Tower name would live on in the deep drilling division. The last annual report under the old Hi-Tower name, for the year ended May 31, 1962, showed a net profit of $394,536 vs. $328,723 for the previous year. Cash flow was up to $846,483 from fiscal 1961's $759,053. It seemed a long way from Doc's first little shot-hole rig. But Doc and his brothers would have a lot further to go.

Those who came over from Hi-Tower discovered that the Seamans ran a tight financial ship. People in the drilling industry tend to develop an almost emotional attachment to their rigs. Toolpushers in particular, who would spend many years with one rig, inevitably developed a bond with their equipment, and solicitously sought to upgrade it with new and better machinery. Doc looked upon the rigs as cash-generators for his wider corporate ambitions. He delegated to B.J. the job of controlling expenditures, and B.J. proved highly effective at it. This inevitably led to the occasional grumble of discontent from the field. Nevertheless, this proved remarkably effective in generating funds for expansion.

Two new directors were appointed at the 1961 annual general meeting. One of them was Sandy Sinclair, who had taken over as president of Charterhouse Canada after Bill Hulton had moved to the Mercantile Bank of Canada. The other was Harry Van Rensselaer, a New York stockbroker, who would play a key role in providing funds for Doc's exploration ambitions. Van Rensselaer became a financial consultant to Bow Valley and eventually joined the company as vice-president of finance at a time when it was developing an almost insatiable thirst for money.

5
The Plunge into Exploration

When Doc Seaman had decided to take the plunge in 1949 and sink his savings into that modest little shothole rig, he hadn't possessed any great masterplan. He certainly hadn't used management theory, which was still in its infancy, as his guide. In any case, no entrepreneur — of Doc's era at least — ever started a business based on theory. Doc just saw the opportunities, gauged the demand, and then acted. Shot-hole rigs had led into full-scale seismic operations and larger slim-hole rigs; the slim-hole rigs had naturally evolved into yet larger oilwell drilling rigs; a desire to keep the rigs busy had resulted in the innovations of turnkey contracts and taking a piece of the wells. Sometimes the bits of the business so created didn't fit together so smoothly, but a corporation, like the human body, inevitably has growing pains.

By the time Bow Valley Industries had appeared on the board of the Alberta Stock Exchange, Doc had clearly evolved one central element of his corporate strategy: the determination to develop his own oil and gas exploration and production as a way of keeping the rigs busy and smoothing out the cyclical ups and downs of the drilling business. That strategy would eventually lead to worldwide exploration success, and to production in areas as diverse as the stormy North Sea and the jungles of Indonesia. But for the moment, it consisted of nothing more elaborate than a few wells in Alberta and Saskatchewan.

The Seamans had drilled their first exploration wells in the shallow gas sands of Medicine Hat, where gas had been encountered by the Canadian Pacific Railway some seventy years previously. These were drilled with modified slim-hole rigs, but they led quickly into full-scale exploration drilling with the big rigs. Doc's first independent oil venture sprang from the company's success with the trailer-mounted Cardwell rigs in southeast Saskatchewan. In 1956 and 1957, the little trailer rigs were doing a roaring business at Weyburn, where they were drilling for a company called Central Del Rio (which evolved into today's PanCanadian Petroleum).

The Seamans' fiscal year ended on May 31, and Doc realized that they would have to pay a fair chunk of taxes unless they found some form of shelter. The most obvious tax write-off was for oil exploration, so he approached Central Del Rio and asked if the oil company had any prospects that Sedco might take on a farm-out, that is, drill an exploration well in return for a portion of any discovery. Doc was told that the company did have a couple of prospects on what it believed to be the edge of the field. Doc took these prospects to a consultant in Calgary whom he had gotten to know, Rod McDaniel (who had taken his first job in the oil business as a roughneck with Ralph Will and whom Will had encouraged to take a degree in petroleum engineering at his old alma mater, the University of Oklahoma). McDaniel was enthusiastic, so Doc took the farm-out and drilled the two "edge wells." The first well struck oil.

Doc did the same thing the following year and gradually developed oil and gas production income. Within a couple of years he was involved as a partner in twenty or thirty wells a year. Doc wasn't a wild-eyed explorationist, or a gung-ho promoter, but he did get bitten by the oil bug. He soon determined not just to expand the exploration side of the Bow Valley operation, but to make it his main corporate goal.

However, for a drilling company it was a problematic goal. Many of the oil companies maintained that such companies had no business exploring on their own behalf. It was felt that there was a conflict, since a drilling company that was also involved in exploration might use the knowledge it had gleaned from its drilling operations to gain an unfair advantage. For example, oil companies frequently "drilled into" land sales, that is, they drilled a well adjacent to a block of land due to come up for auction with a view to gauging the adjacent block's value. If the drilling company they used was also involved in exploration, then that company might use the information from the well to bid for the land on its own account. There were similar feelings about seismic companies becoming involved in exploration on their own account, and this was one of the reasons for the Seamans' break with Mac Baker and Seismotech.

Nevertheless, Doc felt there were great opportunities in exploration and production. The means to exploit them came along in the shape of two men, a young Calgary banker named Harley Hotchkiss, with whom the Seamans were already acquainted, and the New York stockbroker Harry Van Rensselaer.

Hotchkiss and Van Rensselaer

Van Rensselaer was a model of the U.S. East Coast establishment. It was rumored that his forebears had been passengers on the *Mayflower*.

One of the Van Rensselaers was also a commander in the American forces during the war of 1812. His father had been a lawyer turned investment banker who had lost a fortune in the Great Crash. Young Harry was saved from the educational consequences of his father's financial problems by his youthful tennis prowess, which helped see him through Kent School and into Princeton.

After a spell overseas in the air force and some pioneer electronic work in radar and television, Van Rensselaer moved into Wall Street in the early 1950s to work for the Bank of New York as an investment analyst. Among his specialities was the oil industry, and he started to follow activities in Canada. He began to subscribe to the Nickle map service and the *Daily Oil Bulletin* and kept a record of wells drilled in Alberta.

In the spring of 1954, his interest was aroused by activity west of Edmonton in the Pembina area, so he decided to spend his summer holidays in Canada and see what was going on. He visited Drayton Valley — noting with interest that the Royal Bank had set up a branch office in a packing box! — and decided from what he heard and saw that the Pembina field was a major oil play.

After visiting, and falling in love with, Jasper and Banff, Van Rensselaer and his wife returned to New York and he recommended that the Bank of New York invest in three companies with good land positions in the Pembina area. It took some time to unlock the Pembina field's geological key because the "payzone," that is, the thickness of oil-bearing sands, was relatively thin, and discovery wells produced only 200 barrels or so of oil a day. However, what made the field a petroleum bonanza was its size. It turned out to cover 1,000 square miles and thus was the largest oilfield in North America. The stocks Van Rensselaer had recommended all had sizable price increases, which further helped establish his name in the Wall Street community.

Soon he was lured away from the Bank of New York to join the investment firm of Henderson, Harrison & Struthers. He continued to specialize in Canadian oil stocks, and maintained his prowess on the tennis court (He was still ranked in the top twenty in the U.S. at the age of thirty-seven.). It was a combination of his business speciality and sports talent which led him to become much more directly involved in the Canadian oil business.

One day, his doubles partner, Alastair Martin, who was related to the enormously wealthy Phipps family, said that his family holding company, Bessemer Securities, would like to invest some money in Canada. Did Harry know of likely prospects? Van Rensselaer suggested that they go and have a look for themselves, so they set off with their wives for Calgary. There, Van Rensselaer intended to introduce Martin to Harley Hotchkiss, a valuable contact who was running the oil and gas department of the Canadian Imperial Bank of Commerce.

Hotchkiss' background was quite different to that of Van Rensselaer. He had grown up on a small tobacco farm in Southern Ontario. Then he had spent two years in the Canadian merchant marine before returning to a hockey scholarship at Michigan State University. After a geology degree and a spell with Canadian Superior, he went to work for the Commerce and quickly became an assistant manager in their oil and gas department. The Seamans banked with the Commerce and Hotchkiss — who shared their enthusiasm for, and skill at, sports — got on well with them. They would often curl and go duck hunting together.

Hotchkiss had met Van Rensselaer when the Wall Streeter had first come to Alberta to look at the Pembina play, and the two had kept in close contact. When asked about potential investment opportunities, Hotchkiss gave the two men some names, but afterwards he took Van Rensselaer to one side and said he was interested in running the sort of company of which they were thinking. Why didn't he and Van Rensselaer put something together? Over the next few months, the two men worked on a proposal for a small oil and gas company based in Calgary that would use U.S. investment funds. They took their plan down to Bessemer Securities, and also showed it to the giant investment house of Scudder, Stevens and Clark. However, they couldn't quite clinch the deal. Then Hotchkiss told Van Rensselaer about Doc Seaman.

He explained that Doc had a fast-growing drilling company and that he was developing a landspread and production income. If Doc put the Seamans' lands and production income into the company, then it might be easier to attract the Americans. In fact, Doc had been looking for just such a scheme, and so Alcon Petroleums (for Alberta-Connecticut, where Van Rensselaer lived) was set up. Wall Street took a dive in 1959, which contributed to lower American interest in the issue than had originally been forecast, and so the Seamans wound up owning 75 per cent of the company while the remainder was split between Hotchkiss, Van Rensselaer, and a number of American partners.

The basic concept of Alcon was that it would reinvest the production income from the Seaman lands, while also investing money that Van Rensselaer would raise via his blue-chip contacts on Wall Street. The U.S. investors would pay a management fee, while Alcon would also receive an interest in all the projects into which it put the American money.

In his first year as president of Alcon, Hotchkiss had about $150,000 of production revenue from the Seaman lands, plus about $100,000 of U.S. money to invest. He set up an office in two rooms on 8th Avenue, which he shared with Boone Pickens, the colorful American who would one day shake up the entire North American oil industry (and in the process precipitate the takeover of Gulf Oil Corporation by Standard Oil of California), and started looking for deals.

Success was a matter of effort and above all contacts. Hotchkiss was permanently on the lookout for prospects, poring over land maps and taking farm-outs. If the well he was involved in was close enough to Calgary, he would drive out to the well site. There he would peer through a microscope at the cuttings brought up from the well bottom, looking for a trace of oil-bearing rock.

Alcon moved ahead by a number of small successes rather than large ones. Perhaps its largest success was at Crossfield, which proved to be a textbook example of the tenacity required to be a successful oilman. Hotchkiss had heard through his old contacts at Canadian Superior that the company wanted to test a prospect but did not have sufficent funds in its budget. Hotchkiss went over to the Canadian Superior offices and looked at the prospect's geology. He liked what he saw, but it would involve the drilling of a $100,000 well. While he was discussing the prospect with Doc, word came that another company, Amax, had moved in and taken the farm-out. Undeterred, and with Doc's support, Hotchkiss now approached Amax with an offer to take a piece of *their* action. The explorationist he spoke to, however, said Amax wasn't interested in a partner. Hotchkiss, with the bit now between his teeth, told the man that he'd have to go above his head. He phoned the explorationist's boss, who was in New York, and eventually succeeded in gaining a part of the farm-out in return for paying a few per cent extra of the cost. The well was a success and led to the discovery of a field that has produced close to a trillion cubic feet of gas.

The Dilemma of Success

Half a dozen times a year, Hotchkiss would fly down to New York, sometimes with Doc, and they would both stay out at Greenwich, Connecticut with Van Rensselaer. Each morning they would take the New Haven commuter train into Manhattan to update existing investors on — or enthuse new ones in — the potential of Canada's answer to Texas. Van Rensselaer, who had continued his love affair with the Canadian Rockies, would come up each year for his holidays, and would frequently be on the phone to Hotchkiss for news of Alcon's latest ventures and successes.

Doc, meanwhile, was always keenly interested in Alcon's activities, but deliberately avoided looking over Hotchkiss's shoulder. One of Doc's great strengths was his ability to delegate. That did not mean, however, that Doc was less than consumingly interested in the performance of Alcon.

By 1963, when Bow Valley's drilling operations were already among the largest in Canada, Doc was convinced that there was a natural limit on the size of the drilling fleet that a company could handle efficiently. He believed that future increases in profits had to come from the oil and gas side. The 1964 budget was revised to allow for the maximum expenditure on oil and gas properties. In February, 1964, when Alcon's production had topped 1,000 barrels a day, Doc issued a "Manifesto for Growth" which heavily emphasised investment in oil and gas, not just for its own sake but because of the spillover effects into the company's drilling and oilfield supply operations.

Nevertheless, the perceived conflict between a company being involved in both exploration and drilling remained not merely a problem but a dilemma. To trumpet the company's growing exploration efforts was to invite the loss of drilling contracts from oil companies. Yet the company needed to emphasize its exploration efforts in order to raise money in the East because an exploration company was far more attractive as an investment vehicle than a drilling company. On the one hand, board members like Van Rensselaer and Charterhouse's Sandy Sinclair — who knew what enthused the denizens of Bay and Wall Streets — would tell Doc that he had to raise the company's exploration profile. On the other, B.J., who now ran the big rigs, emphasized that to do so would be dangerous. After all, he would point out, three-quarters of their cash flow still came from the rig business. It seemed that the more successful Bow Valley became as an explorer, the less the company could talk about it!

The company resolved to attempt to create two profiles for itself, a contract drilling profile in the West and an exploration profile in the East. Needless to say, this was no easy task. The other relevant innovation Doc had made was to turn Bow Valley into a holding company. A holding company would be more attractive to investors than a drilling company. Also, putting drilling and oil and gas activities into separate subsidiaries would, it was hoped, help "distance" the two operations from each other.

Hotchkiss suggested that Bow Valley should concentrate on building up its own production income so that it would have to rely less on the outside American investors, who also meant a lot of additional paperwork. Nevertheless, the U.S. funds remained of overwhelming importance. By 1966, Bow Valley was spending almost $1.5 million a year on exploration and development. Van Rensselaer, meanwhile, succeeded in pulling in a record $3.7 million that year from his American investors, who were enthused by tales of the major finds made in northwestern Alberta at Rainbow and Zama (in 1967, Van Rensselaer's commissions on attracting drilling funds brought him in almost $63,000, which was more than Doc's salary!).

Oil and gas revenues after payment of royalties amounted to $1,462,566 in 1967, compared to $969,044 in the preceding year and $792,000 in 1965. Between 1963 and 1967 annual production of oil had climbed from 159,532 to 404,559 barrels; natural gas liquids from 6,459 to 22,668 barrels, and natural gas from 195,209 thousand cubic feet (MCF) to 759,640 MCF. In 1967, Bow Valley's oil and gas expenditures rose above $3 million.

However, there was also now a parting of the ways with Harley Hotchkiss — at least from a business point of view and for the time being. Hotchkiss had been approached by Baron Carlo von Maffei, whose family controlled a sizable fortune, about starting up a new oil company with him. The Bow Valley board in any case was involved in tidying up the subsidiaries, so it was decided to buy out Alcon's minority shareholders, the two largest of which were Hotchkiss and Van Rensselaer. An outside evaluation of the 66,972 Alcon shares involved was made and the board agreed to purchase them for $630,000. Harley Hotchkiss went off to manage a new company, set up with Von Maffei, called Sabre Petroleums (which, having been started from scratch, would be sold for $24 million within a decade) and a new manager had now to be found for Alcon. The man Doc chose was Gordon Darling, one of a group of Imperial Oil employees who, discontented with an internal reorganization, had recently left that giant company.

Within a year, Bow Valley had further tidied up its oil interests by selling the 19 per cent equity stake it had acquired in Castle Oil & Gas. This stake had been acquired as part of a joint arrangement with Bruce Watson, an oilman whose association with the Seamans went back to their first Saskatchewan drilling operations, and Phillip Graham, a wealthy Vancouver investor. The three partners controlled Castle through a trust, and Castle in turn controlled another oil company, Canadian Homestead, holding 18 per cent of Homestead's equity. For the Seamans, the Castle-Homestead arrangement was primarily a portfolio investment. They realized a profit of close to $1 million from the sale of the shares.

With the purchase of the Alcon minority and the sale of Castle, the Seamans rounded out the first chapter — and the first decade — of their involvement with oil and gas exploration. Gordon Darling would now be instrumental in moving their horizons beyond the conventional exploration lands of Western Canada and towards the new

Canadian frontiers at a time when virtually the whole industry saw the Far North as the key exploration province of the future. As it turned out, those northern aspirations were to be a frustration for Canada's oil companies. Nevertheless, Bow Valley's shrewd investments in the North were to be a key factor in raising the company's profile and increasing its attractiveness to investors. And, for a company growing as fast as Bow Valley, investors were becoming more and more important.

6
Financing a Burst of Acquisitions

Although drilling operations continued to provide the bedrock of earnings after the Hi-Tower acquisition, and U.S. drilling funds injected more and more cash into Bow Valley's search for oil, Doc's expansive vision consistently outstripped the financial resources available to the company.

The relentless search for new sources of money would lead Doc into business circles far removed from the rough-and-tumble world of the Calgary oilpatch. Just a few years before, New York, Toronto, and Montreal investment dealers and bankers had turned him down. Now he would return to their wood-panelled offices as an increasingly valued visitor. Soon they would come knocking at *his* door.

Of critical importance to any young company is its relationship with its bankers. There always tends to be a creative tension between ambitious risk-takers and their lenders. The risk-taker, especially one with a vision as broad as Doc's, perpetually tests his credit limits. However, once he has established his credentials, then the funds available to him grow correspondingly. Banking — despite the impression bankers sometimes attempt to give of their enterprise being bound by the iron laws of economics — is essentially about trust. Doc and his brothers early on developed a reputation for trustworthiness.

To a large degree, the need for bank funds came from the desire to avoid taxes. If Doc knew that the year was going to be a good one — and from the very start years tended to be good — then he would hasten before the end of his tax year on May 31 to buy new equipment, or look for a farm-out on which to drill a well. Of course the fact that the company was going to do well on paper didn't mean that it had free-floating cash around. So Doc would go to the bank and seek to have his credit limit expanded. He mortgaged himself up to the hilt in order to expand the business. On one occasion, the manager of the main Calgary branch of the Canadian Imperial Bank of Commerce paced up and down his office nervously as Doc sought further loans. Doc had already pledged virtually everything he owned and the banker was worried about over-exposure. At last the banker said, somewhat sheepishly, "I'll need your insurance policies as collateral." "OK," said Doc, and left the branch. By the time he had walked around the corner, the manager — who had obviously had a Scrooge-like revelation — came running out of the side-door and said: "I won't need your insurance after all."

Eventually, Doc switched the company's business from the Commerce to the Royal, primarily because the Royal was prepared to provide more money on better terms than the CIBC. The relationship has survived until this day. Of key importance in the Royal getting Bow Valley's business was its growing skill in oil and gas lending. A banker who doesn't understand the business he is lending to will usually err on the side of conservatism. The Royal could loan more on any specific piece of petroleum industry collateral, be it reserves or an oil rig, because its bankers took the trouble to learn the business. That skill was embodied in men like John Ashburner and Jim Boyle.

John Ashburner was a tall, elegant banker who was in the forefront of making the Royal the leading energy bank in the 1950s and 1960s. A native Albertan, born in Medicine Hat, he had returned from war service to the Royal and — with the exception of stints in Edmonton and Montreal — had spent his entire career in Calgary. After Leduc and subsequent finds, Ashburner travelled to more experienced oil banks in the U.S. to find out "how it was done." He played a key role in pioneering production loans and other energy-lending techniques. The Royal banker who developed an even closer relationship with Bow Valley was Jim Boyle, a low-keyed and soft-spoken man held in the highest regard throughout the oil banking business. Thanks to bankers like Ashburner and Boyle, the Royal at one time held 60 per cent of the oil banking business in Calgary and had almost 80 per cent of the loans to the drilling industry.

However, Bow Valley also needed sources of finance outside the banks. Doc kept in close touch with his old navigator from war days, Tom McGlade, who worked for the investment house Shields & Company Inc. in New York (now Prudential Bache Securities Inc.), but his first real contact with the world of high-finance was Charterhouse's Bill Hulton. Hulton was the first financier to take an active interest not just in the Seamans' financial condition, but also in their financial potential.

Hulton saw something special in Doc from the start, but he realized that he had to be coached in the subtleties of high finance. Hulton started to bring sophistication to that little steel building on 39th Avenue almost as soon as he first arrived there in 1956. He would press the Seamans' associates — Ernie Rice, Mac Baker, and Stan Rokosh — for financial projections and budgets, something they found difficult to get used to.

51

Hulton also insisted that Doc change his auditor, Jack Sasseville — which Doc found hard — and appoint the big-name firm of Price Waterhouse. If Doc was to grow and raise more money, then he had to do the right things and be associated with the right people. Hulton introduced Doc to Bay Street specialists like Bud Willis and Brian Drummond at investment dealer Greenshields. Through Charterhouse, Bow Valley also acquired Sandy Sinclair as a strong, long-term board member.

Harry Van Rensselaer remained Doc's key link with the establishment in New York. From the first time they had met, Van Rensselaer had been enormously impressed by the quiet Canadian. The New Yorker's first interest in Doc Seaman had been as a conduit for U.S. drilling funds, but Van Rensselaer was also, thanks to his Wall Street connections, the pipeline to investment funds of greater quantity, and less specific nature. Doc would always have preferred to raise cash in Canada, but he continued to find it difficult to arouse the investment interests of the denizens of Bay Street. But after Doc linked up with American funds in petroleum exploration via Alcon, Van Rensselaer told him that Wall Street might put more money directly his way. Once Wall Street had given Doc its seal of approval, Bay and James Streets were not far behind.

Risk-takers would almost always prefer to borrow cash than to raise it by selling equity in their company. However, investors also like to have a little of the "cream" if they think a company has high potential; they like to have a chance to purchase its shares, which offer the prospect of capital appreciation far greater than the return on fixed or floating interest-rate loans. As the 1960s opened, Doc had an excellent track record and ran a good, clean, low-overhead operation. Van Rensselaer told him that investors on Wall Street would probably like to have a piece of Doc's action. He thought he could raise a million of fixed interest debt for him, but that to make it really attractive, Doc should attach some warrants to the debentures enabling the debenture-holders to buy his company's shares for an attractive price at a future date. Van Rensselaer had looked closely at the Seaman operation and concluded that a million dollar debenture could be paid off in three or four years from production income alone — without taking the funds from the drilling side of the business into consideration.

Wall Street's Stamp of Approval

Doc agreed over the phone with Van Rensselaer to go ahead with the deal at 10:00 A.M. New York time. By noon, Van Rensselaer had the debenture placed with a number of investment firms and individuals. The participants were the company of which Van Rensselaer was still a partner, Henderson, Harrison & Struthers, for $50,000; the Bank of New York (via its retirement fund and profit sharing system), for $300,000; The Seeing Eye, $200,000; Puritan Fund, Inc., $100,000; Grosvenor-Dale Company,Inc., $225,000; and a number of wealthy individuals from the Martin and Clay families. The debentures paid 7.5 per cent and carried an entitlement to purchase fifty common shares for each $1,000 of debenture at a price of $11.50 a share up to May 31, 1966, and at after that at $15 a share up to May 31, 1973.

The four individuals who took debentures were also involved with the drilling funds that went into Alcon. The Clays — an old Georgia family in the cotton and textile business — would, in particular, retain a strong financial interest in Bow Valley for many years. However, it was the presence of the Bank of New York in the deal that represented the undeniable stamp of approval for the young company.

Bow Valley would gain the support not merely of the Bank of New York, but of its chairman, John Traphagen, a legendary financier who had been like a father to the young Van Rensselaer when he had worked at the bank. Traphagen on one occasion sat on the podium between Doc and Van Rensselaer when the two men gave a presentation to analysts and investment dealers at the India House, a highly exclusive Manhattan luncheon club. For the financiers present, it was tantamount to seeing Doc Seaman sitting at the right hand of the Almighty himself.

In 1961, Van Rensselaer joined the Bow Valley board, and in 1964 he left Henderson, Harrison and decided to move to Calgary. There he continued his fund-raising for Alcon and offered his services to Bow Valley, which accepted him first as a consultant and then as a full-time employee.

In the event, although the $1 million debenture turned out to be a fine investment from the investors' point of view, it proved to be something of a pain in the neck for the Seamans due to the restrictions it placed on Bow Valley's further borrowings. Debenture holders or fixed interest lenders always attach covenants that curtail any actions on the part of the borrower which might endanger the quality of their loan. Indeed, shortly before the placing of the New York debenture, long-term financing from the Industrial Development Bank in Canada had been discussed by Doc's board but rejected because of excessive restrictions the bank wanted to impose on the company's dividends and capital expenditures. There were similar restrictions attached to the debenture. On a number of occasions, however, when the terms of the debenture prevented Bow Valley from doing a deal, the Seaman brothers would step in and personally guarantee the venture. The largest such guarantee, on behalf of a $250,000 loan made to Castle Oil & Gas, involved the brothers lodging 50,000 Bow Valley Industries shares (owned by their wholly owned private company, Seaman Exploration Co. Ltd.) with the Royal Bank. This willingness to put their personal funds at risk for the sake of the company and the minority shareholders inevitably enhanced their reputations with the business community.

In 1963, the Montreal-based Canadian subsidiary of New York's United Corporation made a long-term portfolio investment in Bow Valley through the purchase of 15,000 of its shares at $16 a share. This brought Jack Ahern onto the board. In 1965, the board was further strengthened — and the backing of the Bank of New York further emphasized — by the appointment to the board of bank vice-president Ray Hammell.

By the beginning of 1965, the financial community was really beginning to take notice of Bow Valley. Gross revenues and profits of the company had more than doubled since the Seamans had taken over the business five years before. In the year to August 25, 1964, gross revenues had hit $9.3 million and net profits $637,436.

While the all-important — but still little-publicized — oil and gas exploration side of the business continued to make its steady advances, Bow Valley prepared for a major thrust of public financing. And a major burst of acquisitions. In July, 1965, Greenshields sold 100,000 5.5 per cent cumulative redeemable preferred shares, raising a net $1.9 million for Bow Valley. The following March, Greenshields raised another $4 million for the company through sinking fund debentures.

Since the debenture issue was so well received, Doc wondered if the interest rate hadn't been too high. Nevertheless, the financial men on the board, Hammell, Hulton, and Van Rensselaer, told him that Bow Valley had been lucky to have had such ease in raising that volume of cash. The more conservative board members pointed out that the company had gone to the public twice in a year and should avoid any similar financings for some time to come. Van Rensselaer, ever with an eye on the expansion possibilities of oil and gas, pointed out that new funds would be required if the company encountered a large oil development program. But the board all agreed that the next issue had to be one of equity. Further interest payments on additional debt or preferred shares could make the company vulnerable to a business downturn.

Bow Valley used part of the money it raised in the market to expand its oil and gas operations, but it was also always on the lookout for further acquisitions. These were pursued with twin objectives: to provide further integration of operations on the drilling and service side, and to furnish funds for oil and gas exploration.

A Burst of Acquisitions

Shortly after acquiring Hi-Tower, Doc had been the key figure in bringing together a number of drilling companies to form Western Rockbit, a company that would manufacture drill bits and oil tools locally under licence and thus cut out the middle-man's fees. Doc went to his friends and colleagues at the other drilling companies, men like John Scrymgeour, Paul Bowlen, Jack Storey, and Norm Gustavson, and pointed out that they had enough buying power between them to build these essential drilling supplies themselves. Many people told Doc that the whole idea was too difficult, and that there was too much technology involved. But Doc was not deterred, and went to see a number of bit manufacturers, including the most famous, Hughes Tool, and had no trouble in persuading them to set up a joint operation in Canada.

With Doc as its first president, Western Rockbit took over Hughes Tool's sales organization in Alberta, and started to manufacture bits under licence. Within just a few months, the company was meeting the same quality and production standards as the parent in Houston. Doc set up Western Rockbit as a co-operative, with ownership based on the number of rigs the participating company ran. The company paid good dividends from the start and continues to operate profitably.

As another related diversification, Doc had bought a majority interest in Canadian Oil Tool, a manufacturer of drill bits for the seismic business, from Al Consay and George Cornford. Doc would also sometimes guarantee the debts of those buying rigs in return for gaining their supply business. In August, 1965, Bow Valley bought the assets of Jones & Laughlin Steel Co. — the company for which Bob Phibbs, who now ran Cardwell Supply, had worked — via Cardwell for $1.3 million.

Then, in yet another related burst of expansion, Bow Valley decided to move into aviation. For the drilling business, which often has to operate in remote locations, shifting heavy equipment and crews requires the use of small and large aircraft and helicopters. In 1966, Bow Valley agreed to take a third interest in Northward Aviation, which was run by the famous promoter of northern oil development, Cam Sproule. Northward had been formed as a new commercial airline serving Northern Canada. It operated thirty aircraft, of which it owned twenty. These were small Beavers and Otters, Cessnas, Beechcraft, and a few helicopters. It had facilities at Edmonton and Calgary and throughout the North: at Dawson Creek, Hay River,

Inuvik, Norman Wells, Yellowknife, Cambridge Bay, Resolute Bay, and Fort Smith.

In moving into the aviation business, Bow Valley was going outside its real area of expertise. Northward, which was not well run and which would soon get into financial problems, proved a corporate headache for the company. Despite these problems, however, Bow Valley would expand its air operations in March, 1968, with the purchase of Bullock Wings & Rotors Ltd. Bullock, too, would present its problems for Bow Valley.

To the outside observer, it might appear that the time was ripe for Bow Valley to slow down and consolidate its activities. Indeed, there was a corporate tidying up under way in 1966 and 1967 with the sale of many of the company's extensive property interests and and its stake in Canadian Oil Tool, as well as the purchase of the minority interests in Alcon. But Doc the risk-taker was incapable of putting his mind on hold.

In June, 1966 the company moved its main office to the newly constructed Bradie Building in downtown Calgary, which was partially owned by the Bow Valley pension fund. The plushly furnished edifice on 6th Avenue seemed corporate light-years away from the little steel structure the company had occupied on 39th Avenue just a decade before, but it was a fair reflection of the growth both in the company's size and its sophistication. The construction of the building on 42nd Avenue South East, which the company was now evacuating, had seemed an audacious move, but now that building was simply too small. As the moving vans ferried between 42nd Avenue and the Bradie Building around Stampede Week, 1966, Bow Valley, too, was in a state of corporate transition. The big Greenshields financings of the past year or so had put the company on the financial map, but it was still just a tiny player by the standards of the Eastern financial establishment. Within the next ten years, however, this building would see bank chairmen coming to visit Doc.

As it moved into its new headquarters, a whole new realm of acquisitions was opening up to the company because of of its growing clout with the financial community, and also because of an anomoly that had been discovered by Keith Lazelle in the Income Tax Act.

Looking for the Tax Angles

It has already been pointed out that one of the reasons for U.S. investors' interest in the Canadian exploration business was that they were allowed to write off their expenditures against income for tax purposes. There was no similar provision in Canada either for individuals or, in most cases, companies — except, of course, if they were in the oil business. Mining companies were allowed to write off oil and gas investments, but then Keith Lazelle also discovered that there was a provision for metal fabricators — because of their historical involvement with mining in Canada — to write off oil and gas exploration. Just to make sure, he sought assurances from tax authorities, even going to the extent of hauling a drilling bit, as an example of metal fabricating, into the tax office in Vancouver.

This led directly, at the end of 1967, to the acquisitions of Flame-Master Ltd., an Edmonton-based manufacturer of furnaces and heating equipment, for just under $600,000. Less than a year later, Bow Valley purchased Vancouver-based Mainland Foundry & Engineering Ltd. for $1.8 million. Flame-Master, although not big, was considered a well-run and efficient operation that could, as Doc pointed out to the board, be an "interesting and profitable diversification for Bow Valley." Mainland represented a bigger commitment.

Mainland had been formed by the father of the man who now ran it, Jim Graham. Starting from scratch in an old corrugated-iron building on Vancouver's Powell Street, he had driven out to the Fraser River to hand-load, for 25 cents a truckful, the sand used for mouldings. The sand was not good and produced rough castings, but Graham, with the help only of hammer, chisel, and some old grinding wheels, worked the castings into a saleable form. Out of those humble beginnings in the 1930s, Graham and his son had built the company.

From foundry castings they had expanded into a sheet-metal and fabricating shop specializing in the design, manufacture, and installation of air-collection systems for shavings and dust. From there they had developed a supply side to the business, selling mechanical power-transmission and other equipment to the resource industries. By the end of the Second World War, Mainland's foundry, sheet-metal and fabrication shop and its supply business were generating $500,000 in annual sales. Over the following two decades, branch warehouses were opened and, in 1967, the year before it was acquired by Bow Valley, Mainland purchased 23 acres of land at Richmond, B.C., to house a brand new foundry serviced by both river frontage and a railroad spur.

Meanwhile, Bow Valley had completed its largest takeover to date, that of Bullock Helicopters, for $2.95 million, and had also purchased Connors Drilling Ltd., a diamond-drilling company, for $1 million. A new element in takeover finance had been introduced for the Connors, Bullock and Mainland acquisitions in that Bow Valley, at the suggestion of Harry Van Rensselaer, had paid partially for these companies by issuing shares from its treasury. The Bullock acquisition price was made up of $700,000 in cash and 150,000 Bow Valley shares; Mainland was bought for $1.555 million in cash and 11,150 common shares, while the Connors acquisition was made completely with 80,000 shares. With Bow Valley shares prospering on the stock market, the issue of its stock for acquisitions was a relatively cheap method of financing takeovers. Nevertheless, the cash element of the takeovers, plus the continued expansion of the oil and gas side of the business, meant that larger external financings continued to be needed.

A Trans-Border Financing

In 1967, Doc and his financial advisors decided upon their boldest financing to date: to reduce bank borrowing, they would float an issue of equity simultaneously on both sides of the border. The fact that Bow Valley planned to sell twice as many shares in the U.S. as in Canada spoke volumes about where growing Canadian oil and gas companies had to look for risk capital.

Intensive discussions were entered into with the company's chief investment advisors, Greenshields in Canada and Shields in New York, about the pricing of the issue, while the preliminary prospectus had to be constantly revised to take into account new acquisitions and dispositions. Investors like to have a clear snapshot of companies in which they are going to invest, but Bow Valley under Doc Seaman's guidance was a company that found it difficult to stand still long enough to have snapshots taken.

To understand the logic behind all these acquisitions was to be able to see at once through and beyond them. Amid this bewildering array of drilling equipment of all shapes and sizes, manufacturing and distribution facilities, oil and gas production, fleets of aircraft and helicopters, property development and mining, shone through the simple concept of profitability. To Doc these were not helicopters and rigs but helicopter and rig *businesses,* for the products or services of which there was a demand or potential demand. He saw, therefore, businesses which could generate funds for further corporate growth and expansion and, in particular, for further expansion into oil and gas exploration and production.

For the investor somewhat bewildered by the range of snaps in the corporate family album, the constant that ran through Bow Valley's breakneck growth was a sparkling stock market performance. The price record, adjusted for the stock splits of four for one in 1963 and two for one in 1967, was more than impressive. The annual stock price highs in the years 1963 to 1968 were $2.75, $3.625, $6.875, $9.625, $11.125 and — up to March 22, 1968 — $16.625. For investors, that growth in the share price was the distillation of all they needed to know about Bow Valley's track record, and the fact that Doc and his management team knew what they were about.

From a single modest shot-hole rig, Bow Valley now had a drilling fleet with fifty-four rigs ranging from six 12,000 foot rigs to nineteen seismic rigs — the legacy of Seaman & Warnke. This fleet was operated by three divisions: Hi-Tower, Sedco, and Antelope, which had been acquired, along with its owner, Bobby Brownridge — a personable and popular man who would be important in the further development of Bow Valley's drilling operations — in 1965. A full 75 per cent of the company's employees were still occupied on the drilling side, but the oil and gas exploration facet of the business remained Doc's focus. By the time of the 1968 share flotation, that side of the business was ready to come out of the woodwork, indeed, *had* to come out of the woodwork if the true value of the company was to be recognized by investors.

The share offering was a success, and Bow Valley's sale of 400,000 shares in the U.S. and 200,000 shares in Canada raised $5.15 million for the company. Not only did the sale broaden the market for the company's shares in Canada, but it also led to the creation of a public market in the United States through a listing on the American Stock Exchange. Now, investment analysts had to be courted and the company could no longer play down its long-term oil and gas aspirations. The annual report for 1968 was, for the first time, a glossy affair, with full details of Bow Valley's oil and gas activities at the front.

During fiscal 1969, the company undertook its biggest financing. The massive oil find in 1968 at Prudhoe Bay in Alaska, and Bow Valley's interests in the Canadian Arctic nearby (about which more will be said shortly) led to a further healthy surge in Bow Valley's equity price. The Bank of New York's Ray Hammell pointed out that this share price strength presented an ideal opportunity to sell convertible debentures or preferred shares. The board decided to approach Bow Valley's investment advisors with a view to making a $10 million offering.

Once again, it was New York rather than Toronto that was eager to pick up such an issue. Greenshields tried unsuccessfully for a couple of weeks to sell the issue in Toronto and Montreal. Harry Van Rensselaer managed to sell it in New York in the space of a single morning. The Chase Manhattan Bank and Bankers Trust Company picked up half each of a subsequent $10 million issue of 5 per cent convertible second preference shares.

More Problems of Success

Success and expansion — in particular acquisitions — were meanwhile creating their own problems and concerns for Bow Valley's management and board. While the principles of corporate integration and generating funds for exploration through acquisitions were sound, there were undoubtedly difficulties in administering and monitoring the elements of the growing Bow Valley empire. Steps were taken in 1968 and 1969 to allocate responsibilities for subsidiaries to specific local directors, and also to beef up the head office staff within an overall corporate reorganization. At the board level, Bill Howard suggested that a number of committees be set up to facilitate the directors' execution of their responsibilities.

There was even an element within the board that suggested that a moratorium be placed on acquisitions until the corporate organization had been overhauled. Nevertheless, Doc's view was that acquisitions were a key element of Bow Valley's success. While there would inevitably be problems arising from corporate diversity, the principle remained sound. So the acquisitions continued.

In February, 1969, Bow Valley acquired a 50 per cent interest in Computamatics Limited, a Calgary-based computer software company, and its 83.5 per cent-owned subsidiary, Western Research & Development Ltd., from Rod McDaniel. McDaniel had now not only evolved into one of the country's most respected petroleum consultants, but had also become a key figure within Alberta's tight-knit corporate and political establishment.

Under the well-qualified leadership of Joe Lukacs, Western Research was a technical organization engaged primarily in air and water pollution control, which Doc rightly saw as an area of growing importance. Bow Valley would later buy out Western Research in its entirety.

In July, 1969, in return for $500,000 and 36,000 Bow Valley shares, the company acquired Wonderly & Kershaw Petrochemical Services Ltd. Wonderly & Kershaw operated and maintained gas and sulphur plants on a contract basis, along with the construction of small-diameter pipelines and the transportation of oilfield equipment.

The following couple of years saw a spate of further small acquisitions spread over the Western provinces and down into the United States: Griffith Bros. Drilling Limited in Lac Du Bonnet, Manitoba; Elworthy & Company Ltd. in Vancouver; Dominion Instruments in Edmonton; Atmos Engineering Sales in Calgary; MacPherson Drilling Co. Inc. in Montrose, Colorado.

All these operations fitted into Bow Valley's existing interests.

Elworthy's specialized machinery and control equipment for the saw-mill business complemented the range of products manufactured for and sold to the forest products industry by Mainland. Atmos's heating and ventilating equipment dovetailed with the activities of Flame-Master. MacPherson's diamond-drilling operations enhanced those of Connors.

There were, of course, a number of dispositions: Castle Oil & Gas, Canadian Oil Tool, Northward Aviation, the Australian drilling operation, all of which had proved problematic in one way or another. However, the additions far outweighed the subtractions. This agglomeration of companies sometimes caused a headache for oil industry analysts, but in fact for every company acquired, at least ten more were analysed and rejected. Doc's overall objective remained unchanged: to build up the company's oil and gas interests.

As the go-go 1960s turned into the turbulent 1970s, Bow Valley's reputation as an oil and gas company was to be enhanced first by its deep involvement in Arctic exploration, and second by its bold move into the international arena. The key to its overseas involvement lay in its most important acquisition to date — an acquisition significant not so much for its actual cost but for the exploration commitments into which it would lead Bow Valley. The acquired company's name was Syracuse.

7
Into the Global Arena with Syracuse

By the end of his second decade in the oil business, Doc Seaman had masterminded the creation of a conglomerate with significant corporate clout. Just as the acquisition of Hi-Tower ten years before had taken Doc and his brothers into a whole new corporate realm, so the more numerous acquisitions of the 1960s, and gradual expansion of the oil and gas side of the business, had now taken Bow Valley to corporate heights far above those of Hi-Tower. Gross income in 1970, at more than $44 million, was seven times greater than a decade before; net income, at $2.365 million, was also more than seven times larger over the same period.

At the end of the 1960s, Doc had presented a five year plan to the board entitled: "Blueprint for Growth 1970-1974." In it he indicated that the majority of the company's growth over the period would stem from acquisitions. In the event, the course of the company into the mid 1970s would be set by a single acquisition made in 1971. The target company, Syracuse, was the brainchild of yet another living legend within the Calgary oilpatch, Angus Mackenzie.

Mackenzie was a tall, charismatic Albertan whose parents had come from Scotland's Isle of Lewis. He had had little formal education and for much of his earlier years had been more intent on roistering than on building either a reputation or a fortune in the oilpatch. He did realize, however, that he did not relish working for others. He had gone into partnership with Tate Blanchet, with whom he'd been in the army during the war, in a small company involved in mapping and photo-geology.

It was through this business that he first started dealing in petroleum lands. For a filing fee of $250 and a performance bond of $12,500 (in order to make sure that work obligations were carried out), Mackenzie could secure the rights to 100,000 acres of petroleum and natural gas reservations. He would then go out and peddle these lands to third parties for — he hoped — something in excess of his costs, plus a royalty of 2 per cent to 4 per cent on any subsequent production.

Around this time Mackenzie ran into Jim Palmer, a man who would be his lifelong friend and partner. Palmer had been born in Prince

Edward Island and studied law at McGill and Dalhousie before returning to Charlottetown to article. At the end of 1953, he decided to find a more exciting spot to practise his legal skills and moved to Calgary. Mackenzie met Palmer when the young lawyer was working as a landman for Texaco in Calgary, and started to do business deals with him after he had moved to the law firm of Burnet Duckworth.

Funded by Palmer and private interests based in Edmonton, Mackenzie filed on more and more exploration lands, gradually building up a large, if low-quality, portfolio. "It was like being a junk man," he recalls. Mackenzie's style of operation was also less than grandiose. Living almost on a hand-to-mouth basis, he'd work out of his car, cadging a cup of coffee or the use of a telephone from friends and colleagues. One of these was Bill Siebens, who along with his father, Harold, was renowned for his own impeccable timing and skill in land dealing. Siebens would become Mackenzie's partner in a number of international deals in the following two decades.

Mackenzie realized — or at least assumed — that he'd missed the opportunity of doing the really good deals in Western Canada, the deals executed by the likes of Bobby Brown and Frank McMahon, the legendary czars of Home Oil and Pacific Petroleums. So he decided that the answer was to find some place in the world that had petroleum potential, but which had not been drilled, a place where land rights could be picked up cheaply. He and Jim Palmer decided that the North Sea was such a place.

In 1964, with funds from a deal that he'd done with Bill Siebens' help, Mackenzie and Palmer set off for Europe with almost no money and scarcely any contacts, but with lots of time and almost limitless amounts of chutzpah.

The two men did have one important contact, the Toronto Dominion's London representative, Herb White, to whom they had been introduced by their local Calgary bank manager, Galloway Macdonald. The craggy, white-haired, and charming White proved of great use to the duo, and helped them make the contacts that enabled them to file on some onshore concessions in Hertfordshire in England and on the Scottish border at Roxborough, on land that belonged to Sir Alec Douglas-Home, a future British Prime Minister. Now they had their names on a land map.

Who Are These Guys?

Shortly after they made their first visit to Europe, the Norwegian government announced that it was seeking applications for offshore

63

licences. Mackenzie and Palmer headed for Oslo and announced themselves as holders of significant lands both in Canada and the United Kingdom! When the Norwegian government wanted to see their balance sheet, they had a little problem, since they had no money. They had a geological map of the North Sea prepared by a Calgary geologist, Madeline Suska, whose teenage years had been spent partially in blowing up Nazi installations and partially in prison camp.

The map was a work of considerable imagination, since they did not have access to any of the seismic work carried out by the major companies. Nevertheless, they knew that the big oil companies were interested in the same general area, so they applied for twenty blocks, any two of which they would take. To their astonishment, they were awarded a couple. One of the concessions was adjacent to a block taken by Gulf, and thus considered to have at least some potential.

To bid in company with the Seven Sisters, the corporate rulers of world oil, was an act of almost unparalleled bravado. To some, in particular the big oil companies themselves, it appeared at best as an act of irresponsibility; at worst something close to downright fraud. At the operating meetings, the buttoned-down executives from Gulf or Chevron would look down their noses at Mackenzie and Palmer as if to ask: "Who are these guys?"

Next to Mackenzie's shoestring operation, the smallest company involved in the Norwegian offshore licences was the U.S.-based Phillips Petroleum, which rated as a giant by Canadian standards. Moreover, Angus Mackenzie's victory proved somewhat problematic, for now he had to do something with the land. Specifically, he had to drill a well on it. He steadied himself and reflected that it was just a matter of taking things a step at a time. If seismic work established what appeared to be oil-bearing geological structures, then somebody would surely drill a well for him.

He clearly needed partners to share the project's financial burdens, and was fortunate enough to find a consortium of Norwegian interests headed by Den norske Creditbank, the country's largest bank. Den norske Creditbank's rationale for becoming involved was a long way from exploration roulette. If the North Sea proved to be a major petroleum province, then DnC wanted a piece of the action. They wanted to be involved in exploration to learn the ropes. Mackenzie also found that he was very much of a mind with the bank's head, Johann Melander. Seeking money from the bank, Mackenzie went to see Melander with a rather staid lawyer. The conversation was oblique, with both sides at first skating around the sordid issue of money, until Mackenzie, to his lawyer's horror, said: "How long will it take for your bank to decide about lending some money to Syracuse?" The lawyer, flustered, told Mackenzie behind his hand that he shouldn't press the issue. Mackenzie asked the same question again. "About five minutes," Melander replied. Syracuse had the money.

Another key contact in financing Mackenzie and Palmer's European offshore concessions was Louis Marx, of Marx Toy fame. Mackenzie had been introduced to Marx in New York by Billy McMahon, the son of Frank McMahon, and when he needed some additional funding he simply dropped in to see Marx and his right-hand man, Stan Rawn. The Marx interests were eventually put into a company called Pan-Ocean, the first operator of Mackenzie and Palmer's — and subsequently Bow Valley's — U.K. North Sea acreage.

With the help of the partners, Mackenzie was able to participate in a joint $2 million seismic program and take part in the joint meetings of concession holders, something the majors obviously deeply resented. But his biggest potential hurdle was that of drilling a well. After searching around, the consortium discovered that Phillips had a rig available, and was willing, in return for a 5 per cent stake in the hole, to drill it at close to cost. Conditions were perfect, the sea was calm, and in just two weeks the Phillips rig was able to drill a perfect 7,000 foot dry hole! But the important point was that Mackenzie's consortium had drilled the hole. Now he was indisputably part of the club.

By the end of 1965, Mackenzie was travelling to Europe every four to six weeks and his list of contacts was growing impressively. They included Rupert Hambro, the merchant banker, and Bill Sterling, a notorious Scotsman from a famous aristocratic family. Through Sterling, in turn, Mackenzie met the ruler of Abu Dhabi, an occasional weekend guest at the Sterling's country estate. This, almost inevitably, would lead to Mackenzie gaining land concessions in the Middle East. In the U.K., meanwhile, the aristocratic touch of the Sterlings and the Hambros was useful in gaining concessions from the British government. Unlike Alberta, where land was either issued for cash or put up for auction, the British system was based mainly on negotiations. Charm and connections helped — and Angus Mackenzie soon added the latter to his abundant supply of the former.

Mackenzie, "the big Canadian," with his bristling moustache and his great shock of black hair, became an inveterate globe-trotter, living on planes and prepared, at the drop of a petroleum licence, to head for the Maldive Islands, or Abu Dhabi, or Indonesia. He was not only extremely well read but also was considered to have a brilliant mind, "unclouded," as one of his colleagues pointed out, "by a university education." Everybody liked Mackenzie. He always had a way of making anybody he met feel that that person was important, the man or woman of the moment. But it wasn't just that he was bright, personable, and radiated energy. He also developed a reputation for trust. He wouldn't squeeze the last drop out of oil deals, like many of his compatriots, but would make sure that there was enough left on the table for the other guy. This led people to want to deal with him again.

Meanwhile, the areas in which Mackenzie was operating demanded a certain flair. When dealing with a potentate whose income was $1 million a day, it required some imagination to come up with appropriate gifts that might sway the sheik's generosity in granting petroleum concessions. In one case, Mackenzie "procured" a pure white falcon as a gift. The expenditure was carried on the Syracuse books quite simply, as "a falcon," although Mackenzie hoped that this would be interpreted by the auditors to mean a Ford car! On another occasion, Mackenzie got involved in a no-win bet with the ruler of a Middle Eastern kingdom which resulted in him having to purchase, out of his own pocket, a Rolls Royce for the ruler's energy minister!

Mackenzie and Palmer subsequently parlayed half their European interests into a controlling block of shares in a small Canadian-registered company called Sage Petroleums. It was then that Dick Harris emerged on the scene. Harris was a geologist who had gone straight from the University of Texas, to serve in the U.S. Navy during the Korean War. Then he had joined a Houston-based consulting company before being sent to Alberta to work primarily with the natural gas industry. Young, enthusiastic, exceptionally bright, and a smooth promoter, Harris was considered ideal by Mackenzie and Palmer. He would run Sage and help build Syracuse, the company that would ultimately be taken over by Doc Seaman.

Mackenzie, Palmer, and Harris formed a formidable combination. Harris would read every new geological document available to try and spot likely new exploration areas around the world. Mackenzie would pursue the same objective through his growing list of contacts. Then the two men would sit down together and decide where they might obtain land ahead of the pack. Once they had decided, Mackenzie would simply jump on a plane and go there. Palmer, meanwhile, would apply his outstanding legal mind to the deals, in particular the tax angles.

A South African office was opened in 1967, headed by Fred Wellhauser, an affable and talented young Swiss geologist and geophysical consultant from Geneva. In 1970, Wellhauser moved to London. As a consultant, Mackenzie used Stu McColl a great deal. McColl was a Canadian geologist with widespread experience in Brazil and Europe. He had met Mackenzie in the early 1950s and had run into him over the years as he moved on to work for Imperial Oil and Dome Petroleum. In the late 1960s, when McColl had decided that a corporate career was not for him, Mackenzie had turned up on his doorstep in Oslo. This had led to McColl consulting for Mackenzie and eventually working for him full-time.

In the mid 1960s, Mackenzie had put Sage into Syracuse, which he and Palmer controlled, and taken the whole thing public. By the end of the 1960s, Syracuse had — for a company of its size — a vast international landspread.

The Roots of Merger

The possibility of a link-up between Bow Valley and Syracuse had come up some years before, at around the time Harley Hotchkiss was leaving Alcon to link up with Carlo Von Maffei. The instigator of that deal had been Harry Van Rensselaer, who admired Dick Harris's talents. To Mackenzie and Palmer, Bow Valley was a very sizable operation. The prospect of swapping their interests in Syracuse for the much more solidly based Bow Valley shares was highly attractive. From Angus Mackenzie's point of view, sale was desirable because he liked building companies, not running them. Also, Syracuse was running up hefty debts in the process of building its international landspread.

Angus Mackenzie had first met Doc at the Earl Grey golf course in the early 1950s, and had watched as Doc grew in wealth and stature in the community. Doc had achieved millionaire status before Mackenzie could afford decent suits, but Mackenzie had always been impressed that Doc made time for him. Once Mackenzie decided to become serious about making a success of the oil business, Doc was to discover that the time was well spent. Mackenzie's corporate creation would be the source of a great deal of success for Bow Valley.

In May of 1967, Mackenzie, Palmer, and Harris had been invited to attend a meeting of Bow Valley's board. They thought they had been asked over to consider some form of amalgamation. However, the meeting had been a comedy of errors and misunderstandings. The men from Syracuse had given a brief resume of their operations and their company personnel, whereupon Harry Van Rensselaer had suggested that Alcon could employ the Syracuse personnel and that Alcon could then effectively manage Syracuse. This was not at all the understanding of Mackenzie and Palmer, who said that their ambitions were quite the reverse: that Syracuse would manage Alcon with a view to a merger at some stage in the future. After a lengthy discussion, Mackenzie, Palmer, and Harris left the Bow Valley boardroom, whereupon Bow Valley's directors decided to terminate any further negotiations with Syracuse on the terms that Mackenzie and Palmer wanted.

The international arena was no novelty for Bow Valley, at least when it came to the contract drilling business. With partners or alone, Bow Valley had been involved in drilling operations in Mexico, Australia, and Timor and had looked at possible deals in South America and India. However, those operations were quite different from those of pure exploration.

Bow Valley's oil and gas operations had been growing slowly but surely, and excitement at the end of the 1970s was concentrated on the company's Arctic acreage. Nevertheless, Doc still found the pace of growth frustrating. It was clear that expansion through land purchases and a piecemeal search for farm-in prospects was going to be a long process. Purchasing an existing oil company was one obvious means of acceleration. No company of its size appeared to offer more — or more globally spread — prospects than Syracuse.

One major problem from the Bow Valley board's point of view was the value of Syracuse. Reserves were relatively easy to evaluate, but land on which reserves had not yet been proved was much more difficult. In addition, the form of some of the Middle Eastern concessions, virtually etched on goat's hide, were problematic when it came to the strict legal interpretations of the U.S. Securities and Exchange Commission, to which Bow Valley, with its listing on the Amex, was now subject.

To help evaluate the company, Harry Van Rensselaer brought in Charles Maxwell, a leading oil industry analyst, from the investment house Cyrus J. Lawrence in New York. Also, Lorne Inglis, a well-known analyst with Richardson Securities, and Don MacKenzie, a former Imperial Oil executive with knowledge of the North Sea, were retained as consultants.

Intensive negotiations were held around November of 1970 and it was finally agreed to negotiate a merger on the basis of exchanging one Bow Valley share for five of those of Syracuse. On April 30, 1971, by Certificate of Amalgamation, 1,312,556 shares of Bow Valley were issued in return for the 6.5 million outstanding shares of Syracuse, putting a value of around $20 million on Syracuse. Since established reserves accounted for only around $7 million of this sum, the acquisition represented a considerable act of faith in the value of Syracuse's landspread. The faith would prove well justified.

With the acquisition of Syracuse, Bow Valley of course acquired more than just a global landspread; it acquired Dick Harris and Fred

Wellhauser, who would play key roles in the expansion of Bow Valley's oil and gas interests over the coming decade. Angus Mackenzie would move on to found other companies and expand his global interests, although he would remain very much involved with Bow Valley's North Sea adventures through Sunningdale Oils, another company that he controlled with Jim Palmer. His motto would remain: "Keep it simple. Get the land. Drill the well," although that "simple" approach would lead him through corporate adventures that would strain credibility if written in a novel. He would remain close to Doc and B.J. through their interests in golf and hunting. Fifteen years after the Syracuse merger, Doc and B.J. would still travel almost every year to shoot with Mackenzie at Keir, the Sterling's Scottish estate. For a couple of years, Jim Palmer served as a much-valued member of Bow Valley's board, until he felt that he had to resign because of potential conflict through his other oil interests.

One of the main benefits Syracuse brought to Bow Valley was its very strong natural gas land position in Northern Alberta. These reserves were to play a major part in boosting Bow Valley's cash flows in the 1970s when the company most needed them to finance overseas commitments. Indeed, within just a few years, Syracuse's gas interests alone would justify the takeover. Gas prices in Western Canada would soar in the coming decade, making production much more profitable. These soaring prices in turn were part of a worldwide surge in both oil and natural gas. That surge became associated with an organization that had been founded in obscurity but by the end of 1973 was on the front page of every newspaper and magazine in the world: the Organization of Petroleum Exporting Countries, OPEC.

8
The OPEC Crisis and the Alberta Boom

When he decided to merge Syracuse with Bow Valley, even Doc Seaman had no idea of the magnitude of expenditure, or the scale of exploration success, into which the marriage would lead the company. But neither did virtually anyone in the petroleum business have any idea of the economic turmoil, and resultant political intervention, that oil would precipitate in the coming decade. As the Syracuse merger was being finalized, the writing was already on the wall.

It was clear to Doc Seaman in 1970 that an energy shortage was coming in the United States. This shortage was expected to have a profound impact on the already strong U.S. demand for Canadian petroleum resources. In the event, however, that shortage was to have a profound worldwide effect, and help precipitate economic crises that continued to shake the global economy for more than a decade.

To put the oil crises of the 1970s into perspective, it is necessary to look at the peculiar nature of petroleum as a commodity. Petroleum, from the Latin "rock-oil," had by the nineteenth century been known for several thousand years. The Chinese reputedly piped natural gas in bamboo tubes a thousand years before the birth of Christ; in Biblical times ashphalt and pitch were used as binding and embalming materials; in Alberta itself, long before Europeans appeared, the natives used the material that oozed at intervals from the banks of the Athabasca River to caulk their canoes.

The first great oil boom arose from the discovery that petroleum, once refined, could be used for lighting and lubricating. Lubricating demands grew from the proliferation of steam-powered machinery that drove the industrial revolutions of Europe and North America in the first half of the nineteenth century. Lighting during the same period still depended largely on candles and whale-oil lamps. Pioneering work by a Canadian, Dr. Abraham Gesner, in which ashphalt was turned into illuminating oils helped pave the way for an upsurge both in oil exploration and in technology to find uses for the substance. Over the following century, those twin searches would play a key role in shaping the modern world. Ironically, it was imagined at one time that Thomas Edison's electric light might deal a death blow to the oil business! However, the subsequent development of the internal-combustion engine, the explosive growth of the automobile industry, the advent of air travel, the industrial use of hydrocarbons as fuel, and the development of petrochemicals, slowly but surely hooked the developed world on petroleum.

In the twenty-five years following the end of the Second World War, petroleum consumption continued to double every ten years, as it had done since the 1880s. Astonishingly, however, the wellhead price had actually gone down over the ninety-year period as a result of the enormous success of the major oil companies in finding new reserves, most recently in the Middle East, and in controlling national producers. The major oil companies, or the "Seven Sisters" as they had been dubbed — Exxon, Mobil, Gulf, Texaco, Standard Oil of California, Shell and British Petroleum — saw that their economic interests lay in promoting the increased use of cheap oil. However, this goal inevitably had to come up against the fact that petroleum was a finite resource. The age of cheap oil had to come to an end, and when the end came, it came with a vengeance.

In its earliest days, petroleum had played havoc with the market because of its peculiar nature. Unlike minerals, which had to be laboriously mined, petroleum, once discovered, flowed — often in great abundance — to its grateful discoverer. "Gushers" would flood both the surrounding fields and the economic market. In southwestern Ontario, for example, where the early Canadian oil business was developing even before the activity in Pennsylvania that is now conventionally regarded as the "birth of the oil business," discoveries in the 1860s caused the price of a barrel of oil to drop from $11 to 40 cents within a matter of months.

John D. Rockefeller was the first to seek to control the terrible disorder that a substance with such an unpredictable supply could wreak on "free" markets. He did so through gaining control of the refining and transportation of oil. He was so successful in his market manipulation that he sparked the U.S. anti-trust movement. His Standard Oil Trust was broken up in 1911. However, three of the Standard "children" — Exxon, Mobil, and Standard Oil of California — ranked among the Seven Sisters. In the post-war years, the Sisters' control had become synonymous with cheap oil. In the 1970s, economic forces, clothed in the garb of the nations of the Organization of Petroleum Exporting Countries, were to change all that.

Dependence on Imports

For virtually the first century of the petroleum age, until 1950, the United States dominated world oil production. In 1950, the U.S. produced fully one-half of all the world's oil. Furthermore, the country's production would continue to grow for the next two decades. But by 1965, other huge oil sources had been discovered, primarily in the Middle East. In 1965, Middle Eastern production as a whole outstripped that of the US.

By 1970, U.S. production peaked, but its demand for oil did not. The events of the ensuing three years have been portrayed as a political drama in which the nation's of OPEC suddenly began to flex their economic muscles. They are, perhaps, more an example of the undeniable power of market forces; a tide of rising oil prices on which OPEC bobbed like a gold-plated cork.

OPEC was created in 1960 with five founding members — Saudi Arabia, Iran, Iraq, Kuwait, and Venezuela — in response to the decision by Exxon, the world's largest oil company, to drop the price of oil. The "cartel" had no influence whatsoever on Exxon's decision. When Israel invaded Egypt in 1967, the Arab producers imposed an embargo, but the Shah of Iran broke ranks and the embargo crumbled. Two years later, however, Libya was able to squeeze higher prices out of Occidental Petroleum, a Los Angeles-based company which, under its brilliant head, Dr. Armand Hammer, had broken into the preserve of the Seven Sisters. As the U.S. began to suck in more foreign oil and the world market tightened, OPEC rapidly felt the balance of supply and demand moving in its favor. In 1971, further price increases were imposed under the Tehran and Tripoli agreements. By 1973, the switch from a buyers' to a sellers' market was ready to take place.

In October, Egypt and Syria invaded Israel and OPEC approached the majors with a view to gaining a "substantial" price increase. Shortly afterwards, the Arabs imposed another embargo. This time, thanks to the tightness of the market, it stuck. By December, the price of oil on the spot-market, where oil not under long-term contract is sold, hit $17 a barrel. On January 1, 1974, the official OPEC price was increased to $11.65 a barrel. It had quadrupled in just three months.

Alberta's New Charms

For Canada, where the vast majority of petroleum was produced in Alberta, the implications were profound. Since Leduc, the main

72

problem of Alberta producers had been to sell as much oil as they found. Central and Eastern Canada preferred cheaper imported oil. However, under the National Oil Policy of 1960, the Diefenbaker Tories had created an artificial "Ottawa Valley Line," markets west of which were to be served by Western Canadian oil. As late as 1969, the smaller Canadian companies, such as Bow Valley, represented by the Independent Petroleum Association of Canada, had pressed Ottawa to build a pipeline for Canadian oil into Montreal in the interests of national energy security. They had been turned down. Now, with the quadrupling of the world oil price, Albertan oil suddenly held new economic charms. The issues of pricing and revenue sharing between federal and provincial governments now represented a political minefield. The critical questions were: what should the domestic and export prices be? and how should the revenue pie be split?

For the Alberta government, the answer was obvious. Led by Peter Lougheed, a bright and aggressive lawyer who in just a few years had revived the moribund provincial Tory party and grabbed power from the Social Credit government that had ruled the province for thirty-six years, Alberta saw this as its chance to gain a place in the economic sun.

Mining industries in central and eastern Canada commanded world prices for their commodities, said Lougheed, so why shouldn't Alberta do the same? Pierre Trudeau's federal Liberal government — relying for its power on the oil-consuming provinces of Ontario and Quebec — inevitably saw things differently. How could Albertans side with the rapacious OPEC nations? they asked. The domestic price had to be lower than the OPEC price. However, when it came to exports to the U.S., said Ottawa, OPEC prices should be charged, in which case the federal government would cream off the extra revenue through an export levy. Not surprisingly, Peter Lougheed and the Albertan producers fumed.

For most of 1974, a war of words and rival tax and royalty increases waged between the two levels of government. The battle was greatly complicated both by the complexities of resource ownership and the long-stored historical resentments held against central Canada by the West. The oil industry found itself caught in the middle.

Alberta trebled its royalties on the new, higher domestic prices, which were still held well below OPEC levels. Ottawa responded in the May, 1974, budget by declaring that provincial royalties would be non-deductible for federal tax purposes. It seemed like a classic example of killing the industry golden goose. The industry voted with its exploration dollars and headed for the U.S. border, badly hurting the prospects of drilling companies such as Bow Valley's subsidiaries, Hi-Tower and Sedco. The stock market plummeted. The major oil companies' shares dropped 40 per cent of their value in the final nine months of 1974, but the Western producers' group, which included Bow Valley, dived 54 per cent, helping to drag the entire index down by 27 per cent. For Bow Valley, the timing of the crisis could not have been worse. Not only was it hit by the drop off in domestic exploration, but its involvement in an enormously expensive North Sea well, about which more will be written shortly, brought it to the brink of financial crisis. Bow Valley survived. Moreover, the clouds of political dispute also turned out to have silver linings.

By the end of 1974, it was obvious to both levels of government that their warring was damaging the entire industry, and hence their own potential revenues. First Ottawa and then Alberta made significant concessions, and although it was not obvious at the time, these new concessions, combined with higher prices, would spark a western boom of unprecedented proportions.

Natural Gas: A Boom in the Cinderella Resource

Although Bow Valley would find most of its success in the coming decade overseas, it also participated to the full in this western boom. Despite all the headlines about oil politics and economics both at home and abroad, the real driving force behind the domestic boom of the 1970s was not oil, but natural gas.

Until the mid-1970s natural gas had always been a cinderella resource. During much of Alberta's petroleum past, the gas produced in conjunction with oil had simply been burned off or "flared" at the wellhead. Little effort was made to transport it or build markets for it. The fundamental reason was that, whereas oil was easily collected, stored, and transported, natural gas was bulky and thus difficult to store and expensive to transport.

Despite these drawbacks, in the years after the Second World War, the attractions of natural gas became more apparent. It was not only abundant, but also convenient, clean-burning, and dependable. As a result, a vast network of gas pipelines was built across the U.S. Canada was slower in developing its natural gas resources. Nevertheless, in the 1950s, the business took off with the construction of the TransCanada PipeLine from Alberta to Eastern Canada and the Westcoast Transmission line to the West, as well as export lines to serve U.S. markets. Canadian gas use almost trebled in the 1960s, reaching 917 billion cubic feet (BCF) in 1970, while exports increased more than sevenfold over the same period to 780 BCF. However, natural gas was less than a major moneyspinner for the producers. The gas pipe-lines were government-regulated utilities. Their growth depended on the size of their systems. As their principal interest therefore was in maximizing the volume of their throughput, they had a strong vested interest in keeping prices down in order to promote demand.

At the beginning of the 1970s, gas consumers in Canada were pay-ing an average of 63 cents a thousand cubic feet (MCF) for their gas, but transportation charges made up the bulk of the cost. In most cases, producers received less than 15 cents an MCF. It was this very system of fixed pipeline charges, combined with the practice of pricing gas when it came out of the pipeline rather than when it went in, that were to be the roots of a revenue bonanza once petroleum prices took off.

After Peter Lougheed swept to office in 1971, he had soon picked on energy in general, and natural gas in particular, as the area in which he planned to take a tougher line with central Canada and Ottawa. A report from the Alberta Energy Resources Conservation Board had estimated that natural gas was underpriced at the wellhead by between 10 and 20 cents an MCF. TransCanada PipeLines officials rejected such a price hike, hardly increasing the Alberta premier's already slim regard for the company. However in 1973-74, the federal government decided to link domestic natural gas prices to those of oil by pricing them at 85 per cent of the oil price at the "Toronto City Gate," that is, where TransCanada delivered its gas to the local Ontario and Quebec utility companies. Ottawa also decided to link gas export prices directly to the much higher export price of oil. Perhaps due to the bitter dispute over the oil export levy, Ottawa made no export levy on natural gas.

Due to the fixed pipeline charges, increased prices paid by con-sumers meant much greater increases to producers. If consumers paid 60 cents an MCF and pipeline charges were 50 cents an MCF, then producers would receive 10 cents an MCF for their gas. However, if the price to the consumer doubled to $1 an MCF, while the trans-portation charge remained constant, then producers would receive 50 cents, an increase of 400 per cent! In fact, between 1970 and 1977, when the domestic consumer price for gas increased more than two-and-one-half times, the price to the producer, before royalties and taxes, increased by a factor closer to ten! Export prices increased even more sharply, as did export demand. For domestic explorers and producers, gas was suddenly the place to be, and Bow Valley — thanks in large part to the Albertan lands the company had acquired with Syracuse, and the lands it would soon pick up — was already there.

Bow Valley's exploration and production activities in the first half of the 1970s consisted primarily in finding and bringing onstream additional gas, mainly in the Wandering River area of northeastern Alberta. By 1976, the company had more than eighty gas wells in the area. In May of that year, the initial gas gathering system and compression facilities were completed. These facilities were designed to produce 30 million cubic feet (MMCF) of gas a day, of which Bow Valley's share would be around 20 MMCF. Four months earlier, the company had placed two shallow gas fields in production, at Gough Lake and Edgerton, bringing the company another 5 MMCF daily, while it already had around 5 MMCF a day coming from its major interest in another shallow gas project at Medicine Hat in southeastern Alberta.

While these operations were less than sexy in the eyes of investors, they were Bow Valley's first big petroleum moneyspinners. Largely because of natural gas, revenue from domestic oil and gas operations had increased more than fivefold, to $14.5 million, in the five years up to the end of fiscal 1977. However, Wandering River's first full year of production in fiscal 1977 had a far more dramatic impact on company profits. Until that year, more money had always been plowed back into oil and gas than had been received from it. The service side of the business, dominated as ever by the oilwell drilling operations overseen by B.J. and Don, had provided the vast bulk of revenues — and all the profits. In 1977, however, domestic oil and gas provided pre-tax profits of $5.5 million out of total income before tax of just over $8 million.

These profits could not have come at a better time. Bow Valley's overseas commitments were proving a critical drain on resources, and the area that had just a few years before seemed like the focus of Canadian exploration for the rest of the century — the Canadian Arctic — was about to receive a severe setback.

76

9
Arctic Adventures

Conventional wisdom in the North American oil and gas community at the end of the 1960s — following the huge find at Prudhoe Bay on the North Slope of Alaska — held that the continent's petroleum future lay in the Far North. The Mackenzie Delta and then the Beaufort Sea were indeed Canada's exploration hot-spots for the ensuing decade. But activity was dogged by both exploratory and political frustration.

Bow Valley moved early to become active in the Delta and the Beaufort, and even earlier to participate in the Panarctic consortium set up to drill further east in the Arctic Islands, but it is a tribute to the company's management that it made profits from its Arctic involvement although not a drop of oil had been produced from any of these northern areas by the mid 1980s.

Doc Seaman never got carried away with "northern dreams," as did some of his colleagues. He was also quick to realize the practical difficulties and possible delays in producing Arctic oil. When it came to the Panarctic consortium, although he was one of the first in, he was also one of the first to attempt a graceful exit once he realized that the operation was a financial drain whose returns — if they came at all — could come decades into the future. Finally, and perhaps most importantly, the huge overseas obligations that Syracuse would bring to Bow Valley would not have permitted the company the luxury of further Arctic expenditures anyway. Nevertheless, Bow Valley showed immaculate timing and shrewd husbandry of its Arctic interests at a time when such interests were *de rigueur* for the discriminating oilman.

A key figure in turning the company's attention to the North was Gordon Darling, who had succeeded Harley Hotchkiss in heading Bow Valley's oil and gas operation in 1967. Darling's corporate origins at Imperial Oil were important. One of a group of employees who left the giant in the late 1960s due to dissatisfaction with centralization of the company, he nevertheless came imbued with Imperial's exploration philosophy, and Imperial's philosophy at the time was: "look north."

This philosophy was based partly on the assumption that the Western sedimentary basin was largely played out. For Imperial, a large company with significant production requirements to feed its huge refining and marketing network, the perennial need was to replace reserves. Reserves of sufficient magnitude were considered far more likely to be found in the frontier areas.

Although Bow Valley's situation was quite different from that of Imperial — and although Imperial's move out of Alberta would prove something of a strategic mistake — Doc decided to look north, and in terms of the company's public profile and stock market performance at least, the move paid off.

Bow Valley's first involvement with northern exploration came with the company's participation in Panarctic, a joint venture between a number of Canadian companies and the federal government to explore in the Arctic Islands. Wallace Pratt, the great American geologist, declared shortly after the Second World War that the great frozen desert of the Arctic Islands might cover huge petroleum reserves. Pratt's assessment was of purely theoretical significance, since nobody at the time saw how petroleum could be transported from such a remote and hostile area. However, towards the end of the 1950s, when Doc's exploration interests were still confined to taking pieces of a few "edge" wells in Saskatchewan, Ottawa's Geological Survey of Canada produced a highly optimistic report on the area. In 1961, enthused by the Islands' potential, Jack Gallagher, the smooth and handsome promoter who ran fledgling Dome Petroleum, operated the first well to be drilled in the high Arctic, just 1,000 miles from the North Pole at Winter Harbour on Melville Island. The hole was dry, but the achievement lay in the fact that the well had been drilled at all.

The man who really promoted the Arctic Islands dream was J.C. "Cam" Sproule, another visionary geologist who became obsessed with the North. Doc had been approached by Sproule to participate in the Panarctic consortium he was trying to pull together to invest $20 million in Arctic Islands exploration. Sproule had already persuaded Dome, CP Oil and Gas, and mining company Cominco to join his venture.

Doc's primary interest in the Islands was as a potential job for the company's drilling side, which in concert with Commonwealth Petroleum Services Ltd., which was run by Doc's friend John Scrymgeour, had put together a joint venture specifically to drill in the Arctic. However, since the two companies could not be sure of drilling contracts, Doc realized that this new venture had to be assessed purely on its exploration merits.

Panarctic had committed to its program more than 50,000,000 acres of land in the Arctic Islands and had the exclusive rights to explore on those lands. Seismic activity commenced in March, 1968, and it was planned to follow up with a multi-well drilling program beginning early in 1969. Doc pointed out to the board that the Islands represented one of the last situations where the company might acquire substantial potential oil-bearing lands. The board agreed, and they decided to invest $500,000 for a 2.258 per cent interest in Panarctic.

Commonwealth-Hi-Tower also succeeded in winning the drilling contracts for the consortium and, in 1969, two Commonwealth-Hi-Tower rigs began drilling on Melville Island. The first well, at Drake Point, experienced a gas blow-out — which at least established the presence of hydrocarbons. In the second test, at Sandy Point, the well was dry and abandoned. At the end of fiscal 1969, a third well, Panarctic Marie Bay, was still drilling. A third rig was scheduled to be in operation around November, 1969.

A Timely Farm-In on the Delta

Bow Valley's critical involvement in the Mackenzie Delta came via a well-timed farm-out taken from Numac Oil & Gas Ltd., a company founded by another self-made millionaire and old friend of Doc's, Bill McGregor. McGregor had some 320,000 acres of land in the shallow waters offshore the Mackenzie Delta. The holdings were in a checkerboard pattern and sat close to Imperial's choice acreage. McGregor had originally attempted to farm-out to major oil companies, but approvals for such farm-outs took time to work their way through the majors' inevitably large bureaucratic systems. This was not to be the first occasion — or the last — when being relatively small and able to move quickly gave a Canadian company the advantage over one of its larger multinational counterparts.

McGregor spoke to Darling, who was interested in Bow Valley taking the acreage. Late one afternoon, Darling received a call from McGregor offering the farm-out to Bow Valley. Darling, in turn, went into the office of Harry Van Rensselaer, whom he knew to be an enthusiast of the Far North. Van Rensselaer recognized that investor interest was turning to the Arctic frontier, and believed that an Arctic landspread could only help Bow Valley's share price. He quizzed Darling about the geology of the area and then the two men went in to see Doc. Doc listened to Darling's geological prognosis and Van Rensselaer's assessment of the investment attractions of such a deal. Then he told them to call McGregor back and take it. As they left the office, Darling told Van Rensselaer he'd call McGregor first thing in the morning. Van Rensselaer said:"Perhaps you'd better go and do it now." It was just as well he did, for within less than an hour a major company had called to seek the farm-in. A month later, Prudhoe Bay was discovered and Harry Van Rensselaer was in New York to see Bow Valley's stock jump on the news.

The massive find in 1968 at Prudhoe Bay on the North Slope of Alaska galvanized interest in the North. Although Prudhoe Bay was some 350 miles to the west of the Mackenzie Delta, it was close enough to arouse geological excitement. Most Canadian companies now had little chance of gaining acreage, but the wealthier foreign-owned companies were told by their head offices to get up there and buy into the action. Bow Valley, through its well-timed farm-in, now found itself in the middle of the action. Suddenly, the corporate suitors were standing outside Doc's door in the Bradie Building. By the time the 1969 annual report appeared, 26 companies had approached Bow Valley with a view to farming-in on its Mackenzie Delta acreage.

That winter season, the major players in the Delta, Imperial, Shell Canada and British-American (Gulf), drilled three wells. Although two were abandoned and one was suspended, the excitement hardly abated. Soon, Imperial made its discovery at Atkinson Point, and then, in 1971, it announced further discoveries at Mayogiak and Taglu, both of which were less than ten miles from the nearest Bow Valley acreage. Taglu, in particular, would turn out to be a major gas field.

The impact of the Taglu field on Bow Valley's share price is clear from the fact that Harry Van Rensselaer named each of the yachts he was to buy in the years to come *Taglu*.

Imperial soon successfully followed up on its Taglu find and made a further multi-zone gas discovery at Mallik just three miles from the nearest Bow Valley acreage. Meanwhile, Gulf and Mobil had made an additional discovery further south on the Delta. During the 1972-73 drilling season, more than a dozen drilling rigs were active after freeze-up on the Delta. Even more important, Imperial announced plans to build two artificial islands in shallow waters close to Bow Valley's acreage.

Meanwhile, although negotiations with parties interested in a farm-in continued, Bow Valley carried out a seismic program to evaluate its valuable acreage and played its cards close to its chest. In its 1972 annual report, the company declared: "While Bow Valley's management is keenly aware of the deep interest which the company's shareholders have in arrangements which will be made for the exploration and, in the event of discoveries, the development of Bow Valley's Delta acreage, it is not deemed in the company's best interests to say anything further at present beyond the statement that discussions are currently in progress."

In 1973, Bow Valley increased its Mackenzie Delta interests by buying out Christopher Explorations, which belonged to Townsend Martin, one of Harry Van Rensselaer's blue-chip New York investors. Meanwhile, Shell Canada announced two further discoveries, as did Gulf Canada as operator on behalf of the group containing both Imperial and Shell.

The majors were now confident that they would, in a few years, establish commercial quantities of natural gas production. Thoughts turned to transportation systems and a consortium of companies, known as the Canadian Arctic Gas Study Group, was formed to work on plans for a pipeline. Bill Wilder, the former chief of Toronto-based investment giant Wood Gundy, was drafted to head the group. Soon a plan was hatched to build a massive dogleg line — soon touted as the world's most expensive privately financed project — to pipe gas from the Prudhoe Bay field via the Delta, where it would "piggyback" Canadian gas.

Despite the political trauma of 1973 and 1974, the economics of the OPEC crisis — involving a quadrupling of oil prices within a matter of months — appeared excellent news for the Far North. Meanwhile, Bow Valley's service activities in the area were boosted as the company shipped Hi-Tower's new 20,000-foot Hercules Tranportable rig to the Delta to work for Imperial Oil. Bow Valley's 1974 annual report featured *Delta #1* perched on one of Imperial's artificial islands in the shallow waters of the Delta.

A Timely Farm-Out

Negotiations over a farm-out, meanwhile, were coming to a head. Doc and Dick Harris had by now talked to a great many companies, and had received attractive offers from Imperial and Texaco. However, the company most willing to pay the highest price in terms both of cash and drilling commitments was Sunoco E&P, the subsidiary of Philadelphia-based Sun Oil Co., which had pioneered tar sands production in Canada with the construction a decade earlier of the Great Canadian Oil Sands plant.

One of Bow Valley's problems, however, was the company with which it had shared its farm-out from Numac, Arctic Coast Petroleums. Arctic Coast was controlled by the Clay brothers, Harris and Landon, the enormously wealthy Americans who were a key part of the group brought in by Harry Van Rensselaer. The Clay brothers sat at the negotiating table, and every time a deal appeared close, they seemed to want more. Now, however, Sunoco was becoming exasperated. Suddenly, when Dick Harris happened to be away on an overseas trip, Sunoco announced that unless a deal was concluded that night, they were going to walk away. Doc, flanked by the re-calcitrant Clays and his legal advisors from Bill Howard's law firm, finally managed to pull together an agreement. The exhausted parties closed the deal at 2:00 A.M. For Bow Valley, it turned out to be an excellent one.

Bow Valley and Arctic Coast agreed to farm-out to Sunoco in return for a payment of $3.5 million to cover seismic and other technical data carried out by the partners, plus $1 million a year for eight years, subject to certain conditions. Under the terms of the deal, Sunoco had to drill a minimum of three wells. To earn an undivided 45 per cent working interest in all the partners' Delta permits, Sunoco would have to drill a minimum of twelve wells at the rate of at least two a year. In addition, there was a call upon Sunoco to provide non-recourse development finance for the lands in the event of commercial finds.

It was an outstanding deal, that not only provided several million dollars in cash to Bow Valley but also released it from all further financial commitments in the Delta. The deal still left Bow Valley — in the event that Sunoco exercised all its options — with a 27.5 per cent stake in the Delta lands. Within just a few years, Bow Valley would use the same technique to even greater advantage, and when the need for finance was much more urgent, in the North Sea.

When it came to the Arctic Islands, meanwhile, Doc had quickly lost enthusiasm for the project, and thus had also been keen to farm-out, or simply sell, Bow Valley's interests. Bow Valley was also once again having problems with the Clay brothers.

In 1970, Bill Clark, another disillusioned former Imperial employee, joined Bow Valley as senior landman. Almost as soon as he arrived, he inherited a crisis. A junior landman had neglected to renew permits for the company's acreage in the Arctic Islands. The Clay brothers sued Bow Valley and demanded financial reparation. Bow Valley's only hope was to get the permits restored, so Clark, Harry Van Rens-selaer — who had some government experience through his activities with the Independent Petroleum Association of Canada — and Dick Harris, who had just joined the company with the Syracuse merger, began to make frequent pilgrimages to Ottawa. In the end, Doc and Harry Van Rensselaer managed to gain audience with Jean Chrétien, Minister at the Department of Indian and Northern Affairs, and his senior officials. Doc explained that they were virtually being held to ransom by the Clays over the issue. Chrétien sympathized with their circumstance and finally the permits were effectively restored. The Clays, who had been financially reimbursed by Bow Valley, were now forced, under the terms of the reparation, to return the money.

This experience further dampened any ardor Doc may have felt for the Islands. In addition, Gordon Darling brought the Imperial Oil view of the Arctic Islands to Bow Valley. The corporate giant was much less enthusiastic about the eastern than the western Arctic. Darling persuaded Doc that, despite Cam Sproule's enthusiasm, the Islands had little potential. As a result, Doc had suggested to the board as early as 1971 that the company's interests there should be sold. In mid-1973, a sale of half the company's interest in Panarctic to Home Oil had been considered, but this deal had fallen through.

Doc persisted with his attempts to sell, however, and soon came up with what appeared to be an excellent deal. He reached an agreement with the provincially-owned Quebec oil company SOQUIP (Société Québécoise d'Initiatives Pétrolières) for SOQUIP to buy Bow Valley's stake in the Arctic Islands for $7.9 million, plus the assumption of all Bow Valley's remaining exploration commitments to Panarctic.

Doc took great care to explain his intentions to his fellow consortium members, but the federal government in the end vetoed the deal, apparently unwilling to share federally controlled lands with any of the provinces.

The company had now clearly gone off Panarctic. The Arctic Islands consortium traditionally gained the working capital it required for exploration by the periodic issuance of shares to its consortium members. When it came to the March, 1975 issue, Bow Valley declared that it would not be participating. Doc had determined that further exploration expenditure in the Islands appeared to be throwing good money after bad. Subsequent events would seem to prove him correct.

In any case, Panarctic had, since Prudhoe Bay, been a much less attractive prospect than the Mackenzie Delta and the Beaufort, if for no other reason than that the Western Arctic areas had the financial muscle of the big multinational companies behind it. However, all the financial muscle in the world proved powerless in the face of the national paranoia and political upheaval unleashed by the first OPEC crisis.

Pipeline Politics

In early 1974, Canadian Arctic Gas Pipelines Limited, the successor to the Canadian Arctic Gas Study Group, filed an application for a forty-eight-inch, $7 billion natural gas pipeline from Prudhoe Bay via the Mackenzie Delta. The scheme appeared a model of corporate logic and seemed to dovetail neatly with the Canadian federal government's northern aspirations. The Liberal government clearly favored a pipeline down the Mackenzie Valley, and seemed to support the more general principle of pipeline corridors to link Alaskan supplies of oil and gas with the lower forty-eight states.

However, in 1973 and 1974, relations with the U.S. deteriorated in the wake of the OPEC crisis. There was a feeling that U.S.-owned companies — and thus by extension the U.S. in general — had duped Canada over the true extent of Canada's petroleum reserves, exaggerating them in order to justify large exports south at "cheap" prices. Meanwhile, in the U.S. there was bad feeling because of Canada's rejection of a "continental" approach to energy problems, and its decision to charge OPEC prices for its oil exports to the U.S., and OPEC-linked prices for gas. The Americans would also be offended by Ottawa's creation of the Foreign Investment Review Agency (FIRA).

Coincidentally, there was an upsurge in ecological and environmental concerns over northern development. These political and environmental facts were to turn the northern pipeline debate into a morass.

The "winner" of the debate was Robert Blair, the head of Alberta Gas Trunk Line. Blair had been a somewhat reluctant member of the Canadian Arctic Gas consortium, but had then left it to hatch his own rival schemes. Blair, a highly complex man, was motivated by a profound Canadian nationalism and a desire to revitalize the sagging fortunes of the provincial pipeline system that he headed (and on whose board Doc Seaman sat).

Blair first came up with an all-Canadian "Maple Leaf Line," that would merely bring gas down the Mackenzie Valley without linking it up with Prudhoe Bay. Then, after he left Arctic Gas, he formed his own consortium and soon hatched a scheme to bring Prudhoe Bay gas to the lower forty-eight states via a pipeline which followed the route of the Alaska Highway. This "Alcan" proposal planned to link up Delta gas via a spur line that would come southwest from the Delta to link up with the main line. Blair took great care to court environmental and native groups.

The Arctic gas sponsors initially regarded Blair more as a nuisance than a rival. But they had failed to take due note of the power of politics. In May, 1977, a bombshell report on the impact of the pipeline was produced by Justice Thomas Berger, a judge who had been appointed by the federal Liberal party and who was well known for his radical views and support of native groups. Berger dealt two crushing blows to the Arctic Gas consortium. He recommended a moratorium on all Mackenzie Valley development for ten years, and he condemned altogether the notion of a pipeline across the Arctic National Wildlife Refuge, which was on the route from Prudhoe Bay to the Mackenzie Delta.

Shortly afterwards, the National Energy Board in Ottawa, which had also been holding hearings on the pipeline issue, dealt the final blow to Arctic Gas, coming down in favor of a modified Alcan line. But Blair's victory proved pyrrhic. Within half a dozen years, gas finds in Alberta and the impact of U.S. gas price deregulation on U.S. domestic supplies would undermine the need for expensive northern gas, which would in turn confirm the considerable body of expert opinion that maintained from the beginning that the Alcan line was unfinanceable.

The Beaufort Dream

Meanwhile, as Blair was in the process of winning his pipeline victory, the third distinct area of Canadian Arctic exploration, the Beaufort Sea, was being brilliantly promoted by Jack Gallagher's Dome Petroleum in a way that also relied heavily on politics.

Through persuading the federal government to introduce a system of "super-depletion," or uniquely generous tax write-offs for highly expensive frontier drilling, Dome was able to attract huge amounts of money into its Beaufort activities, and, not coincidentally, earn hefty profits from the innovative drilling fleet it had installed in the Beaufort in 1976.

Bow Valley, which had early on acquired Beaufort acreage, and maintained its interests there, allowed its Panarctic stake to decline following its decision not to put further money into the venture. On the Delta meanwhile, although Sunoco had made some finds whose flow-rates would have been very impressive if discovered in the south, the uncertainties over northern transportation caused activity to wind down.

Exploration in Canada's North thus proved a frustration for all concerned. Bow Valley, by well-timed farm-outs which allowed it to preserve its interests at no additional cost, by speedy decisions not to commit further funds where it saw little prospect of returns, and by emphasizing its drilling activities, was one of the few companies that came out ahead. In any case, with the Syracuse acquisition, Doc Seaman had firmly set the company's exploration sights elsewhere. It was in the international arena that it was to achieve its most important successes, and find its resources most severely strained.

10
A Foothold in the North Sea

Bow Valley's experience in the North Sea was complex and convoluted, but it was undoubtedly successful. Within just a few years of taking over Syracuse — the company which brought it its North Sea interests — Bow Valley achieved spectacular exploration success. The first couple of wells in which it was involved discovered commercial fields at Heimdal and Brae. However, the cost of drilling those wells, in particular the Brae discovery well, placed a great strain on the company's financial resources.

Bow Valley extricated itself from that crisis by a farm-out with Ashland Oil of Kentucky. This farm-out, which was similar to that negotiated with Sun in the Mackenzie Delta, not only released it from further financial obligations in the development of the all-important Brae field, but also ensured that Bow Valley would receive significant cash from the field as soon as the oil started flowing.

The farm-out was essential not only because of its financial structure, but also because of its timing; Brae proved to be a much more complex geological detective story than was at first apparent. The gap between the granting of the exploration licence beneath which the Brae field sat and the production of the first oil was one of thirteen expensive and frustrating years. Nevertheless, Brae remains, at the time of this book's publication, Bow Valley's most significant exploration success.

Evolution of an Oil Province

Small oil and gas discoveries had been made onshore Great Britain as early as the 1930s, but it was not until the 1950s that radically changed geological thinking, and exploration success on the European side of the North Sea, accelerated interest in the area.

In 1959, the Groningen gas field, ranked as the world's fifth largest, was discovered in the northern Netherlands. At around the same time, geological thinking was being revolutionized as a result of the theory of plate tectonics, which asserted that the Earth's crust, far from being stable, consisted of huge plates which, as they moved against or away from each other, created massive pressures and faulting. It was believed that these pressures had resulted in constant changes in the surface characteristics of the northwestern European continental shelf which resulted in ideal conditions for the generation of hydrocarbons. Geological movements over the previous 200 million years had created thick sedimentary basins beneath what was now the North Sea.

Nevertheless, there were a number of dampeners to enthusiasm about North Sea exploration. Firstly, the sedimentary basins lay in water depths of 300 or more feet, where drilling had never been attempted before. Moreover, the Sea itself was one of the most deadly of the Earth's navigated waters, where wave-heights of 100 feet and winds of 150 knots were not inconceivable. Finally, there were legal quibbles over offshore jurisdiction. It was not until the late 1960s, almost a decade after the first United Nations' Law of the Sea Conference, that these disputes were settled. The technical problems, in turn, were solved by the evolution of sophisticated offshore drilling equipment, in particular the semi-submersible rig, a giant floating rig much closer in size to a ship than to its seemingly puny land-locked cousin.

In 1962 and 1963, the first marine seismic work in the North Sea was carried out by a joint venture of BP, Shell, and Esso. Named "Operation Seashell," it was based in the East Coast fishing and holiday resort town of Great Yarmouth. In 1965, the first offshore success came with the discovery of the West Sole field. However, the triumph was tinged with disaster, when, less than a week after the find's announcement, the operation's rig, the *Sea Gem*, tilted and capsized with the loss of thirteen lives. It was perhaps the North Sea's warning that her petroleum riches would not be easily won.

In 1969, the first oil field, Montrose, was discovered by BP's rig *Sea Quest* while drilling for Amoco about 135 miles east of Aberdeen. When the rig sensed a high-pressure zone, the well-testers automatically assumed that it was gas, since conventional wisdom held the whole area to be gas-prone. They were, it was reported, so unprepared for an oil discovery that they had no container for the sample. The first North Sea oil was brought ashore in an empty pickle jar from the rig's galley!

In fact, the Amoco discovery generated little excitement at the time. OPEC oil was still $1.80 a barrel, so the field was only marginally economic. It might have been drilled only because Amoco was able to offset its cost against profits elsewhere. Other factors were that the company was concerned both about the forced relinquishment of the land if it was not drilled, and about not being given attractive lands in future rounds if it failed to meet its exploration commitments. But

87

within a few years, the vise-like tightening of the world oil market, personified in the notion of OPEC "muscle," was to make the North Sea both economically and politically highly desirable.

Meanwhile, at about the time of the Montrose discovery, another, far more significant, field was being uncovered by Phillips Petroleum in the Norwegian sector. Three wells confirmed a structure about 10 miles long and 5 miles wide. It was named Ekofisk and contained more than a billion barrels of recoverable oil.

Astonishingly, Sir Eric Drake, then chairman of BP, predicted early in 1970 that no more major fields would be found. It was all the more astonishing because later the same year his own company made one of the biggest finds, that of the Forties field, where there were an estimated 2 billion barrels of reserves. In February, 1971, Shell/Esso found the small Auk field south of the Forties. Five months later, the partnership of giants had its greatest success at Brent. Much further north than the Forties field, Brent contained 2.2 billion barrels of oil and 3 trillion cubic feet (TCF) of gas.

The discoveries of the giant Forties and Brent fields in the U.K. sector of the North Sea, and that of Ekofisk in the Norwegian sector, confirmed the area as a major exploration province. It would soon become obvious that North Sea reserves were of a magnitude similar to those of OPEC members like Libya and Abu Dhabi, and twice the size of those of a Venezuela or a Nigeria. Bow Valley, or rather its latest takeover, Syracuse, had just managed to get in under the wire with its licences. Not long before the merger, in June, 1970, Syracuse had secured exploration licence P.108. That licence alone would be worth many times what Bow Valley paid for the company. After 1971, the competition for North Sea lands really heated up.

The British government had divided up its sector of the North Sea into administratively convenient blocks of ten minute intervals of latitude by twelve minutes of longitude. Licence P.108 included blocks 16/3 and 16/7 which sat, corner to corner, about 75 miles north of the Forties field and directly between the Forties and Brent finds.

That the company should have been in such a risky and techno-logically demanding play seemed questionable, but that such a tiny organization as Syracuse had gained licences in the face of competition from the majors was almost astounding. Once again, it went back to Angus Mackenzie's nerve, but also to the system the British had adopted to distribute licences, which permitted smaller companies — if they had a plausible enough story to tell — to sit at the table with the big boys.

Once jurisdictional boundaries had been settled, the British gov-ernment had set out to examine how they would regulate exploratory activity in their sector of the North Sea. Governments usually issue drilling rights on land in one of two ways, either on an auction basis, or by direct issuance — under which system the companies involved normally have to make financial or non-financial commitments. Oil companies didn't like the auction system, because it meant they often had to lay out large amounts of money up front. They therefore pressured the British government to issue exploration licences directly.

The British government, for its part, was eager to see the North Sea developed. The U.K. was almost entirely dependent on imports for the oil that supplied around two-thirds of its energy needs, a situation which exacerbated its chronic balance of payments problems. If oil could be found to substitute for imports, the government wanted it found and produced as quickly as possible. Whitehall realized that the major oil companies were the only ones who could do the job and do it quickly, so it agreed to go for a direct licencing system. Perhaps paradoxically, it was this system that allowed smaller companies with enough daring to gain a piece of the action.

An auction system would have completely excluded smaller companies, which, like paupers at Sotheby's, would have been outbid by their giant counterparts. Ironically, one of the reasons Mackenzie, Harris, and Palmer had turned their attention to the international arena was that discoveries in Alberta in the middle and late 1960s — such as those at Rainbow Lake, Edson, and Mitsue — had, under the provincial auction system, driven land prices out of sight. An issuance system opened the way for more subtle diplomacy, involving personality and contacts, and Angus Mackenzie was a master at such diplomacy. Direct issuance meant that someone had to do the issuing. If you could persuade that person that you could do the job, then you stood a chance of winning a licence. The man whom Angus Mackenzie had to persuade of his abilities and his intentions was a career British civil servant who shared his first name, Angus Beckett.

The Target of Diplomacy

Beckett, a geographer by training and a former schoolmaster, had joined the Civil Service in 1940. In 1947, he had been posted to the petroleum division of the Ministry of Power, and, in the early 1950s became the petroleum attaché to the British Embassy in Washington. He was involved with the North Sea from the start, helping to determine boundary lines with Britain's European neighbors. Then, as under-secretary at the Ministry of Power and subsequently at the Department of Trade and Industry, he was given the responsibility for doling out exploration licences. The important thing about being on good terms with Beckett was not that he was likely to show you special favors, but that he was likely to assist you to tailor your bid to fit in with government priorities.

Instead of allowing a free-for-all on applications for licences, the British government had decided that it would invite applications in a number of "rounds," in which specific sections of its jurisdiction would be offered. The criteria for applications were fairly loose. Priority would be given to those bidders who planned rapid exploration and exploitation; applicants had to be incorporated in the U.K. and be U.K. taxable; if the applicant was foreign-owned, then its home country had to offer equitable treatment to British companies; the company had to present a suitable work program and have the resources to carry it through; and finally, it had to make a contribution to the development of resources both on the continental shelf and the U.K. in general.

For the smaller participants, presenting a suitable work program and showing that they had the resources to bring it to completion were obviously the most difficult criteria. In an area where even Shell and Esso felt they should have a joint operation, it was obvious that the only hope lay in the consortium approach. Even then, however, exploration commitments could prove an enormous drain on financial resources. The secret when it came to bidding, however, was to express supreme confidence, and at this Angus Mackenzie was an expert.

The third round of bidding in the U.K. sector of the North Sea came up in 1969. It was far larger than the first two rounds and the first time that the more northerly areas had been opened for bidding. Previously, interest had been confined to the more southerly sections of the North Sea, "jack-up rig country," where the waters were less than 300 feet in depth. Mackenzie, Dick Harris, and Stu McColl had all seen a report prepared by Shell that suggested there might be a petroleum basin further north than the present focus of exploration. They knew they didn't have a chance butting heads with the majors further south. There appeared to be the requisite "big bumps" shown in the seismic work that had been carried out on the more northerly areas, so they decided to take a flier. McColl selected the blocks.

Mackenzie's enthusiasm was critical in finding partners for the deal. Syracuse's corporate associate with the deepest pockets was the New York-based Pan Ocean, which had joined in Mackenzie and Palmer's first venture in Norway. The other partners that became involved were: Hambros, the merchant bank, whose stake would go into the flotation of Bill Siebens' British company, Siebens Oil and Gas U.K.; and Saga, a Norwegian-based concern. Bill Sterling indirectly held a small stake and Angus Mackenzie and Jim Palmer retained a separate interest in Brae after the sale of Syracuse through Sunningdale, a company named after the famous Surrey golf course. Under the terms of their bid, the partners had agreed to carry out seismic work and drill a well. Where Angus Beckett's advice had been invaluable was in persuading them to offer a 20 per cent back-in on the licence to Britain's National Coal Board. This may well have swung things in their favor in gaining exploration licence P.108. As it turned out, P.108 contained the motherlode.

Syracuse originally held a 35 per cent interest in licence P.108. When Bow Valley acquired Syracuse within a year of the award, it had no idea of the licence's value. Marine seismic surveys were now carried out and interpreted, and Bow Valley and its partners began to formulate drilling plans for the properties. Dick Harris had wanted Bow Valley to be operator of the field, but Pan Ocean insisted on filling this role.

The partners would meet at the old Bristol Hotel in Londons's West End because the Pan Ocean office wasn't large enough to accommodate them. The meeting area for their top-secret negotiations was separated from the hotel coffee shop by a curtain! Here they hammered out their strategy. In fact, once the consortium had obtained its own seismic work, the prospects didn't look enormously exciting. A well was obviously going to be expensive. One alternative for the partners was to farm-out straight away, before any significant expenditures had been made, but the authorities frowned on that idea.

In the London office, Fred Wellhauser decided that he needed help with the growing mound of work, so he put an advertisement in the paper for a geologist. One of those who replied was a young Englishman, Clive Randle. Randle had graduated from London University's Imperial College at the time of BP's crucial West Sole discovery. He spent his first eight years in the oil business trotting the globe with a well-site service company, but when that company was taken over, he started looking for a new job, preferably based in England, where he had recently married. He saw Bow Valley's ad and decided to apply. He had heard of the company because he knew it was involved in building a semi-submersible rig in Norway, so he went to see Fred Wellhauser at the company's little office at 26 St. James's. Fred Wellhauser painted exciting pictures of the company's prospects all over the globe, from the Maldives to the Mediterranean. Randle liked the sound of the organization and joined up in February, 1973, as chief geologist for the U.K., Africa, and the Middle East. When Wellhauser went to Calgary in 1976 to become head of worldwide exploration, Randle would take over the London office. The company's involvement in the Brae field was to provide some trying times for Randle, requiring all his tenacity and sense of humor.

The *Odin Drill*

When the consortium partners sat down to plan strategy for blocks 16/3 and 16/7, they knew they had to drill a well. This aspect was of special significance to Bow Valley because the company was engaged on the other side of the North Sea in its most ambitious exploit in the drilling business: it was a partner in the construction of a giant semi-submersible rig. This exploit followed Doc's long-term strategy of combining drilling and exploration activities wherever possible. When the first well was drilled on block 16/7, it was drilled by Bow Valley with its own rig, *Odin Drill*.

Semi-submersible rigs had developed as a refinement of submersible rigs, which had been designed to be towed to an offshore drilling location and then positioned on the sea bed. Semi-submersibles were designed to drill in deeper waters by utilizing a system of flooded pontoons and anchor moorings. They were more sophisticated than their land cousins, and much more expensive, but they also had to drill in much more difficult conditions. The North Sea was one of the most testing drilling locations in the world.

Bow Valley had looked several times at moving into offshore rigs before the Syracuse merger, and had considered joint ventures with the U.S.-based Offshore Company. Such a move would have been a natural extension of its onshore drilling operations. However, the Syracuse merger brought a new rationale for moving offshore: in granting exploration licences, governments would probably look favorably on a company with offshore drilling capability. The building and operation of a rig would also clearly demonstrate the company's commitment to the area.

For Doc, a key contact in the development of the company's offshore operations was Emil Dinkla, an eminent Norwegian marine engineer and consultant. He introduced Doc and Don Binney — who would assume responsibility for the *Odin Drill* — to the Norwegians who would become their partners in the deal. The key man in Norway was Martin Siem, a former war hero and managing director of the giant Fred Olsen group, which, among many other interests, controlled the Aker shipyards that would eventually build the rig.

Doc brought in Home Oil, which was still controlled by the legendary Bobby Brown, as a Canadian partner, and Martin Siem introduced him to the principles of two Norwegian companies who would become partners in the deal: Hagb. Waage and Wilh. Wilhelmsen. Largely for tax and legal reasons, Waage wound up with 40 per cent of the rig, and Bow Valley, Home and Wilhelmsen with 20 per cent each. However, Bow Valley was to manage the joint venture. In

August, 1971, Don Binney outlined the benefits of the deal in a memo to Bow Valley's board. Not only would the company share in the profits of the venture, but it would also receive a management fee. Operating the rig would enable drilling personnel to be reassigned to the North Sea from Western Canada, where operations were somewhat depressed. It would strengthen the company's hand when bidding for licences in both the British and Norwegian sectors. The exploration side of the company would guarantee one year's work to the rig, as would Home Oil — which also had North Sea interests. Binney foresaw that there would be no shortage of work for rigs of this type in the coming ten years. In this latter assessment, Don Binney was slightly optimistic, but that should not detract from his role in overseeing the construction of the rig and making yet another ambitious scheme a hard, metal reality.

Late in 1971, Bow Valley joined its partners in committing themselves to the construction of a $32 million offshore rig. By 1974, the self-propelled vessel would be completed and ready to drill the first Brae well.

11
Brae: The Sweetest
Farm-Out

The first well on the Brae block, 16/7-1, was spudded on September 19, 1974. It proved to be a long and painfully expensive hole, dogged by some of the worst weather experienced in the North Sea and extremely difficult drilling conditions. *Odin Drill's* blow-out preventers failed tests; several times tools were lost down the hole requiring expensive "fishing" jobs; in December an anchor chain broke during a fierce storm; in February 3,000 feet of drill-pipe became stuck in the hole when the well encountered unexpectedly high pressures; in March and April there were a series of frustrating equipment problems. By the time the *Odin Drill* recovered its anchors and moved off the drill-site on May,10, 1975, the hole had cost U.S.$16 million, making it one of the most expensive drilled in the North Sea — or, indeed, anywhere — up to that time. That well severely strained Bow Valley's resources. The company's share of its costs, for a time, swallowed all its discretionary cash flow. To top it all, when Pan Ocean, the Brae operator, sent a telex to its partners on the well's results, it announced that the hole was dry! The shows of hydrocarbons coming up from the well during drilling had not been encouraging.

However, disappointment turned to joy when electric logs were taken and testing began. They revealed 500 feet of "gross pay interval," that is, potentially oil-bearing sandstone. When the well was tested, it flowed a whopping 22,000 barrels a day. In its first North Sea well, Bow Valley as both exploration partner and driller, had struck the motherlode. The field was immediately declared commercial, named Brae, and the British Coal Board exercised its purchase option, thus reducing Bow Valley's stake to 28 per cent. On July 11, *Odin Drill* spudded a second well on the same block about 4.5 miles west of the discovery. This well reached 7,997 feet and tested oil at a rate of 4,023 barrels a day. Gas was also tested "at substantial rates" from a separate geological stratum. What the consortium was hoping for was that the second well would show the same geological characteristics as the first, thus indicating a continuous field. However, the second well had obviously hit a separate, shallower reservoir.

On October 8, 1975, a second Brae appraisal well, 16/7-3 was spudded in 340 feet of water some 3.7 miles southwest of the discovery well. It was another gusher. The well encountered 1,000 feet of continuous gross payzone in the Upper Jurassic sandstone. Production tests yielded 14,000 barrels of oil a day. The results were announced in March. It was hoped, and indeed initially thought, that this well was on the same structure as the first well, indicating a giant reservoir of perhaps a billion barrels — an exploration "elephant" among the largest in the North Sea. However, this third well again turned out to be on a separate structure from both the first and second wells. Nevertheless, whatever the precise form of what lay below, these wells were all world-scale. Nothing of their magnitude had ever been found in Canada (and would not be until the Hibernia find off Newfoundland in 1979). They promised to take Bow Valley into the petroleum big time.

In fact, Brae proved to be one of the most complex finds in the North Sea. The structure that would be developed as the South Brae field would not be hit until the eighth well on the block. In the end, it would take more than a dozen wells to determine what lay under 16/7. But perhaps fortunately for Bow Valley and its partners, neither they nor those looking to buy-out or farm-into the consortium knew that at the time.

The significance of Brae to Bow Valley was not recognized immediately. In the event, Brae would contain a number of separate fields, the total development costs of which, by 1984, would be estimated, in as-spent dollars, at more than U.S.$10 billion. Bow Valley's share of those costs would come to U.S.$1.4 billion. For reference, in 1975, the entire Canadian oil industry would spend a total of $4 billion. Expenditures of the size necessary for Brae development would have given companies much larger than Bow Valley corporate trauma — but for one detail: Bow Valley negotiated the sweetest farm-out deal in its history. Under that farm-out, which was very similar to that negotiated on the Mackenzie Delta with Sun, it would never have to contribute another cent of its own to Brae costs.

The Price of Success

Syracuse's foreign landspread had taken Bow Valley into huge exploration commitments. By the middle of 1973, eighteen months before the Brae well was drilled, the board was already expressing concern over anticipated foreign oil and gas expenditures. From the time he joined Bow Valley, one of Dick Harris's main preoccupations had been finding companies that might ease these financial commitments by taking farm-outs on Bow Valley lands.

As a matter of exploration priorities — as well as because of doubts about the pace of Arctic oil development — Bow Valley had already farmed-out its acreage in the Mackenzie Delta and was trying to sell its stake in Panarctic. Nevertheless, the cash saved in the North was still far short of the overseas exploration requirements. The first Brae well brought these financial commitments to a burdensome level.

Largely because of North Sea costs, it was predicted that the company would suffer a cash deficit of from $3 million to $5 million for 1975. Drastic measures had to be considered. Exploration expenditures were cut by $1.5 million for the remainder of 1975. It was decided to approach Sun, the company that had taken Bow Valley's Delta farm-out, with a view to Sun buying either Christopher Explorations, which Bow Valley had bought a short time previously because of Christopher's interests in the Delta, and/or purchasing Bow Valley's stake in Panarctic. Doc thought for a while he had managed to sell his Panarctic stake to Quebec-owned SOQUIP, but this sale was frustrated by the federal government.

In addition, the company decided to try and find a buyer for some or all of its foreign interests outside of the North Sea. Dick Harris was dispatched to sell this "foreign package." It was proposed that an equity financing be attempted. The sale of *Odin Drill* as well as Arctic drilling operations and Bow Helicopters was considered. Doc even approached federal energy minister Donald Macdonald with a view to the government becoming financially involved in return for access to secure foreign oil.

Once the first three wells had been successful, the nature of Bow Valley's financial problems changed, but they became no less pressing. The costs of success in the North Sea were almost as daunting as the price of failure. Further delineating and development costs were likely to be far more than Bow Valley's relatively frail resources could sustain.

The crisis was exacerbated by Harry Van Rensselaer's choice of this particularly bad moment to leave the company. Shortly before he left, Van Rensselaer had taken a lengthy "dog and pony show," the term for a series of promotional presentations, to U.S. investment specialists. As usual, his presentations had been impressive, and had led to a number of U.S. investors taking up Bow Valley stock, or adding to their holdings. This buying interest in turn helped lift the Bow Valley stock from the doldrums of the latter half of 1974, when the Ottawa-Alberta dispute had severely depressed markets. But when these U.S. investors subsequently saw Van Rensselaer not only leave

*From the left, Doc, Don, and B.J. show early indications
of corporate aggression as they stand guard in front of
one of their father's tractors!*

Doc in his Royal Canadian Air Force days.

One of the Seamans' first seismic rigs outside their
supplier's office.

Ralph Will

Big moment on the Amex. From the left, Len Quigley, Bow Valley's New York lawyer, Ray Hammell, Harry Van Rensselaer, B.J., Doc, and Jack Ahern watch as Bow Valley appears on the board of the American Stock Exchange.

Post-Amex celebrations in Manhattan. Standing from the left: Harry Van Rensselaer, Marg Howard, Don Binney, B.J., Bill Howard, Ray Hammell, and a member of the bar's staff. Seated from left to right: Sally Binney, Eleanor Seaman, Keith Lazelle, Helen Lazelle, Doc Seaman, Evelyn Seaman, another staff member, Tom McGlade, Don Seaman, Sue Van Rensselaer.

Jim Palmer (left) and Angus Mackenzie strolling down Piccadilly on one of their first jaunts to Europe to talk their way into the North Sea.

Aboard the semi-submersible Dan Queen *in the South China Sea. Standing (from left to right): Dick Harris, Angus Mackenzie, Dr. Dao Duy Chu from the South Vietnamese government, Fred Wellhauser, Ray McBeth of Calgary's Tri-Ocean Engineering, Lloyd Flood, unidentified member of the Canadian Embassy staff from Peking, and Dave Williams of Westburne Industries. Squatting are, on the left, Arthur Menzies, the Canadian Ambassador to Peking, who also held responsibility for Vietnam, and Ray Gould of Siebens Oil & Gas.*

The South Brae jacket under tow from Ardersier in Scotland.

The South Brae platform being hooked up. On the left of the platform is the accommodation vessel Safe Holmia. *On the right is the crane barge* DB100.

Clyde Goins and Doc at Bow Valley's coal operation. Between Doc and Clyde in the background is Bill Tye.

Bow Valley's coal-processing facilities in Bell County, Kentucky.

(Above) *Delineation drilling in Indonesia at Ramba with the Dawas River in the background.*

(Right) *Aboard the Bow Drill One in Halifax harbor. Facing the camera, from the left: Don, Doc, B.J., (the now Reverend) Don Binney, and Henry Popoff.*

*Bow Drill 3 tied up at pier 19 outside Saint John Shipbuilding & Dry Dock,
New Brunswick*

Don at the wheel of a Western Star truck.

From the left: Sandy Sinclair, Bernie Sank, a Hi-Tower toolpusher, and Lord Michael on the rig floor.

Gerry Maier addressing the assembly at the high-tech, official dedication of the South Brae Platform.

the company, but sell his holdings; and when Bow Valley shares lost half their value in the fall of 1975, some of them rapidly lost confidence both in Canada and the stock.

Van Rensselaer was a mercurial and impulsive man, and there was no doubt that he became increasingly disillusioned with the federal-Alberta dispute over energy and its impact on energy policy. He could also sense the growing nationalistic sentiments that would result in the Foreign Investment Review Agency. Finally, he simply felt burned out from millions of miles of corporate travel. Nevertheless, his exit prompted several of the major U.S. shareholders, who had been part of his original blue-chip group, to pull out. With these investors gone — the second largest stock-holding group after the Seaman brothers themselves — Doc felt himself vulnerable to takeover. Stock sales had depressed the share price, but the North Sea prospects made Bow Valley an attractive acquisition target. Doc went across the country tying into his now considerable establishment contacts in search of a new large shareholder. Eventually, he found his new major share-holder via a route that took him back to Brae.

Among the potential large investors Doc visited was Leo Kolber, the man who ran CEMP, the holding company for part of the Bronfman family interests. CEMP had held a large interest in Pan-Ocean when it had been sold to Marathon. The Bronfmans liked the North Sea involvement, so they took part of the proceeds from the sell-out to Marathon and invested them in Bow Valley. The relationship was to prove highly beneficial to both sides. From Bow Valley's point of view, the Bronfman representatives on Bow Valley's board — first Leo Kolber, and later Arnold Ludwick and James Raymond — not only provided valuable advice, but also added significantly to the company's financial credibility. CEMP, meanwhile, would have no reason to regret its stake in the company (which today stands at 11 per cent). By the middle of 1976, Bow Valley's shares would have doubled from their 1975 low. By mid 1979 they would have doubled once more on their way to yet a further doubling early in 1980. Nobody could now claim that Harry Van Rensselaer had painted a false picture in 1975. The only regrets came from those — like Van Rensselaer himself — who subsequently sold the stock!

With the Bronfmans having taken a stake, Doc now had his new strong partner. However, that still left the issue of financing Brae. The first alternative was to seek non-recourse financing from the banks, that is, loans that would be repaid out of Brae's production with no recourse to Bow Valley's other income or assets in the event that the field did not produce up to expectation. By the time of the Brae discovery, BP had financed the Forties field and Occidental

Petroleum had financed the Claymore field with bank finance. However, radical Tony Benn's arrival on the scene as U.K. Socialist energy minister created political nervousness among the bankers.

Another concept considered by the Brae group was to bring in an operator to take over the field's development and give the existing partners a "carried interest." However, the notion of a group-approach to the field's financing disappeared when Pan Ocean sold out to Marathon Oil of Findlay, Ohio, in 1976.

Bow Valley wanted a deal similar to the one the company had with Sun Oil in the Mackenzie Delta. They wanted reimbursement for the money they had spent so far on the field, and then — in return for half their interests — they wanted the company farming-in to assume all their financial obligations for the remainder of the field's life. Bow Valley would repay its share of these costs out of production. However, the company wanted to make sure that its whole income from the field wasn't swallowed up in repaying costs. Bow Valley's pitch was that although the major portion of the proceeds of production would go towards repaying the development costs born on its behalf, it should, from first production, receive 30 per cent of the oil free and clear. Dick Harris did most of the leg work in trying to sell the deal. He went to see Shell and Esso and Mobil and Gulf, and the European national oil companies. None would bite on what Bow Valley considered acceptable terms. The majors also had doubts about the Brae field's geological potential.

Marathon, once it had bought Pan Ocean, was an obvious candidate to take a farm-out from Bow Valley. Harold "the Hoop" Hoopman, Marathon's strong-willed, hip-shooting chief executive, invited Doc and Dick Harris and Fred Wellhauser down to his headquarters in Findlay, where they made their farm-out pitch. A week later, Hoopman and his top brass came to Bow Valley's offices in Calgary. Hoopman wanted to buy Bow Valley out, a proposition that, given Bow Valley's tight financial position, was attractive. However, in the end Doc and the Bow Valley explorationists decided that they should hang on for a farm-out in order to maintain an interest in the field. Hoopman would eventually negotiate a deal with two of the other partners — the Norwegian Saga group and Bill Siebens' company — similar in structure to the deal that Bow Valley would soon make. That deal resulted from one of Doc's now very large list of executive friends and contacts.

A Trip to Florida

For some time, Doc had been talking to Ashland Oil of Kentucky about the possibility of Bow Valley taking over Ashland's Canadian interests. He had met Ashland's U.S. head, Orin Atkins, socially and, realizing that the U.S. operation appeared crude-short, he suggested that access to North Sea oil would be of great value to them. Why not take a piece of Bow Valley's action?

Dick Harris's first presentation to Ashland in Calgary was not propitious. Ashland seemed less than enthusiastic about Bow Valley's desire to earn profits as soon as production started and be carried financially forever. However, Orin Atkins liked the sound of the deal. Doc was asked down to a meeting in Denver. There, in the Stouffers Hotel outside Denver airport, he met with Atkins, Earl Joudrie, the head of Ashland Canada, and a raft of Ashland top brass. At the end of the meeting, Doc and Atkins shook hands, which in the oil business meant the deal was effectively done. However, Atkins had formally to take the deal to his board, and that would require a more structured presentation.

Doc called Harris and Wellhauser, who were in Manhattan pitching the farm-out to a major oil company, and told them of Ashland's commitment. Shortly afterwards, Atkins called up Dick Harris and told him that the main Ashland board was to meet at the Breakers Hotel in West Palm Beach, Florida. Could Harris come down with his maps and his geological models and make Bow Valley's pitch? Harris said yes and Atkins said he'd send the company plane to pick him up. Harris travelled to Florida and gave his complete presentation — now all the smoother for the fact that he had practised it so many times!

Neither Doc nor Harris could afford to let Ashland know just how desperately Bow Valley needed the farm-out, because then they would hang tough and drive a harder bargain. In fact, Brae was swallowing around $1 million a month, that is, all Bow Valley's "spare" cash. Atkins offered to fly Bow Valley's head of exploration back to Calgary, but Harris told him that he was off to see another company, clearly implying that if Ashland hesitated, they might lose the deal. But the important feature was that the handshake had already been made. Soon Atkins called to tell Doc that the board had agreed to go ahead. Bow Valley had its farm-out.

In fact, there was to be a great deal of often tough negotiation before a final agreement was reached, and relations between the two sides were not always cordial. There were also political and tax considerations. Not only had the agreement to be acceptable to the U.K. government, but there was also the thorny issue of government "participation" — to which somewhat nebulous concept the U.K.'s Socialist government had committed itself. Another major potential stumbling block to the Ashland farm-out was that it was at first declared liable to U.K. capital gains tax, which would have given Bow

Valley a hefty tax bill and undermined most of the financial benefits of the deal. However, in the end Britain's Inland Revenue took a highly understanding and accommodative attitude.

On May 28, 1976, Bow Valley announced the signing of a letter of intent with Ashland Oil under which Bow Valley assigned half its 28 per cent interest in blocks 16/7, 16/3, and 16/2 — the last of which, awarded more recently than the first two blocks, sat next to them — to the U.S. company. In return, Ashland had agreed to pay Bow Valley some $15 million to recover their costs, and loan Bow Valley an additional $7.5 million to pay for Bow Valley's share of estimated future exploratory and appraisal drilling on the licences until the development stage was reached. It was agreed that this loan would be repaid out of production income.

The most important aspect of the agreement was that Ashland would loan Bow Valley its entire share of development costs for the field, including the expensive installation of production platforms and transportation facilities, until production revenues had enabled Bow Valley to pay back all loans. The Ashland loans were non-recourse, that is, they would be repayable only from production on the licences. Ashland would receive 70 per cent of Bow Valley's 14 per cent share of net proceeds from production, but Bow Valley would receive the remaining 30 per cent until the loans were paid back. Then the entire 14 per cent would go to Bow Valley's coffers. The deal was universally recognized as an excellent one for Bow Valley.

Although Bow Valley had managed to release itself from further direct investment in Brae development, it retained a keen interest in both that development and other factors affecting its Brae interests. One of these was participation. The government had declared that it wanted a 51 per cent majority interest in producing fields. The nature of this interest was the subject of long and acrimonious debate with North Sea producers, and the group of which Bow Valley was a member was no exception.

One of the difficulties of negotiation over the Brae block was that the state oil company had already inherited 20 per cent of the field through its acquisition of properties from the National Coal Board. The consortium's other, and related, problem, was the zealous nature of the government's negotiators.

Government Participation

The man with whom the group had to negotiate over the issue of majority British participation was a bearded and bushy-haired young

bureaucrat who shared the name but none of the free-enterprise lean-
ings of the head of Ashland. His name was Robin Atkins. He was a
protégé of Lord Kearton, the former chairman of textile company
Courtaulds and the first head of the newly created BNOC. Like other
men in similar positions — and the Canadian energy bureaucracy was
later to prove no exception — Atkins sometimes appeared to see
himself as a knight in shining armor defending the national interest
against the depradations of foreign-owned oil companies who sought
only to ravage the country of its resources. Needless to say, this
attitude did not make for easy negotiation. The Brae negotiating team
was led by Bill Swales, a big, witty, generous, cigar-smoking Marathon
executive.

Some of the meetings the group had with Atkins at Stornaway
House on London's Green Park amounted almost to physical torture.
The partners sometimes felt that Atkins deliberately positioned himself in the west-facing windows of the meeting room so that they
would be blinded by the afternoon sun! One of the strangest meetings
occurred when Atkins turned up at the meeting with a cricket bat!
He might of course have been going off to a cricket match, and to
suggest that he brought it as an act of intimidation seemed like paranoia. Still, it left a strange feeling among the participants.

In the end, the issue of participation turned out to be a storm in a
teacup. The form it eventually took — although it may have met the
U.K. government's political objectives — amounted to a very tame
thing: the British National Oil Corporation secured the right to purchase 51 per cent of the crude produced from any field at market
prices. Compared with the geological problems of establishing a commercial field and the costs of bringing it into production, participation
paled into insignificance.

The massive prospective costs of Brae delineation and development
created corporate upheavals for all the Brae partners, leading each
either to seek a farm-out partner or — as in the case of Sunningdale
and Pan Ocean — to sell the entire company (Sunningdale was taken
over by Kerr-McGee). In terms of the development of the field, the
most important piece of corporate musical chairs was the purchase
of the field's operator, Pan Ocean, by Marathon Oil.

Marathon had begun its life as the Ohio Oil Co. in 1887, the result
of an amalgamation of a number of independent oil producers. Within
twenty-five years, the company had become the largest oil producer
not only in the state of Ohio, but also Indiana and Illinois. By 1936
it was producing also in Wyoming, Kansas, Texas, Oklahoma,
Louisiana, Arkansas, Kentucky, California, Montana, and New Mexico. Its greatest success was as a majority shareholder in the giant
Yates field of West Texas, which was discovered in 1926 and which

101

produced an astounding 225 million barrels of oil in the years between 1929 and 1936.

Marathon saw Brae as a chance to get in on the ground floor of the development of a North Sea field. The haul was to prove a long one.

Geological Jigsaw Puzzle

One of the reasons it took so long to delineate the Brae field was because of disagreements about the shape of what lay below. As Wallace Pratt said, "Oil is found in the minds of men," and the oil found in the minds of the consortium's geologists for quite a while did not correlate with what was actually there.

A geologist's skill lies in re-creating in his mind's eye the Earth as it existed hundreds of millions of years ago, in seeing the lay of primeval rivers and oceans; in spotting where sediments may have been laid down and buried to form traps for the transmuted hydrocarbons that would become petroleum.

Marathon, Ashland and the other companies that became involved with Brae were hoping they had found one large oil-bearing structure. Subsequent drilling established that this was not the case. The first two wells that Marathon drilled after acquiring Pan Ocean — and following Bow Valley's Ashland farm-out — were dry, indicating that the reservoir did not extend as far west as had been hoped. The next two wells, drilled further east, were also disappointing. The eighth well hit the South Brae structure but it was not until the thirteenth well had been drilled on the block that the nature and proportions of the field finally took shape. Ray Dafter, the *Financial Times* of London's energy expert, summed up Brae by saying: "For an industry commentator this has been one of the most baffling of finds to evaluate, denoting, no doubt, its complex structure."

What Brae turned out to have been in far-distant prehistoric times was a giant cliff off which a number of rivers had poured their waters and their sediments. These sediments had then built up in a number of fan-shapes which sometimes overlapped each other. They accumulated over millions of years into great cones that were later covered by shale. They became "fanglomerates." North American geologists had had such trouble with the concept because they had simply never seen anything quite like it before.

Instead of the single, long structure hoped for, the Brae field was thus discovered to contain a number of structures strung out like fans on a rope. South Brae was the most southerly of these. After the first three wells, the Brae find had initially been touted as potentially one

102

of the North Sea's biggest oilfields. Subsequently, it had been regarded as one of the area's biggest disappointments. Once the geological key to the area had been unlocked, it appeared that the gambles taken by the likes of Marathon and Ashland had been worthwhile. Nevertheless, Doc Seaman and the Bow Valley management and board breathed many hefty sighs of relief that the company had pulled off the Ashland deal when it did.

New Partners

Over the years following the successful conclusion of the Ashland farm-out, the Ashland stake in Brae was to undergo a number of changes of ownership. Almost as soon as Bow Valley's agreement in principle had been made with Ashland, Ashland in turn farmed-out 45 per cent of its participation to another U.S. company, Louisiana Land and Exploration, in return for LL&E paying 45 per cent of Ashland's obligations. This left Ashland with 7.7 per cent and LL&E with 6.3 per cent of the field. Then, primarily for tax reasons, 1.4 per cent of Ashland's stake was lodged with its Canadian subsidiary, Ashland Oil Canada. In October, 1978, Kaiser Resources took over Ashland Oil Canada for $482.4 million, acquiring with it the Brae stake. Then Kaiser bought out the remainder of Ashland's stake. Kaiser in turn sold all its oil interests to Dome Petroleum, although it maintained its holding in Brae. Following further convoluted corporate dealings, including an abortive attempt to sell its stake to the Swedish national oil company, the Kaiser stake wound up with the British Columbia Resources Investment Corporation (BCRIC). Thus, by the time the field eventually came into production, Ashland itself had long departed and the 14 per cent that Bow Valley had farmed out was divided 7.7 per cent to BCRIC's British subsidiary, Westar Oil U.K., and 6.3 per cent to LL&E.

During all these dealings, Bow Valley's concern was that as its farmed-out stake passed on, it fell into corporate hands strong enough to maintain the financial commitments associated with it. The fact the agreement was kept "whole" during this period was regarded as a tribute both to the Bow Valley staff and legal advisors — like Howard Mackie's Jim Mackie and Edd McRory — who drew up the original deal and shepherded it through its subsequent reincarnations.

The farm-out's value to Bow Valley during the development phase of Brae was clear. By the end of 1983, the year in which the first oil flowed from Brae, Bow Valley had received advances of U.S.$334 million from the partners to whom it had farmed out. Moreover, these partners were still obliged to loan Bow Valley the considerable sums that would be needed to delineate and develop other parts of the Brae field. There would be a number of times during the development phase of South Brae when Bow Valley's farmees must have questioned the scope of their involvement. But for Bow Valley, the deal only looked sweeter and sweeter.

12
Bringing Brae Onstream

By the fall of 1978, Marathon was busily preparing to make its submission to the U.K. Department of Energy on the Brae field's development. It was not a friendly field.

At 13,000 feet, the reservoir was one of the deepest found in the North Sea. This depth in turn contributed to another problem. The oil sat under enormous pressure — at around 7,000 pounds per square inch — and at great heat — around 120°C. In addition, the oil possessed a higher than usual concentration of gas, primarily carbon dioxide, dissolved within it, forming carbonic acid. As a result, the petroleum from South Brae would spurt from the pipe as a seething, gaseous, corrosive liquid. The costs of piping and taming this oil would add considerably to the final bill for the production system of U.S.$2.4 billion.

The size of the field's recoverable reserves also turned out to be less than hoped. After Brae's first three wells — and since the field lay directly between the giant discoveries of Forties and Brent — figures of a billion barrels or more had been bandied about. Subsequently, Marathon's president and chief executive, Harold Hoopman, had landed in hot water with Lord Kearton, the head of BNOC, for suggesting to U.S. investment analysts that the field could contain over 500 million barrels. In the end, the recoverable reserves of South Brae were pegged at 292 million barrels of oil and gas liquids and 150 billion cubic feet of natural gas. While this did not rank South Brae among the giants of the North Sea, it certainly placed it among the major commercial pools. Marathon's studies indicated that the viable life of the Brae field was around fifteen years, with a peak production of 112,000 barrels a day between 1984 and 1987. From Bow Valley's perspective, that level of production would have a dramatic impact on its oil revenues and its overall earnings. Its 14 per cent share of the peak production would bring it 15,680 barrels of oil a day. In 1975, the year the Brae discovery well had been drilled, Bow Valley's total daily oil production had been under 2,000 barrels. Now this figure would make a quantum leap, and the impact on earnings would be truly dramatic. Of course, 70 per cent of that oil flow would go to paying off development costs, but those development costs would, in turn, bring further fields into production, leading to higher and higher revenues for Bow Valley.

Moreover, as Marathon's development plans were being considered by the British government in 1979, the renewed spectre of an oil crisis and rapidly rising prices made the value of that production all the greater. The British government had committed itself to world pricing and world prices were once more on the increase. Between January, 1979 and January, 1980, the official OPEC price of oil doubled — from U.S.$13.34 to U.S.$26.00. Of course such increases were likely to — and indeed did — lead to a renewed assault on profits by the British government. Nevertheless, 15,680 barrels a day at the prevailing world price meant annual pre-tax and royalty revenue to Bow Valley of U.S.$148.8 million. Brae was rightly regarded as a "company-maker." However, that flow of wealth depended on Marathon's ability to bring the field in on time.

Because of the extra equipment needed to process the oil and gas, South Brae demanded one of the heaviest production platforms in the North Sea. Marathon's development plan called for a single huge structure close to the site of the eighth Brae well. From that platform, fourteen production wells would radiate down and outwards up to a radius of two miles from the platform to drain the field. In order to maintain reservoir pressure, and thus the flow of the oil, it was realized that facilities would also be needed to inject as much as 200,000 barrels a day of water back into the field.

Oil from the platform would eventually be pumped seventy-four miles by submarine pipeline to join up with production from the Forties field and from there be piped to Cruden Bay on the Scottish coast. The crude, having been treated, would eventually wind up at the Hound Point terminal on the Firth of Forth, where the Brae partners would "lift" their shares by tanker.

A Platform for all North Sea Seasons

A North Sea production platform is a beast of gargantuan proportions. The Brae "A" platform would be no exception. Sitting in 367 feet of water on eight huge legs, its helicopter deck would rise 237 feet above sea level. Its twin drilling rigs would tower another 160 feet above that. The "jacket" on which the whole vast conglomeration of drilling, production and processing equipment, and crew quarters sat would weigh 21,000 tons. Some of the modules that would be fitted onto its deck like pieces of a giant Chinese puzzle would weigh

2,000 tons. To hold it in place, steel piles 7 feet in diameter would be driven from its 4 corners 240 feet into the seabed.

The contract for the platform jacket was placed in June, 1980, with the McDermott yard at Ardersier, northeast of Inverness. It was worth £47 million. To accelerate production, twenty-four sub-contractors were hired to contribute the steel for the jacket, twelve in Europe and twelve in Japan. The remainder of the platform was also a truly international affair. Production and drilling modules were built in Newcastle and Lowestoft in England, while the living quarters, helideck and module support frame were under construction at two Spanish yards.

To keep the project on time and on budget was a mammoth task, overseen at every stage by Marathon. In the summer of 1981, one of the world's largest pipelaying barges, the *Semac 1*, took just eight weeks to lay the seventy-four-mile line that would link Brae to the Forties pipeline system. In May, 1982, the huge jacket was pushed onto the *M44* launch barge and secured for its journey to Brae. On the morning of June 7, four tugboats began hauling the barge and its towering, rust-colored burden away from the shipyard, into the Moray Firth, and then out to sea. Just thirty hours later, at sunset on the evening of June 8, the barge arrived at its site. Waiting for it was the semi-submersible crane, *Hermod*, where a specially prepared control room had been set up as the command centre for the installation of the platform. On the *Hermod* also were the senior executives of most of the partners involved in the project.

None of them, even the senior executives of Marathon, had ever been involved in a project of this magnitude. For many of them, it would be the highlight of their corporate careers. They stood at the high altar of the most advanced offshore technology. The event they were witnessing would have enormous significance for the financial standing of all their companies; and yet this was a time not for thoughts of engineering specifications or profit and loss statements. It was a time of emotion, a time to marvel at the fruits of men's minds and the rewards of risk-taking on a massive scale.

During the brief North Sea summer night, the pinpoint flames of acetylene torches flashed around the fastenings where the jacket was attached to the barge. Ballast tanks at one end of the barge were filled, tilting the vessel so that the jacket could slide into the water. Early the following morning, the observers on the *Hermod* stood in a chill wind as the jacket slid slowly, majestically into the water, almost disappearing beneath the waves before bobbing back up. For the workers on the *M44* launch barge, the experience was somewhat different. The jacket looked like a skeletal mammoth taking a slow dive into the freezing waters. They stood mesmerized as the round soles of the creature's tree-trunk legs disappeared. Then they realized that the tidal-wave-sized backwash might sweep them into the sea too, so they all ran for it.

The next crucial step was the tipping of the jacket onto its seafloor location. The rig had to be positioned to within just a few feet of a predetermined point directly on top of the wellhead, so as to link up with the submarine pipeline to Forties. This was achieved with the help of radio transponders on the four corners of the platform, and on the wellhead and pipeline. These in turn were linked with the computer in the *Hermod*'s control room. Experts were swung aboard the platform to operate the valves that, over a period of hours, brought the platform to a vertical position. Then more valves were opened and the platform sank to the seafloor. Marathon had wanted to make sure that the platform was positioned within thirty feet of its target and oriented to within five degrees. The final position was within three feet and two degrees.

Over the following eleven days, the thirty-six piles that would hold the platform in place — weighing almost 10,000 tons — were driven into the seafloor. It was the fastest such installation seen in the North Sea. The job, however, was far from over. Next came the much more intricate and demanding task of installing the platform's topside modules. For this job, the size and strength of the crane-barge *Hermod* was crucial.

Hermod is one of only two such vessels in the world capable of lifting 2,200 tons offshore even in rough weather. Because of this capacity, it became possible to bring modules to the jacket in a much more finished condition than had been the case with other North Sea platforms. In early July, these modules began arriving from the shipyards on Britain's east coast and from Cadiz and Almeria in Spain. By August 6, the last module was in place atop the jacket. Once again, the installation, at fifty-seven days, was a record for a platform of the size of the Brae "A." Now came the most labor-intensive part of the operation, the "hook-up."

Another semi-submersible crane vessel, the *DB-100*, was moored alongside the platform to provide accommodation for over 700 workers and storage space for materials. By mid-October, crew quarters for another 240 men were ready aboard the platform itself. The platform and the *DB-100* were connected by a movable bridge across which workers commuted. At the best of times this bridge would have ranked with the scariest of fairground rides; at the worst, it was forced out of action completely by frequent North Sea gales.

Because the weather was forcing delays in the tight construction schedule, Marathon decided in November to increase the workforce. Another semi-submersible accomodation unit, the Swedish *Safe Holmia*, with living-space for a further 525 people, was tethered to the platform. In the summer of 1983, the *DB-100* pulled away to be replaced briefly by the *Safe Holmia*'s third successor, the *Safe Felicia*, which remained in place until the platform was operational.

The hook-up of the rig presented tremendous logistical problems. Between November, 1982, and June, 1983, there were as many as 1,900 men working on the platform. These welders and electricians and scaffolders and painters each had tiny pieces of the great jigsaw puzzle to put into place, each had small but significant tasks that all had to dovetail into the great task. Moreover, every fourteen days, virtually the entire team would be helicoptered ashore to be replaced by their alter egos on the other shift, all of whom had to be briefed on progress, modifications, and re-scheduling.

Due to the lack of space on offshore installations, the logistics of equipment supplies rank with those of a small war. It was crucial that each of the hundreds of thousands of pieces of the final platform, from welding rods to multi-million dollar turbine and pumping units, arrive on time and in sequence.

A key factor in the Brae "A" platform's 32,000 ton topside weight was the equipment needed to tame the field's petroleum, which, by the time it reaches the surface, is still under pressure of 3,500 pounds per square inch. The gas element was to be removed in three stages at progressively lower pressures. The gas from the second and third stage separations was to be returned to the main stream from the first separation, and then this whole stream was to be cooled to condense out the gas liquids — gasoline, butane, propane — which were then to be introduced back into the crude oil stream that would be piped ashore via Forties.

The highly-corrosive separated gas, meanwhile, had to be cleaned via a 4,000-ton Selexol unit, the first such unit used offshore. Selexol is an absorbent substance that soaks up carbon dioxide and hydrogen sulphide under high pressure and releases them under low pressure. The "cleaned" gas would be reinjected into the reservoir below until some way could be found of economically producing it. The carbon dioxide and hydrogen sulphide would be separated from the Selexol and flared. Because of the corrosive nature of the gases, which could eat through steel in a matter of weeks, all the equipment in the gas separation plant had to be made of Incaloy, an expensive nickel/chrome alloy.

Another North Sea first would be that electric motors would be used to drive all the major pumps, compressors, and rotary machinery. The generators were to be driven by four Rolls Royce turbines, producing enough power to supply electricity to a city of 100,000 people.

The First Flow

Finally, on July 12, 1983, the big moment arrived. At 2:41 A.M., the last choke valve was opened on the platform's computer-bedecked control room and oil began to flow from more than two miles beneath the ocean floor. The great platform, with its twin orange and white rigs and its flare booms projecting like antennae, looked like some exotic marine monster. That impression was increased as flames from the flared-off gas suddenly burst from the end of the booms, shedding their light and heat on the platform workers below. The president of Marathon's U.K. subsidiary, Bill Kinney, a man much admired both in his own company and among the Brae partners, summed up the feelings of that moment: "I must confess to feeling a lump in my throat as the first oil flowed. There can be no greater feeling of excitement and sense of accomplishment." That feeling of excitement and accomplishment was fully reflected throughout the Bow Valley empire.

Two months after the oil started to flow from the field, on September 14, Bow Valley made its historic first lifting of Brae oil from BP's terminal at Hound Point. The *M.V. Finny*, an 850-foot-long tanker, picked up its cargoe of 526,466 barrels of oil and transported it to the Milford Haven refinery of the purchaser, Gulf Oil, in South Wales. A month later, Gulf's cheque for more than $15 million represented the first reward from a venture that had started with Odin Drill's 16/7-1 well more than eight years before.

There to see the first lifting was a man who symbolized Bow Valley's status within the British community, the chairman of Bow Valley Exploration (U.K.), Lord Michael Fitzalan Howard.

Doc had clearly seen from Angus Mackenzie's example that key British contacts were vital in establishing the company's status and in winning concessions. Bow Valley director Bill Howard had remained deeply involved in the Canadian army over the years, and, in his capacity as representative for the Canadian Territorial Army, had met Lord Michael when the latter was head of the Commonwealth Association of Territorial Armies. Lord Michael was not merely the brother of the Duke of Norfolk — whose family seat is at Arundel Castle — but he had also been Marshal of the Diplomatic Corps and a member of the Queen's household. Bill Howard thought that he would be an ideal director, so he arranged for a meeting between

Lord Michael, whose official residence was St. James's Palace, and Doc. The two men got on well and not long after the drilling of the first Brae well, Lord Michael became a director of Bow Valley.

Along with the the bluest of blood and the best of connections, Lord Michael also possessed a shrewd mind and a dry British sense of humor. He was the quintessential English gentleman. As such, he shared Doc and B.J.'s passion for hunting. On one occasion, the brothers invited him goose-hunting at Peace River in Alberta. At 5:00 A.M., as the other hunters — mostly roughnecks and local farmers — gathered, bleary-eyed and in blue jeans, to drink coffee, they were treated to the sight of Lord Michael in immaculate tweed jacket and tie!

After a couple of years, Lord Michael's other commitments forced him to resign from the full Bow Valley board, but Doc persuaded him to stay on as non-executive chairman of the U.K. operation.

North Brae: Another Mammoth is Born

The delivery of the first Brae oil coincided with another major event in Bow Valley's North Sea involvement. Following the delineation of South Brae, drilling around the site of the first Brae well, 16/7-1, determined another commercial structure, North Brae. Early in June, 1983, Marathon announced on behalf of Bow Valley and its other Brae partners that it planned to place a second platform on the Brae field, some eight miles north of the South Brae platform, to tap the North Brae field. It was anticipated that the total cost of the project would be £1.7 billion. The plans submitted to the U.K.'s Department of Energy called for platform installation in 1987 and first production late in 1988. It was expected that the peak production rates from the platform would be around 75,000 barrels daily, with sales of dry gas beginning some nine years after the start-up of condensate production. It would be the first North Sea condensate field, and would use a sophisticated gas-cycling process to achieve maximum liquid recovery. Recoverable reserves of the field were estimated at more than 200 million barrels of condensate and 600 billion cubic feet of dry gas.

In October, 1983, the Department of Energy approved the plan and the contract for the detailed design of the platform's jacket was awarded to Brown and Root. Another giant project was under way, and Bow Valley was a part of it.

For a company of its size, Bow Valley enjoyed enormous success in the North Sea, and the Brae field's development will continue for the remainder of this century at least. However, not all its North Sea activities were unqualified successes. Bow Valley had been involved during the Brae delineation and development in two other major ventures in the North Sea: the discovery and development of the Heimdal field, and the part-ownership and operation of the semi-submersible *Odin Drill*. Both proved to be somewhat frustrating experiences.

13
North Sea Frustrations: *Odin Drill* and Heimdal

For Bow Valley, *Odin Drill* was at once a source of intense pride and financial disappointment. The semi-submersible developed an excellent reputation in the demanding North Sea oilpatch, but at the same time, problems with Bow Valley's partners in the rig, combined with soft markets, made it at best a marginal proposition.

Between 1974 and 1978, *Odin Drill* was used to drill the discovery well and eight others on Block 16/7. It also drilled several wells on other blocks, most notably for Bow Valley's partner, Home Oil. After three and one-half years in the North Sea, *Odin Drill* was on its twelfth well. Its total footage up to the completion of the eleventh well had been 126,480 feet, almost twenty-four miles of penetration into the Earth's crust at a rate of 112.4 feet a day for every one of its 1,125 days on location. Only eighty-five days had been lost due to bad weather and forty-nine due to mechanical breakdown.

A good deal of the rig's operational success was attributed to its stable international workforce. Of the ninety crew, the drillers tended to be predominantly North American, the sailors Norwegian, and the caterers British, although Europeans had taken over a number of the drilling jobs. Ken Lord, who managed the rig for Bow Valley, held the responsibility for following up on contract prospects, establishing rates, supervising staff, and keeping an eye on costs. His job was made no easier by the fact that he was surrounded not merely by the usual myriad of technical and logistical matters, but also by the enormous complexities of jurisdiction and taxation involved in a jointly owned international operation. Nevertheless, like most men in such positions, he developed a fierce pride in the rig's performance. The problems, however, were not ones of performance, but of money.

The top priority with a piece of expensive drilling equipment like the *Odin Drill* is to keep it working. There had been difficulties from the start with Pan Ocean's reluctance to use the rig. To persuade Pan Ocean to use it for the third well on block 16/7, it had been necessary for Home and Bow Valley to finance some of Pan Ocean's expenditures. This had cost Bow Valley an additional unbudgeted $1 million.

As well, Bow Valley and Home had given their Norwegian partners exceptionally good terms on the financial operation of the rig. Each Canadian company had committed to take the rig for one year of its initial four year contract. If rig rates went down, it was the Canadian company that had to bear the losses, because the Norwegian parties' day-rates were guaranteed. Since day-rates for rigs were large, any depression of rates could involve a large financial drain.

The *Odin Drill* needed a rate of around $23,000 a day to cover its operating, depreciation, interest and debt-amortization costs. If it could only command $20,000 a day, then that meant an effective loss of $1 million a year. The operation had been profitable in its first two years, but in 1977, markets had turned weak as a wave of newly constructed semi-submersibles had flooded into the North Sea. In addition, the varying corporate objectives and problems of the rig's partners were now inevitably driving them apart.

When it came to the Norwegian partners, Wilhelmsen's major reason for involvement had been to gain experience in offshore drilling. This they had now achieved, and they were running three semi-submersibles of their own. They were quite happy at the prospect of a sale. Waage meanwhile had run into severe financial problems in its shipbuilding activities. Indeed, the only asset the company owned in the end was its 40 per cent stake in the *Odin Drill* operation. Home, too, wanted to sell out.

By the beginning of 1978, while the *Odin* was still working on appraisal wells on block 16/7, the source of future work looked uncertain. Although there was a possibility that Marathon would want the rig again in another three months or so, there was no guarantee that this would be the case, nor that the *Odin Drill* could find an acceptable job in the meantime.

There were considered to be some brighter prospects on the horizon. All the new rigs under construction were expected to be in service by January of 1978, with no more coming into commission until 1980; the fifth round of licences was due to be worked in 1978; it was felt that the bottom of the slump had been reached; and finally it was regarded as likely that opportunities were bound to open up — as they indeed did — on the east coast of North America and other offshore oil provinces throughout the world. In the North Sea itself, the British government had declared its intention to issue licences on a more regular basis, which would, it was felt, help sustain a more even but higher level of activity. Meanwhile, other exploration areas around the U.K., such as the Western Approaches and the English Channel, were also thought likely to be opened up.

Nevertheless, stacked rigs whose owners were in many cases strapped for cash were sure to exert a downward influence on day-rates for the immediate future, while operating cost projections were rising fairly sharply due to inflation. One particular problem was wages. The Norwegians had introduced a law in 1977 reducing the average work week offshore to thirty-six hours. This meant that five crews were needed to service the rig instead of four. The Norwegian Seaman's Union was also expected to negotiate a sizable wage increase.

The view from Bow Valley's U.K. rig-managers was that although *Odin Drill* would lose money in 1978, it would return to profitability in 1979 and make hefty profits in 1980 and 1981. But the picture looked less rosy once requirements for servicing the debt on the rig, and also the requirement to have the rig inspected (and thus out of commission), were taken into account.

The suggestion of the U.K. operating group was that Bow Valley should consider buying out its partners and setting up a U.K.-based operation with cheaper U.K. labor. In the end, however, Calgary decided that the best solution was to sell the rig, and in October, 1978, the rig was sold to Global Marine.

For Bow Valley, *Odin Drill* had been a bitter-sweet venture. But if in the end it had not met the rigid demands of the bottom line, it had at least given the company valuable experience in offshore drilling operations. Within just a couple of years, Bow Valley would be back in the offshore drilling business again, but this time in a much bigger way.

Odin Drill had provided its frustrations, but had been a learning experience for Bow Valley. The development of the Heimdal field, however, provided a much more complex and convoluted learning opportunity.

The Heimdal Experience

If Brae delineation and development had been difficult, then the evolution of the Heimdal field could be classified as labyrinthine. However, the complexities were not geological, but rather those of energy politics. The inter-consortium dealings at times seemed like nothing so much as the politics of a sixteenth-century Italian duchy.

In June, 1971, Bow Valley's consortium had been awarded block 25/4 in the Norwegian sector, approximately eight miles south of the large Frigg gas discovery. The first North Sea well that Bow Valley participated in was on block 25/4 in December, 1972. It hit paydirt, testing at a rate of 33.8 MMCF of gas and 545 barrels of condensate a day.

Further success came on the block when a second well, drilled three miles northeast of the original discovery, hit hydrocarbons in the same

115

formation as the first well, indicating a sizable, potentially commercial field. Preliminary engineering and financial studies indicated that this field, named Heimdal — which was about 100 miles off the Norwegian coast in 375 feet of water — could be in production by early 1978.

The discovery was particularly gratifying, and also perhaps something of a relief, to Dick Harris. Syracuse's vast land spread, and its exploration commitments, were a hefty burden for Bow Valley. Harris was under pressure to produce the goods. Heimdal was the goods. It was the first major success on the old Syracuse lands, although it certainly wasn't the last. But the Heimdal field would provide many headaches for Bow Valley and its partners before it finally entered the development phase.

From the start, the Norwegian government had taken a much more interventionist and gradualist approach to North Sea development than its U.K. neighbor. Because the Norwegians had neither the domestic petroleum demand nor the balance of payments problems of the U.K., their needs for development were less pressing. Statoil, the national oil company, was also to emerge as a much more active partner in consortia in the Norwegian sector. These factors meant that the oil companies in general experienced more frustration in their dealings with the Norwegian government than with Whitehall. Although Syracuse had — prior to its acquisition by Bow Valley — established itself in Norway and developed good relations with both the banking and government sectors in Oslo, the Norwegian government would later cool on involving smaller companies in development. Meanwhile, the politics of natural gas sales and transportation would further complicate an already complicated picture.

The non-government partners in Heimdal felt themselves part of a game of smoke and mirrors, in which the geology or economics of the field played second fiddle to behind-the-scenes negotiations on larger issues of politics and the pace of hydrocarbon development. In 1975, the Norwegian state oil company, Statoil, exercised its back-in to the Heimdal field, reducing Bow Valley's share of costs and production from an original 15.2 per cent to 8 per cent. Soon after its first two wells, Heimdal was projected by the Norwegians to contain between 1.7 and 2 TCF of gas and 28 million barrels of recoverable condensate. The condensate figure would be on the low side, but the much more important natural gas reserve figure proved to be optimistic. Moreover, the field's condensate was problematic, since it had either to be stored or transported via pipeline, thus increasing the development costs of the field.

By the end of 1975, when the excitement at Brae was dominating the company's interest, it became clear that Elf Norge A/S — a subsidiary of the French national oil company — was now much less

116

optimistic about the field's development. However, the extent to which this resulted from pressure on the part of the Norwegian government, which did not want to rush development, was not clear. In January, 1976, Elf delivered a much less optimistic appraisal of the field's prospects to the stunned members of the consortium. Costs, they said, were going up, reserves were going down, and the whole commercial viability of the field was being brought into doubt. Statoil's back-in had seemed to support the field's commerciality, but now, for whatever reason, that burst of enthusiasm appeared to have dissipated.

When the field had initially been declared commercial, a gas purchase contract had been outlined with the British Gas Corporation. It was planned that the gas from the field would flow north through a new line to link up with the Frigg system — which would come into production in September, 1977 — for delivery in Scotland. After the bleaker economic picture painted by Elf in January, 1976, however, the contract seemed in serious doubt. Officially, the consortium made a statement that the first production from the field was likely in 1981-82 rather than the original forecast of 1978. But then the political winds began to change for the better.

Early in 1978, the Norwegian government publicly announced incentive proposals to encourage the development of small offshore fields, and made specific mention of Heimdal. In June, Bow Valley was part of the group that met with the Norwegian government to discuss these proposals. The field had now effectively been in limbo for a couple of years.

In October, 1979, Elf was authorized by its partners to commission a feasability study to re-evaluate the field. Bow Valley's estimate of total Heimdal reserves was 1.7 TCF of gas and 49 million barrels of condensate. The company estimated that production of 350 MMCF of gas and 10,000 barrels of condensate a day would cost around $760 million to develop. However, a fifth well on the block early in 1980 led to a further reduction of reserve estimates. Bow Valley's share of proved reserves was estimated to be 95.4 BCF of gas and 2.4 million barrels of condensate (These estimates would subsequently be reduced to 93.6 BCF and 2.2 million barrels). Costs were also to rise sharply again. Nevertheless, in the minds of the non-government consortium members, it was still politics rather than economics that was holding up development. At this stage, however, politics suddenly began to work in their favor. Transportation plans for the gas now changed dramatically, and in fact became the key factor in the decision to develop the field.

More Pipeline Politics

The Norwegian government wanted natural gas from Statfjord, a field far north of both Heimdal and Frigg, to be piped via Norway — and there processed — before moving on to its final destination at Emden, West Germany. Along the way — after leaving Norway again, it was to link up with gas from the Ekofisk field and its satellites, which lay as far south of Heimdal as Statfjord lay north of it. This line would be known as Statpipe. However, it was discovered that there would be a shortfall in the Ekofisk portion of the line around the mid-1980s. Hence a plan was hatched by Statoil and the Norwegian government to link in Heimdal reserves, which would join up with gas from Statfjord after the Statfjord gas had been landed and processed in Karsto, Norway.

Bow Valley tried, unsuccessfully, to become a partner in the pipeline spur that would link Heimdal gas with the flow from Statfjord on the way to Ekofisk, but was rejected by the Norwegian government.

Of crucial importance to development was the signing of sales contracts for the field's gas. At the end of 1980, a consortium of gas buyers from continental Europe had outlined an offer to buy the field's gas. Then Elf and Statoil had offered to buy the gas. Then the British Gas Corporation, hoping to win the gas for Britain and have it piped via the Frigg system, re-entered the fray with a higher offer. There were frantic negotiations in the first two weeks of January, 1981, but the Heimdal group, which although operated by Elf was dominated by Statoil, decided — not surprisingly — to go with the Statoil pipeline plan. That inevitably meant that the gas would finish up in continental Europe rather than the U.K. Production, meanwhile, was now not expected to commence until 1986 at 307 MMCF of gas and 7,700 barrels of condensate a day. Developments costs, including escalation and contingency, had now risen to U.S.$1.2 billion.

The costs of financing the project were now foremost in corporate minds. Financing, in turn, inevitably revolved around sale of the gas — and the concept of project finance.

Project financing had evolved in step with massive energy projects such as those in the North Sea. The size of these projects frequently dwarfed their sponsors — or at least would threaten them financially if they failed — and this inevitably forced bankers to take a new perspective on funding them. Instead of looking at the cash flow and collateral of the borrower, as in traditional lending, the banks now had to look primarily at the financial viability of the project itself. If it was thought that the project could stand on its own feet, generating enough cash to repay both interest and principle — with a healthy risk cushion — then the banks were prepared to "project finance" it, often on a non-recourse basis, thus eliminating virtually all risk to the sponsor. This was the form of the deal eventually worked out by Bow Valley for its share of the costs of Heimdal.

Ralph Mackenzie, who had joined Bow Valley as controller of its oil and gas division in 1970, had been sent to the London office in 1976 to deal with the intricacies of North Sea finance. His first job had been the negotiation of the original sales contract for Heimdal gas with the British Gas Corporation. That contract, however, had fallen into abeyance as the field's development became mired in politics. Mackenzie (no relation to the peripatetic Angus) would play a role in selling the Brae farm-out package, but his main task became the negotiation of the early stages of the Heimdal financing, which in turn was inextricably connected with the pre-sale of its gas. Another key figure in the negotiations — particularly after Ralph Mackenzie left the company in 1981 — was Peter Owens, an Englishman with an accounting background who had had two years experience with Thorne Riddell in Calgary before joining Bow Valley just as the Ashland financing was being completed in 1977. Clive Randle, head of the U.K. operation, retained overall local responsibility for the tough negotiations ahead. The head office men most involved at the later crucial financing of the project were Bill Tye, who had been appointed Bow Valley's chief financial officer in 1980, and Larry Mackwood, the company's treasurer.

Project finance was heavily dependent on the security of sales contracts. Fortunately, the French national oil company appeared to want the gas very badly. It wanted it so badly that it approached Bow Valley with an offer the Canadian company couldn't refuse. If Bow Valley would sell Elf its gas, then Elf would not only provide interim finance for the company, but it would help negotiate a limited-recourse deal with the banks. BVI agreed and appointed merchant bank Rothschilds as its financial advisor.

As all this was going on, the issue of the disposal of the field's condensate was also having a bearing on development costs. The original plan had been to pipe the condensate via Mobil's Beryl field, but Mobil subsequently decided that it did not have enough capacity to accommodate the production. A new plan was adopted to ship the condensate via the South Brae platform southwest of Heimdal. Costs were further increased when it was decided to raise the system's capacity by 10 per cent, bringing production up to 337 MMCF of gas and 8,290 barrels of condensate a day.

119

Nothing Is But What Is Not

Elf's parent, Société Nationale Elf Aquitaine, (SNEA), agreed to provide bridging loans to Bow Valley pending a definitive agreement with the banks. However, negotiations, most of which took place in Paris, became bogged down in myriad legal and technical details, which involved phalanxes of corporate and bank lawyers. Under the agreement being negotiated, the only recourse to Bow Valley for financing was in the case of cost overruns. At the time, in 1982 and 1983, there was international jitteriness over the health of both the banking system and the energy sector. Dome Petroleum, with more than $6 billion in debt, was threatening to become the world's largest bankruptcy. That situation increased nervousness about Canadian oil companies in general. There was one particularly memorable meeting with dozens of participants in the Paris offices of the bank Credit Lyonnais. There were no windows and no air-conditioning in the negotiating room, which became cramped and stifling. The complex technical arguments were beginning to take on an almost surreal quality. Tempers were becoming frayed. One of the Elf lawyers leaned back in his chair, and reflected, quoting Macbeth: "Nothing is but what is not."

The following day, there was another inconclusive meeting at Elf's offices. Elf, Bow Valley and their Rothschilds' consultants felt that the banks were being picayune and unreasonable. At 5:00 P.M., when the banks were refusing to budge on the intricate but highly important issue of remedies to them in the case of technical default, the Elf-Bow Valley team, much to the banks' astonishment, stood up and walked out. The move had not been pre-arranged but had a highly salutary effect on the bankers, who virtually chased their potential customers out of the door in an attempt to get them to return. The following day, the phone hardly stopped ringing as Bow Valley and Elf were cajoled back to the bank.

In the end, it was agreed that the participants had virtually to lock themselves in one location until the technicalities of the deal had been ironed out. They all spent close to a month in the Hilton Hotel in Amsterdam. Although the words were Shakespeare's, they seemed more in the spirit of Lewis Carroll, when one of the bankers decided to call the corporate vehicle that would hold the banks' security NIBWIN, which stood for: "Nothing is but what is not."

In November, 1983, the deal was signed in Paris under which Bow Valley borrowed U.S.$145 million as its share of Heimdal development costs. Although it would be a number of years before the field would start paying cash to Bow Valley, the important point, once again, was that the loan was non-recourse to the company's other assets.

In July, 1984, the Heimdal platform, which had taken two years to construct, was towed out to its site. By the end of August, installation had been completed and the at once mammoth and intricate task of installing the topsides began. First production was anticipated in mid-1986.

Heimdal had presented a much longer and messier experience than Brae, but it had now been brought to a successful conclusion. Although the fruits of the field were some way down the road, Bow Valley had increased the scope of its international activities, the breadth of its corporate experience, and its stature within the international oil and financial communities.

But Bow Valley had hardly been standing still while the long and demanding tasks of delineating and bringing the South Brae and Heimdal fields onstream was underway. Indeed, during that period, the company had made massive strides elsewhere. It had enjoyed hard-won success — and even met magnificent failure — in its other overseas exploration activities; it had made a major acquisition south of the border; it had been involved in an important uranium find in the Seamans' home province of Saskatchewan; and it had made an enormous commitment to drilling and exploration offshore Canada's East Coast.

14
Adventures in the Orient

It Is Not Good For The Westerner's Health
To Hustle The Asian Brown,
For The Westerner Riles — And The Asian Smiles
And He Weareth The Westerner Down.
And The End Of The Fight
Is A Tombstone White
With The Name Of The Late Deceased
And The Epitaph Drear:
"A Fool Lies Here
Who Tried To Hustle The East."

— RUDYARD KIPLING

Although the subsequent development process had been long and arduous, Bow Valley had met success in the North Sea with its first couple of wells. Its first wells offshore Abu Dhabi were also successful, although development there was to be marked by many frustrations. Success in the other parts of the world was to take longer. In Indonesia, which would ultimately rank second only to Brae in importance, success took more than a decade, and in Vietnam, it did not come at all. However, the company had some remarkable experiences in the process of failing!

One of the key men in Bow Valley's Far Eastern activities was Lloyd Flood, a fellow Saskatchewaner and old friend of the Seamans who took to the Orient like a duck to water. Where most westerners never succeed in fully understanding the inscrutable and oblique ways of the region, Flood — a man with an enormous sense of humor — rejoiced in them.

Flood had known the Seaman brothers at the University of Saskatchewan, and became particularly good friends with Don. For a time, B.J. had been Flood's drafting instructor. Flood became a geologist with a subsidiary of Canadian Superior. He ran into the Seamans again in 1956, when he was working in Calgary for the oil arm of Monsanto Chemical, and Doc came to visit him to bid on some of the company's drilling work.

Flood then moved out of oil and gas for some years to become a partner in a computer data processing business. He eventually fell back into the Seamans' orbit when Bow Valley bought him and his partners out in 1971. When Doc asked him if he wanted to stay with computers or move back into oil and gas, he decided to move back into oil and gas. Shortly after he joined Bow Valley, the Syracuse merger brought both Dick Harris and many exotic properties into the company. Harris asked Flood if he'd ever been to the Far East. Flood hadn't, but soon found himself in Sumatra looking at some land prospects, which he acquired for Bow Valley. "Now you've got it," he was told, "you might as well manage it." In 1973, he moved his family to Jakarta.

While the bane of business in North America and Europe was an ever-growing mound of complex legislation, in the Far East things were equally intricate but far more subtle. When dealing in Indonesia and Vietnam, what was needed more than an army of lawyers was a fine sense of nuance. Flood learned Eastern languages and Eastern ways and became a master of the art. But whatever the negotiating skills needed, the bottom line always remained the discovery of petroleum. It took more than a decade for Bow Valley's — and Flood's — efforts to be rewarded. The successes were hard won, but the failures too were, in their own way, magnificent.

Vietnam: The Magnificent Failure

Bow Valley's involvement in Vietnam had its origins — as does so much activity in the oil patch — over a few drinks. In the spring of 1972, Lloyd Flood was in the bar of the Goodwood Hotel in Singapore with Wilf Bailey of Asamera, the company with which Bow Valley would later enjoy success in Indonesia. Bailey casually asked if Bow Valley might be interested in an oil play off Vietnam in the South China Sea. If it was, then perhaps he could provide some contacts in Saigon. The Vietnamese War was in full swing, but Flood dutifully passed this information on to Dick Harris. As it happened, Angus Mackenzie, Harris's former partner, was also looking — via Sunningdale — at the area at the time. Offshore production in the southwest part of the South China Sea, offshore Malaysia, had met with considerable success, and it was only a matter of time before companies started looking farther north, offshore Vietnam's south coast. Stu McColl, who was now president of Mackenzie's Sunningdale, was particularly interested in the area. Over a few more casual drinks at a hotel in Oslo, McColl had offered Dick Harris and Fred Wellhauser a quarter share in any action they might obtain offshore Vietnam. Harris and Wellhauser had agreed on the spot.

The two groups started to look at putting together a consortium to apply for an exploration licence. They obtained some non-exclusive seismic work that had been shot over the area, and also reports produced by a geological service company run out of Singapore by a man named Jim Blake. They also acquired key contacts in Vietnam, the chief of which was an American named Hank Mucci. A former colonel in American intelligence, Mucci had tremendous connections in Saigon. If the partners wanted a car, or a typewriter, or an English-speaking secretary, he could fix it up in a matter of hours.

As partners, Bow Valley and Sunningdale brought in Bill Siebens — who had known Mackenzie and the Seamans for a long time, and who was already involved with them in the North Sea — and the U.S. contract drilling company, Santa Fe.

All the early day-to-day negotiation with the Vietnamese was carried out by Mackenzie. His charm worked once more and, on July 14, 1973, South Vietnam's National Petroleum Board announced that the consortium had been awarded two concessions, covering 3.4 million acres, 180 miles south of Saigon. Bow Valley was to become operator of the venture and a 2,000-mile marine seismic program was planned for late 1973. All this, however, was subject to the signing of formal concession documents.

On Monday, August 13, 1973, Angus Mackenzie called from Saigon to say that the Vietnamese National Petroleum Board wanted to sign final documentation on August 21. For the four partners, this meant panic stations. They had just a week to organize appropriate wholly owned Vietnamese subsidiaries, register branch offices, line up letters of credit through the Bank of America in Saigon, and perform the myriad other legal and financial requirements for companies operating overseas.

By Wednesday, the 15th, a courier was on his way to the South Vietnamese embassy in Washington with the relevant documents from Bow Valley, Sunningdale, and Siebens. There he linked up with a representative from Santa Fe, and the information bundle was notarized by Vietnamese officials. That Saturday, the 18th, lawyer Bob Newby from Jim Palmer's law firm was on his way with the bundle to Saigon to sign on behalf of the four companies.

In July, Bow Valley's board had made a $1.5 million, six-year commitment to a Vietnamese venture. By September, they would be asked, and would agree, to make a second commitment for a similar amount to cover an increase in the planned seismic work. Instead of the originally planned 2,000-mile program, a 4,000-mile program was carried out between late January and early March, 1974. Bow Valley supervised the acquisition and processing of data, and then set to work to interpret it. The results looked good. There were major anomalies beneath the acreage that could be giant oil traps. Drilling was scheduled to begin in 1975.

In May, 1974, a 35 per cent interest in one of the concessions was farmed-out to the French company Aquitaine in return for exploration commitments on the block. Aquitaine then, in turn, farmed-out half its interests to the petroleum arm of the Japanese company Mitsubishi. In February, 1975, the South Vietnamese government approved the new arrangements. However, it was by now becoming clear that new arrangements of a more sweeping nature were in store for the South Vietnamese government itself. The Americans had begun to withdraw from the country in the latter half of 1974, and the North Vietnamese had begun to move in very quickly. In March, 1975, Lloyd Flood had made a trip to Saigon. Late one evening he had been standing on the balcony of the Caravelle Hotel in the South Vietnamese capital when he heard a tremendous barrage of artillery fire in the distance. Hank Mucci was in the room. "Henry," said Flood, "I can hear the guns going off out there tonight. Does it mean very much?" Mucci told him not to worry, that it was just the nightly barrage. But it turned out to be something more.

Flood left later that week, declaring that he would be back closer to the start of drilling. But by the end of the month, as the American pull-out gathered momentum and the North Vietnamese moved from strength to strength, it was obvious that Saigon was in danger. The consortium was forced to pull out its personnel. The last man out was Mucci, who left at the end of April. He made his dramatic departure via helicopter from the roof of the U.S. Embassy. Shortly afterwards, the North Vietnamese tanks rolled into the South Vietnamese capital.

Fears of the "domino theory" now ran rampant throughout Southeast Asia. The original Vietnam exploration consortium disintegrated, and a few months after the fall of Saigon, Flood returned to a meeting in Calgary of the Canadian joint-venture partners. Bill Siebens said that some of his people had talked to North Vietnamese representatives in Paris, and that the situation didn't seem hopeful. However, Flood, through his extensive Far Eastern network, had met some Frenchmen in Singapore who thought that it might just be possible to get back into Vietnam and deal with the new government. They had already made visits back to Saigon. Flood was asked by the group to pursue that approach. Siebens declared, somewhat less formally: "I'll kiss your ass if you get us back in." Despite that threat, Flood returned to Singapore to give it his best shot. In its 1975 annual report, Bow Valley stated with a typical resoluteness: "Bow Valley and its partners are of the opinion that a resumption of operations, on terms and conditions acceptable to the group, is entirely possible, and efforts to contact the new Vietnamese administration are in progress." That rather antiseptic assessment did no justice to the heroic nature of those efforts.

Into the Heart of Darkness

Flood discovered via his contacts that the North Vietnamese had a small mission in Singapore involved in non-strategic trade with the West. He arranged to see the head of the mission, explained what his group had been doing in Vietnam, and said that he would like to visit the North Vietnamese capital of Hanoi to discuss the resurrection of the agreement to drill on the South China Sea acreage.

After several more meetings, the head of the trade mission suggested that Flood could go to Hanoi to discuss his proposition. "How?" asked Flood. The North Vietnamese told him that he could go via Vientiane in Laos and that they would warn their embassy there to expect him. Flood was well aware that nothing in South East Asia was ever so straightforward. Might he, he asked, be graced with just a small letter of introduction to the ambassador in Vientiane? Armed with the letter, he set off on the circuitous trip to Hanoi.

His first stop was Bangkok, where his old friend Henry Mucci had now set up shop. Mucci helped him obtain a visa for Laos, and, after a couple more days, he took off for Vientiane in an old DC-6B, with oil dripping from its wings. When he approached the North Vietnamese ambassador in the city, he was not at all surprised that the man had never heard of him. He presented his letter of introduction and, after another delay, was given a visa to visit the North Vietnamese capital. Soon he was aboard a Russian-built turbo-prop headed for Hanoi.

The day in November, 1975, that Lloyd Flood stepped onto the tarmac in the communist capital, he had a very keen sense of walking into the heart of darkness. The terminal was filled with grim-looking soldiers wearing baggy uniforms and red-starred Mao caps, all sporting their Russian AK47 rifles. Flood should have been at home preparing to celebrate his twenty-fifth wedding anniversary. Instead, he was one of the first Canadian businessmen into Vietnam after the fall of the South. As he looked around the terminal, he said to himself: "Flood, you stupid fool! You're forty-eight years old. What are you doing here?" Apprehensively, Flood cleared customs and immigration and was met by representatives of the trade ministry, Techno

Import. He climbed into a car for the six-mile trip to Hanoi. As the car pulled away from the airport, suddenly the road was filled with honking buses and weaving cyclists, and carts pulled by water buffalo. By the side of the road, peasants pounded away at their rice. Flood's tension eased. He had held the image of brutally efficient North Vietnam, but it appeared just like the rest of South East Asia: organized chaos!

Half a world away, in Calgary, Bow Valley worried both about Flood and their investment. Ralph Mackenzie, who was by now specializing in financing the company's international petroleum activities, would try to glean information from the Department of External Affairs in Ottawa, but he never discovered a better source of information on Vietnamese affairs than the *New York Times*! Flood meanwhile was led through a maze of meetings with people whose identities were not always clear. He was quizzed about the nature of the consortium's agreements with the South Vietnamese, about the work that had been carried out, about the group's activities in Saigon, and about the geological nature of the structures they wanted to drill.

On the afternoon Flood was due to leave Hanoi, he was approached by one of the officials with whom he had held numerous meetings. The official, a Dr. Chu, spoke a little English. He thanked Flood for his directness, and informed him that they knew that everything he had said was correct. The reason they knew this was that, three days after Saigon had fallen, they had taken possession of all the documentation in the consortium's Saigon office! The official concluded by saying that in due course they would meet again to discuss co-operation and matters of mutual benefit.

The Longest Yard

It would take three years for Bow Valley — as head of a new, all-Canadian group — to win back the licences. During that period, Lloyd Flood would make almost fifty trips to Vietnam. Depending on the stage of negotiations, Fred Wellhauser or Angus Mackenzie would be brought in, like fresh players off the bench in a long and gruelling game. Angus Mackenzie would bring his towering frame and charismatic persona to the table, waving his arms about and waxing lyrical. Fred Wellhauser, more soft-spoken and subtle, would speak to the North Vietnamese in English via the translator until they reached a sticking point. Then he would switch into his own perfect French. Status was very important to the North Vietnamese. In 1976, Flood was concerned that they seemed to think his rank not high enough.

As a result, Bow Valley reorganized a subsidiary and made Flood its president and Wellhauser its chairman. The North Vietnamese congratulated Flood on his elevation and the talks began to progress once more!

Apart from the difficulties of negotiation, there were also the physical hardships, at least by Western standards, to overcome. The employees in the London office, who were involved in the complex and often acrimonious meetings over Brae development and government participation, looked on with amusement as their colleagues prepared for Far East trips like big game hunters going off into the bush. Flood, Mackenzie, and Wellhauser and whoever else was going along would trek to Fortnum & Mason in London's Piccadilly and stock up with "survival kits" of tinned foods of all sorts.

The principal sticking point in the negotiations was that the North Vietnamese wanted the consortium to accept a low fixed rate of return on their venture; what the Communists believed to be a "fair economic rent." Their point of view was not out of line with that of many socialistically inclined governments in the developed world. Indeed, those who would frame Canada's National Energy Policy in 1980 were the philosophical soul-brothers of the North Vietnamese! Bow Valley for its part attempted to explain that under such regulations, no activity would take place. If there was insufficient prospect of profit, there would be no exploration. If there was no exploration, there would be no oil. If there was no oil, there could be no government revenue.

One could sympathize with the attitude of the North Vietnamese negotiators. Their intellectual appreciation of free-enterprise capitalism came from Marxist text books. Their direct experience of the West had come out of the bomb-bays of B52s. Bow Valley's representatives had a great deal of trouble trying to explain that they had to deduct the costs of the capital they invested before they could calculate their return on investment. Interest rates were high and these costs were large. At one stage, one of the North Vietnamese negotiators declared earnestly to Fred Wellhauser that interest rates were too high and that he should go to the Canadian government and insist that the rates be brought down. Wellhauser said that he entirely agreed with him, but that he didn't think that he'd have much success!

The final deal with the Vietnamese was hammered out by Flood and Rod DeLuca. DeLuca, a graduate of the Colorado School of Mines and a Harvard MBA, had joined Syracuse in 1969, where he found himself primarily involved in warding off the company's creditors! He joined Bow Valley with Syracuse and, between 1971 and 1979, played a key role in the company's foreign acquisition activities. In

1976, he had set up office with Flood in Singapore, assuming responsibility for all areas outside Flood's primary bailiwick of Indonesia. As such he covered a territory that stretched from New Zealand to Korea, from the Seychelles to the Philippines.

Flood decided that the two men should employ the white hat/black hat, or good cop/bad cop, approach. DeLuca was to don the black hat, assuming the role of the hard-line official consortium representative; Flood was the good guy. On one day during the intensive negotiations, the Vietnamese suggested a little recreation. They took Flood and DeLuca to Vung Tau — a former resort centre where Bow Valley's supply base would eventually be sited — and suggested that they swim and relax. However, it was clear that some of the Vietnamese officials were less keen on relaxing than others. DeLuca suddenly found himself confronted by several of the Vietnamese as they stood in five feet of water. He regained his swim's recreational status by slowly edging further out into the water until the shorter Vietnamese were forced to tread water and, out of breath, head for shore!

After a final session of hard bargaining in Ho Chi Minh City (as Saigon had now been renamed) in July, 1978, a deal was finally struck. The momentous occasion was recorded at a semi-official lunch at the restaurant of the Happy Dragon Hotel. Flood appeared with his trademark, a bottle of Johnny Walker Black Label, and everybody congratulated each other and themselves. In return for a commitment to spend $15 million over three years, Bow Valley and its partners would receive a percentage of production.

In September, 1978, at a grand event in the conference room of the former U.S. Embassy in Ho Chi Minh City, Dick Harris and Fred Wellhauser and Lloyd Flood for Bow Valley, and representatives of the other partners, including Angus Mackenzie, met for the official signing. The event was broadcast on national television, and the local producers organized the official group so that they would be filmed entering the room. Flood and Wellhauser slicked back their hair and adjusted their ties, but by the time they entered the room, the cameras had stopped shooting!

The Final Frustration

After such a negotiation and such a signing, the discovery of oil seemed almost a formality. Nevertheless, the logistics of drilling were extremely difficult. The North Vietnamese were still official "enemies" of the U.S., and American authorities were none too keen on the Bow

Valley consortium's agreement. They applied direct and indirect pressure to thwart the operation at every turn. The American members of the crew of the semi-submersible *Dan Queen*, which would be used to drill the wells, were threatened by U.S. representatives with reprisals if they worked in the South China Sea. The same representatives attempted to cut off services and supplies to the venture by similar tactics. Bow Valley circumnavigated the first problem by crewing the *Dan Queen* with Canadian, Australian, and British crew. They dealt with the second by obtaining supplies through third-party agents who were either British or French or Australian.

Despite all the difficulties, two holes were drilled to about 5,000 feet early in 1980. The first was completed on March 2, the second on March 24. They were perfectly dry. The consortium was deeply disappointed. However, it had to drill holes to fulfill its exploration commitments. But now new, human factors, had appeared. The Vietnamese invaded Cambodia in late December, 1979, which alienated world opinion. In addition, there was the tragedy of the boat people. Drilling with both the boat people and military craft around became virtually impossible. But in any case, the geological disappointments of the first two wells meant that the consortium was not keen to drill further.

If Vietnam produced no drilling success, it did, however, produce one personal triumph. In Laos, Flood had found a young Vietnamese, Nguen Ngoc Phai, who acted as his local guide and expediter. Phai had been recommended to Flood by a flamboyant local Frenchman in Vientiane. The displaced Vietnamese was an expert at obtaining airline tickets when there were no seats available, as well as attending to a thousand other chores. However, when a pro-North Vietnamese government took over in Laos, Phai, who had not only worked for Westerners but who was also a Christian, was obviously in danger. He fled with his family into Thailand, but was arrested and put into a refugee camp. From there he wrote to Flood in Singapore asking if he could help.

Flood contacted the United Nations High Commission for Refugees and established that if Phai could be guaranteed a job in Canada, he would be allowed to leave. Flood spoke to Fred Wellhauser, who of course knew Phai through his own travels to the Far East, and Wellhauser said that he would fix the Vietnamese up with a job in Bow Valley. In September, 1978, Phai and his family arrived in Calgary with no money and only the clothes in which they arrived. Until they found a place of their own, they stayed in Lloyd Flood's house. Today Phai, who changed his name to Richard Van Nugent, works happily for Bow Valley.

Vietnam had been a magnificent failure that had taken seven years of Bow Valley's — and more particularly Lloyd Flood's — time. However, the company had several other exploration irons in the fire. In Abu Dhabi, it had met early success tinged by subsequent frustration. The crowning achievement of Lloyd Flood's long love-affair with the Far East would come in an area different from, but no less exotic than, Vietnam: Indonesia.

15
Middle Eastern Frustration and Far Eastern Success

Bow Valley's exploration efforts in Indonesia, like the North Sea, took more than a decade to come to fruition. However, whereas in the North Sea the first well had appeared commercial, and the delays had been due to geological complexity and the scale of development, in Indonesia it simply took a decade to find anything worthwhile. During that period, Bow Valley spent close to $50 million, a tremendous commitment for a company of its size. Its efforts were, however, well rewarded in the end.

Bow Valley's original Indonesian acreage had come to the company once again through Syracuse. In 1969, Syracuse had picked up two production-sharing contracts covering three contract areas of around 30 million gross acres, mainly offshore. However, these blocks, the Karimata and Mentawai, proved disappointing.

Further exploration acreage came to Bow Valley via an American named Dave Robinson, who had worked for Texaco in Indonesia in the 1950s and 1960s. After leaving Texaco he had filed for exploration licences on some lands that had once belonged to Shell. His original intention was — in concert with Calgary-based Asamera — to put these lands into a new North American public company. This plan had fallen through and so he then turned his efforts to farming-out the lands. It was while trotting the globe on this mission that he had pitched his scheme to Dick Harris. Fred Wellhauser and Lloyd Flood sat down to examine Robinson's prospects. It seemed perhaps presumptuous to be re-exploring lands that the mighty Royal Dutch-Shell had already explored. However, Shell's exploration had taken place before 1936, when techniques were less sophisticated. Wellhauser and Flood saw oil potential in the 68,000-acre Suban Jerigi block in South Sumatra's Palembang basin. Financially, this venture wasn't going to stretch the company, particularly if partners were found, and they believed that with superior exploration techniques they might find some oil that Shell had missed.

Bow Valley originally took a 40 per cent interest in the venture with four partners — Western Decalta Petroleum Ltd. (20 percent), Pacific Lighting Exploration Co. (20 per cent), Corexcal, Inc. (10 per cent), and Petrorep (Canada) Ltd. (10 per cent). The consortium then farmed out a quarter of its interest to the Japanese company, Toyo Oil Development Corporation. Three wells were planned for the block. One of the wells, Kampong Minyak No.1, was an oil discovery. Two of its four delineation wells were completed as oil wells. However, the following year it was decided that reserves were insufficient and the block was abandoned.

For Lloyd Flood, this failure was particularly disappointing. He had grown to like Indonesia and feel at home with Indonesian ways. Everything depended on social contacts, and although the word "bribery" was never used, it was essential to know how to dispense entertainment expenses strategically if anything was to get done!

Greasing the Wheels of Commerce

After the unsuccessful drilling at Suban Jerigi, Flood found that $300,000-worth of the company's casing had been stolen. Through his contacts, he discovered that it was sitting by a railroad siding at a village. Cigarettes were bought for a local military policeman out of gratitude for hearing Flood's report on the stolen casing; a trip for the local militia lieutenant's wife to the city of Palembang was arranged; the stationmaster was tipped for the use of his railyard; and a restraining order was finally secured so that the casing would not be moved. Inquiries in Palembang — as well as Bow Valley's sponsorship of a trip by a local official's daughter to a music contest in Jakarta — got Flood a sympathetic hearing there. Eventually, in return for further considerations, Flood managed to have the casing recovered and delivered in army trucks!

The former employees alleged to have stolen the casing were apprehended, but one of them maintained that it was really Flood who had arranged the whole thing! Flood met with the state prosecutor before the trial came to court and exonerated himself in a typically Indonesian way. In the West, priority might have been given to establishing innocence. In Indonesia, however, a different tack was needed. Flood demonstrated that if he had wanted to steal the casing, he could have done so in a much simpler way. This was an argument that the state prosecutor, who had also been entertained in Jakarta, could understand.

When the case eventually came to court, Flood, at the judge's request, arranged fees to cover the burdens imposed on the Indonesian

legal system. Unfortunately, he misunderstood the judge's requirement. He thought that he had to pay a total of $3,000 for the incon-
venience attached to prosecuting the two alleged culprits. However,
the judge had wanted $3,000 each. As a result, one of the culprits
was convicted and the other released. Bow Valley was thereupon
fined a further $3,000 for false accusations! The bottom line, however,
was that Bow Valley had retrieved its casing at a cost of only $25,000.
A few months later, Flood received a copy of the letter from the
insurance company which would have had to pay for the casing if it
had not been recovered. In it, the company rejected more than half
of Flood's expenses as ineligible. Flood sent the letter back to the
insurance company with a note attached: "The next time the _____
casing is stolen, I'll send a letter advising you, and you can come and
get it yourselves."

Success in the Corridor

Apart from the lack of exploration success and the problems with
the casing, there were also growing political problems for the foreign
oil companies at this time. The Indonesian government had spent
itself into crisis, and sought to boost its revenues by increasing its
share of oil production profits. This precipitated a mass retreat by the
oil industry. In July, 1976, Bow Valley closed its Jakarta office and
Lloyd Flood moved to Singapore, which was also felt to be a better
location both for communications and supply logistics.

Bow Valley restricted its Indonesian involvements for the next few
years. However, in 1980 it returned once more to lands that had been
acquired by Robinson. In a separate deal at the beginning of the 1970s,
Robinson and his partner Asamera had put together another land
package — the so-called Corridor block on Sumatra — and farmed
this out to StanVac, a joint subsidiary of Exxon and Mobil. Between
1971 and 1976, StanVac spent some U.S. $22 million to find a little
natural gas — obviously a disappointment. Then they returned the
lands to Asamera. Dave Robinson had now left the scene and Asamera
began looking for new partners. Flood had discussions with some of
their people in Singapore. Meanwhile, Fred Wellhauser was negotiating with senior officials of the company back in Calgary. He suggested that Bow Valley invest as much as Asamera had in the lands
so far — that is, "equalize" their costs — in return for 50 per cent of
the acreage. Asamera wanted to give only 40 per cent on those terms.

This was originally considered too steep. But then the world oil-price outlook began to change.

In 1979, following the fall of the Shah of Iran, world oil prices began to rise rapidly once more, thus increasing the attractiveness of what had previously been considered marginal exploration risks. Bow Valley returned to the bargaining table and, in October, 1980, concluded a joint venture to earn 40 per cent of Asamera's acreage on the Corridor and Tempino blocks (Tempino was a smaller block that sat north of the Corridor) in return for spending U.S. $11 million in 1980 and U.S. $10.5 million in 1981.

Part of the money was to be used to re-evaluate the data obtained by StanVac, and also to carry out new seismic work. With the price of oil having doubled to more than U.S. $25, the exploration strategy was to look for smaller pools in the 10 million to 25 million barrel range rather than searching for "elephants." Ten wells were drilled in 1980 and 15 wells were drilled in 1981, but although oil was found, its quantities were marginal. Bow Valley's average production in 1981 was 318 barrels per day. During 1982, Bow Valley planned to drill 21 wells and invest $17 million. Results continued to be disappointing. Bow Valley had reached the third year of the agreement and had spent all the funds it had committed without success. Six prospects remained to be drilled. If none of them was successful, then Bow Valley was going to have to abandon the area.

Head office in Calgary was by this time understandably growing a little twitchy about the Indonesian play. Lloyd Flood was going to bed each night a worried man. Then, one morning in July, 1982, at around 4:00 A.M., he was woken by a call from Bow Valley's local exploration manager, "Buddy" de Luna. "Wake up Lloyd," said de Luna, who shared Flood's sense of humor," I've got no bad news for you today."

Then de Luna read Flood the test results of the wildcat well, Tanjung Laban 1. Bow Valley had found what it had been seeking.

In one formation, the Talang Akar, sweet oil had flowed at 1,320 barrels a day. Oil had also flowed from the Batu Raja formation, although rates had been affected by formation damage. Further seismic work was done on the structure and appraisal drilling was planned. Two and one-half miles northeast of Tanjung Laban 1, meanwhile, Asamera and Bow Valley were drilling another wildcat well, Ramba No. 1. This well too hit paydirt. Learning from the problems that the Tanjung Laban well had had with the Batu Raja formation, special techniques were used to test the formation. Sweet oil flowed from it at 1,720 barrels a day. Stabilized flow rates from Tanjung Laban meanwhile had surpassed 2,000 barrels a day.

Not only were these excellent flows of oil, but the discoveries were both just a few miles from existing pipelines. Unlike the North Sea, where discoveries implied huge additional development expenditures, discoveries onshore Sumatra meant cash almost immediately. By early December, five delineation wells drilled on the two discoveries had all been completed as oil wells. The three Ramba delineation wells flowed at between 1,060 and 2,400 barrels a day; two on Tanjung Laban flowed at 480 and 850 barrels per day.

Activity in the Corridor and Tempino blocks now concentrated on the Ramba and Tanjung Laban fields. Pertamina approved a plan to develop the central portion of the Ramba field and gross production from the Corridor and Tempino blocks in 1983 totalled 6,240 barrels a day, with the major constraint being pipeline capacity. However, access to two other eight-inch lines was secured and production increased rapidly. Towards the end of 1984, production had hit 19,000 barrels a day, and was expected to reach 22,000 barrels a day in 1985.

By the end of 1984, more than forty wells had been drilled to delineate and develop the reserves of the Corridor and Tempino blocks. Recoverable reserves — under primary recovery — of around 37 million barrels had been established for the fields. The introduction of secondary recovery over the following two years were expected to increase reserves significantly.

Bow Valley and Asamera's joint exploration agreement on the Corridor and Tempino blocks, which was due to expire in 1990, was superseded in 1983 by a twenty-year Production Sharing Contract with Pertamina for the undeveloped acreage of the Corridor block. Under this agreement, the partners committed to spend U.S. $10 million a year over six years.

By early 1985, Indonesia had become a major contributor to profits and cash flow. In 1983, Bow Valley was granted further acreage offshore Java and, in April, the Jakarta office was reopened.

Success in Indonesia had taken a long time in coming, and had come as a welcome reward to Lloyd Flood's decade of efforts in the area. But Bow Valley's third principal area of overseas exploration success — the Middle East — provided an altogether reverse experience: early success followed by longer-term disappointment.

Success and Problems in the Gulf

Bow Valley's first overseas success had come in the stomping grounds of the major companies, the Middle East. Once again, it came on lands acquired with Syracuse. Through the aristocratic Sterlings, Angus

Mackenzie had been introduced to the ruler of Abu Dhabi. Subsequently, he had flown to the Trucial state and, in typical fashion, made friends with both the ruler and his key advisors. In June, 1970, a group in which Syracuse was a 20 per cent-participant acquired an oil concession of 778,381 acres in Abu Dhabi's shallow offshore waters.

When Bow Valley acquired Syracuse, a comprehensive geological study and marine geophysical program had already been carried out. The first well drilled on the block, Zaboot No.1, was dry and abandoned. Further marine seismic was shot and the jack-up rig Gusto was then contracted to drill a second well. Bow Valley had by this time farmed-out 50 per cent of its stake to Canadian Superior. The well was spudded on August 4, 1973. This and a subsequent well tested oil in excess of 4,000 barrels a day. A third well on the block found more oil and the field was named Arzanah.

A fourth well, the most successful to date, was completed on Arzanah in December, 1975. By early 1976, the engineering and design of the production facilities had been let. The field was expected to be onstream by January, 1978, at an initial rate of 25,000 barrels a day. Project financing on a limited recourse basis was arranged by Bow Valley.

The operator of the field was the American company, Amerada Hess. Bow Valley's experience with Hess as the field's developer was the reverse of that with Marathon at Brae. Arzanah was to develop one problem after another. Amerada's grandiose development scheme ran into hefty cost escalations, while the field itself developed production problems that required expensive stimulation.

Bow Valley's exploration expenditures in Abu Dhabi for the year to May 31, 1978, at $9.3 million, were close to those for all of Canada, and second among foreign expenditures only to those in the North Sea. By the end of fiscal 1978, seven wells had been tested in the field at rates of up to 10,000 barrels a day. Proven reserves were estimated at 79.5 million barrels and peak production of 35,000 barrels a day was anticipated by the summer of 1978. An offshore production platform was planned, from which oil would be piped to Arzanah Island, processed, and then transferred to tankers.

Arzanah Island was the tip of a giant salt dome that rose from a depth of more than 20,000 feet to an elevation of 200 feet. It sat, barren of trees or foliage, about 20 miles offshore Abu Dhabi in the sparkling waters of the Gulf. The cost of the facility was originally estimated at $140 million. By the end of fiscal 1978, however, the cost had escalated to $185 million, and although peak production estimates had been raised to 40,000 barrels a day, production was not now forecast to commence until mid-1979. By the end of 1978, estimated costs of the project had hit $283.5 million. Peak production was back down to 35,000 barrels a day, the projected figure for 1980.

The field eventually came into production in September, 1979. The cost of the project to the end of 1979 had been U.S.$288 million with a further U.S.$44 million budgeted for 1980. The field averaged 26,000 barrels a day to the end of 1979, but then the partners were notified that, effective March 4, 1980, production would be temporarily pro-rated to 20,000 barrels a day. Subsequently, the field would not be able to produce even to that level without stimulation.

During 1981, production averaged only 11,550 barrels a day. Four water-injection wells were scheduled to be drilled during 1982, and pressure maintenance facilities were to be installed in mid-1983, whereupon it was projected that production of 20,000 barrels a day would once again be possible. However, production in 1982 averaged only 10,000 barrels a day, and in 1983 only 8,510 barrels a day. Injection of 35,000 barrels a day of water began in September, 1983. Nevertheless, the field has continued to produce beneath earlier forecasts, a problem exacerbated by production constraints within OPEC.

16
Flying Diamond

In the 1960s, a great deal of Bow Valley's corporate energy had gone into acquiring drilling, service, and manufacturing businesses. This was partly to expand on existing interests, but also to generate funds for further oil and gas exploration. In the 1970s, that emphasis changed. Although the service side of the business continued to grow and generate the bulk of the company's profits, the majority of Bow Valley's creative talents were concentrated on financing its global oil activities. The masterpiece among those financings had been the Ashland farm-out. Not only had that deal removed a significant burden from Bow Valley's corporate shoulders and promised significant growth in oil production, it had also freed the company for new ventures.

Bow Valley had already moved into U.S. oil and gas in a small way in the spring of 1977 by joining an exploration group in the Gulf of Mexico. It soon after became active in further exploration activity in Louisiana, Texas, and Oklahoma. Although Abu Dhabi, Indonesia, and the North Sea would all become big producers for Bow Valley within half a dozen years, the first oil produced by the company outside of Canada came, in January, 1978, from Oklahoma. By then, however, the company was in the midst of a much larger move into the U.S. market.

As with so many phases of the oil business, the deal that Bow Valley ultimately did started out with a personal contact — in this case once again one of Doc's, a man named Henri Moreault. Moreault was an investment specialist who had been born into a well-heeled Ottawa family but had spent most of his working life in the United States. He had worked for several major New York investment houses and had started up the New York office of the rapidly expanding Canadian investment house Gordon Securities.

He had come into contact with Doc in the mid-1970s as a specialist in "interlisted" stocks, that is, stocks traded on both the U.S. and Canadian exchanges. Because of Harry Van Rensselaer's groundwork, and the trans-border share issue in 1968, Bow Valley had acquired a following on Wall Street. Moreault began to follow the company's exploits and became a corporate fan.

Moreault's last job in New York was with investment house

Oppenheimer, where he was in charge of foreign trading. One day over the phone Doc mentioned to him that Bow Valley was interested in expanding into the United States. He asked him if he had any ideas. At the time, Moreault had no specific suggestions. However, a couple of months later, the financier was in the office of Martin Davis, the tough number-two man at Gulf & Western Industries (in 1984, after he had taken over as chief executive at G&W, Davis would be named to *Fortune* magazine's list of "The Toughest Bosses in America"). Moreault was pitching for a role for Oppenheimer in G&W's next U.S. takeover. In the course of the discussion, Davis mentioned that G&W was interested in getting out of the natural resource business, specifically, selling its 39.6 per cent stake in Flying Diamond, a Utah-based petroleum, coal, drilling, ranching, and property company. Moreault's mind clicked.

A few days later, he gave Doc a call and said he might have an acquisition for him. Doc asked Moreault to send him more details. The Wall Streeter rounded up Flying Diamond's financial reports and Securities and Exchange Commission filings, and sent them off to Calgary. There, Bow Valley's corporate analysts went to work.

Early in 1977, Moreault persuaded Doc to come down to New York and speak to some institutional clients. Doc travelled to Wall Street and gave a presentation. He mentioned to Moreault that Bow Valley's staff was still looking at Flying Diamond. In fact, the company had looked briefly at almost a hundred U.S. companies, and in some depth at three or four, but Flying Diamond soon emerged as the most likely candidate. In May, 1977, Doc called Moreault again and told him that Dick Harris would be coming down to New York to meet with him and Martin Davis. Harris established that G&W was a willing seller and returned to Calgary to discuss the purchase further with Doc.

One factor that was to provide some complication later was that Moreault had now left Oppenheimer. He felt that he had had enough of the Manhattan rat-race, and, in November, 1977, he went to work for Dean, Witter Reynolds in the infinitely more placid surroundings of Sun Valley, Idaho (which incidentally dovetailed nicely with his status as a former champion skier). There would subsequently be some contention over which company should receive the finder's fee for the deal.

Locking Horns with Bluhdorn

The plan that Doc, Harris, and the Bow Valley corporate team worked out was that they would make a cash offer of $30 a share to

140

G&W for its 39.6 per cent stake in Flying Diamond, and then make a similar offer to the remaining shareholders. This would cost around U.S. $120 million, making it, at the time, the largest Canadian takeover of a U.S. oil company. The next crucial step was to find the money.

Trevor Legge, who had come to Bow Valley with the acquisition of Cardwell Supply at the beginning of the 1960s, was now the company's treasurer, and played a key role in the company's relations with the banks. The Royal had remained Bow Valley's principal bank, and Jim Boyle its principal banker. In the latter half of 1977, Legge met with Boyle and told him that he wanted to discuss the financing of a takeover. For an hour, Legge went through Flying Diamond's corporate statistics without mentioning the purchase price that Bow Valley had in mind. He knew that the company wanted an amount that would represent the largest loan of its kind in Canadian banking history. Bow Valley already owed the Royal around $125 million, at the time a sizable exposure.

Eventually, the low-key and unflappable Boyle asked the key question: "How much do you want?" Legge took a deep breath and said the company wanted U.S. $120 million for the acquisition, plus another $5 or $6 million to carry the investment for a while. Boyle's only reaction was to say: "Perhaps we'd better have a cup of coffee."

Legge could sense that Boyle would do the deal. Within a couple of days, project finance specialists had been called in from the Royal's Montreal office, and within three weeks or so, the Royal had agreed to go ahead with the financing, assuming, of course, a share price of $30. But that was Bow Valley's assessment of Flying Diamond's worth. Gulf & Western had other ideas.

The haggling over price came down to head-to-head negotiation between Doc and Charles Bluhdorn, Gulf & Western's head. Bluhdorn, like Doc, had founded and created his company, and nobody negotiates like an owner. But Bluhdorn made the mistake of thinking that Bow Valley's offer was merely a negotiating stance. When Bow Valley refused to go higher, Gulf & Western's chairman — a man used to having his way — called Doc in Calgary and proceeded to launch into a tirade about how his company couldn't possibly let its stake in Flying Diamond go for less than $40 a share. Such was the decibel level of Bluhdorn's harangue that Doc had to hold the phone away from his ear. When the American had finished, Doc told him that his staff had done their homework, and the homework said that Flying Diamond was worth $30. Bluhdorn hung up. Just to double-check that his staff had done their homework, Doc called Dick Harris, who was on business in Paris. Harris, as a former consultant, was particularly adept at valuations. He told Doc that $30 was definitely Flying Diamond's worth. That was good enough for Doc.

A short time afterwards, Bluhdorn called back in a more reasonable tone and suggested that Gulf & Western might be prepared to take some Bow Valley stock as part of a higher-priced deal. Doc told him that Bow Valley shares were undervalued in the market and that he didn't want to issue any more at the moment. The deal was $30 a share — in cash. This sent Bluhdorn once more into a fury. But when, after some minutes of ranting and raving, it became clear that Doc wasn't going to budge, Bluhdorn said: "Alright, you can have our stake for $30 a share. You're the toughest goddamn Canadian I've ever dealt with."

On December 16, 1977, Bow Valley announced its agreement to purchase Gulf & Western's stake in Flying Diamond for approximately $50 million, and its intention to offer the same price, $30 a share, to its other shareholders. By April 14, Bow Valley held 90 per cent of the U.S. company's shares. At the end of May, 1978, Flying Diamond was merged with a wholly owned subsidiary of Bow Valley.

Coal: The Hidden Treasure

Flying Diamond was a diverse company, based on mineral rights acquired by a man named Clive Sprouse in the wake of the oil boom in Utah and Colorado at the beginning of the 1950s. In 1968, Clive's son Gary organized these rights — along with other mineral rights he had acquired with his partner, Holmes "Mac" McLish — into Flying Diamond. The company then played a leading role in developing the Altamont-Bluebell oil field. In 1974, Flying Diamond merged with Ray Resources, the creation of James Ray. Ray's father and grandfather had both worked on oil rigs and James Ray moved into the drilling business with his own rig in 1947. Joined by his brother, Rex, he had expanded the business and, in 1968 had formed Ray Resources Corporation. The company by now had six rigs. It expanded through a number of small acquisitions and then, in 1972, made what would be its most significant acquisition, a tract of coal lands in Kentucky that had belonged to the Sigmond family.

When Bow Valley took it over, Flying Diamond's annual revenues were more than $50 million. It was producing around 1,800 barrels of oil and 11 million cubic feet of gas a day, as well as conducting drilling and some pipeline-laying activity. It also had real estate interests. When a number of analysts heard of the deal, they said BVI had paid too much. But they were just looking at the oil and gas. The real treasure in Flying Diamond lay in its coal, and in the man in charge of the coal division, Clyde Goins.

Flying Diamond's coal operation consisted of underground bituminous mining on an 8,000-acre tract south of Harlan, Kentucky. Most of the property was worked via "drift" mining, that is, tunnelling into horizontal seams and then transporting the coal from the rockface via conveyor belt. Goins, a stocky Kentuckian with a wry sense of humor was a "good ol' boy" who lived for his mines and his miners. Born in the heart of Appalachian coal country, he moved to Harlan, close to the coal operations he would one day run, when he was sixteen. In his late teens he had moved to Dayton, Ohio, where he held down two jobs as well as attending business school at night. He then returned to Kentucky and sold mining equipment until, in 1952, the illness of his son and the need to pay hefty medical bills forced him to seek a better-paying job. He wound up in the bowels of the Earth at the coal face. His original intention had been to pay off the bills and then return to a job closer to the daylight, but he found that he enjoyed the work. In the following years, he worked for several companies and gradually moved up the corporate ladder to the top, learning just about every job — and operating every piece of equipment — involved in the coal mining business.

Under Goins, Flying Diamond's non-unionized coal operation had developed a reputation as one of the most efficient in the area. After Bow Valley acquired it, it would expand rapidly. Goins' greatest coup was in securing long-term coal contracts that both helped insulate the company from cyclical demand, and ensured its longer-term growth.

The year that Bow Valley acquired Flying Diamond, Goins' coal operation entered into two major long-term sale contracts. Goins could see the trend developing towards "unit" trains that were automatically loaded and used exclusively to ferry coal from the supplier to the user. With long-term contracts and regular rail shipment, the company would no longer be subject to the fluctuations of the coal "spot" market.

In February, 1978, Goins negotiated a new sales contract with the South Carolina Public Service Authority, replacing a shorter-term contract it had signed the previous year. Under the contract, Flying Diamond was to deliver 500,000 tons of steam coal (that is, coal with very little cleaning or preparation) annually for ten years.

The same month, the company also entered into a steam coal sales contract with Florida Power Corporation for 425,000 tons annually over ten years. The prices prevailing in both contracts were subject to fluctuations in operating costs and the wholesale price index. Goins negotiated a new contract — to take effect on January 1, 1980 — with the South Carolina Public Service Authority to double shipments to 1 million tons a year by 1986, while the term of the contract was also lengthened for 20 years. Shortly afterwards, the contract with Florida

Power was increased to 850,000 tons a year for 15 years. This meant that coal production by 1986 would be 2.85 million tons annually compared with 1.115 million in 1977. New acreage was leased both at Harlan County and at Bell County, 30 miles west of Harlan.

Although 1983 sales were slightly below those of 1982 because of a cutback in shipments under one of its contracts, Goins' operation sold more than twice the volume of coal that it had in 1977. Coal revenues for 1983 were $110 million. In 1984, they climbed to $134 million. Goins was operating 14 underground and 2 surface mines on a total of 33,000 acres in the green rolling hills of southwestern Kentucky, and employing around 500 workers.

But if the coal operations of Flying Diamond were a great success, oil and gas activities in the U.S. proved a disappointment. The existing holdings tended to be somewhat fragmented — often with a great many working-interest partners. Also, sweeping management changes were found necessary following the discovery of potential conflicts of interest in their private oil and gas dealings. In September, 1979, Bow Valley sent Rod DeLuca down to Denver to assume the presidency of Flying Diamond, which had now been renamed Bow Valley Exploration (U.S.) Inc. DeLuca had worked all over Bow Valley's empire and was in London setting up a foreign acquisition unit similar to the one he had worked on in Singapore when he received the call to move to Denver. Over the following few years, Bow Valley spent a considerable amount of money on exploration in the U.S., although it tended to continue to concentrate on smaller, more diverse prospects. Oil and gas continued to be somewhat disappointing, but coal remained the jewel in the crown.

Excitement North of the Border

Apart from the completion of the Flying Diamond acquisition, 1978 saw a number of other significant corporate developments. While the value of the company's mining interests south of the border were perhaps not yet fully realized, enormous excitement surrounded its mineral interests in Canada. A prospect in which it was involved with Imperial Oil and Bill McGregor's Numac at Midwest Lake in northeastern Saskatchewan proved to be a major uranium strike. An extensive exploration program established gross reserves of around 38 million pounds of uranium oxide recoverable by open-pit mining. Bow Valley held a 20 per cent interest in the play, reducing to 12.5 per cent after it had recovered its investment. Production was originally planned to start by 1984, however, a weak market for uranium led to the deferment of development plans.

The company also came to within a whisker of completing by far the largest acquisition in its history. Doc had for some while been looking at the possibility of acquiring Ashland Canada in order to boost the company's Canadian oil and gas side. He was close to the heads of both the Canadian company and its U.S. parent because of the negotiations over the Brae farm-out. In mid-1978, he thought he had Ashland in the bag. Doc and his negotiating team were staying in Toronto's Four Seasons Hotel, and thought they had negotiated a cash and share-swap package for Ashland that would have cost close to $400 million. However, the Ashland negotiators, Orin Atkins and Earl Joudrie, were dealing simultaneously with a rival group from Kaiser Resources, who were staying at the Harbour Castle Hotel. Doc felt 90 per cent certain that he had a deal. In the end, Ashland chose to accept Edgar Kaiser's all-cash offer. Within just a couple of years, Kaiser would have flipped most of the Ashland Canada assets at a profit of more than $200 million.

Although Ashland was obviously a disappointment, Bow Valley had little to be disappointed about in terms of its own financial results. In 1978, when Bow Valley changed its fiscal year to coincide with the calendar year, revenues totalled $232.5 million. Net income of $14.3 million was greater than the previous three years combined. Production of oil and gas liquids during 1978 increased — largely due to the Flying Diamond acquisition — a whopping 125 per cent to 3,795 barrels daily, while gas production increased by 46 per cent to 63.2 MMCF a day. And the best — in the form of the North Sea and Indonesia — was yet to come.

17

Changes Without and Within: The NEP and New Management

The early 1980s were years of intense activity at Bow Valley, of major corporate and management changes set against a background of international oil upheaval and domestic political turbulence. World oil prices once again took off, while at home the National Energy Programme, one of the most controversial policies in Canadian history, was introduced.

The 1970s had been years of spectacular boom for Alberta and its leading oil companies. The main engine of that boom had been the increase in petroleum prices. Between 1973 and 1980, the average wellhead price for crude oil in Western Canada rose from $3.40 to $15.41 per barrel. The price of natural gas rose even more spectacularly, from 17 cents an MCF to $2.20. The impact on exploration was enormous. Total net cash expenditures of the petroleum industry in Alberta rose from $1.5 billion in 1973 to $11.5 billion in 1980. Bonus payments at the province's land sales rocketed from $76 million in 1973 to more than a $1 billion in 1980. The number of wells drilled in Western Canada, and most were drilled in Alberta, more than doubled between 1973 and 1980, leading to the drilling of 6,445 miles of hole in 1980.

The impact on the price of — and trading in — oil shares was even more dramatic. In a stock market that was becoming increasingly infatuated with oil shares, Bow Valley was one of the darlings. The value of the trade in its shares in 1978, at $255 million, ranked it fifth among publicly traded Canadian oil companies, just behind the mighty Imperial Oil. In 1979, the value of trading in Bow Valley shares more than doubled, to $604 million. In 1980, it more than doubled again, to $1.4 billion. And although Gulf Canada, Dome Petroleum, and Imperial Oil traded a greater volume among the oils, Bow Valley was now out-trading Canadian giants like Alcan Aluminum and Bell Canada. Its volume on the Toronto Stock Exchange was twice that of the nearest bank, the Bank of Montreal. After allowing for a two-for-one

146

stock split in 1978 and a three-for-one split in 1980, Bow Valley's shares had risen from a low of less than $2 in 1975 to hit $27 in 1980.

In 1979, events in the international arena, most notably the fall of the Shah of Iran and the accession of the Ayatollah Khomeini, led to a renewed crisis in the oil markets and a further large increase in prices. It appeared that the cycle of wealth was about to go through another rotation. Canadian prices would follow world prices; Alberta and Canadian oil companies would enjoy a further surge of revenues and profits. However, that prospect did not please everyone; in particular, it did not please the federal Liberal government, which, following a few brief months in the political doldrums, had returned to power in 1980.

The 1980 federal election was a matter of the Tories losing power rather than the Liberals gaining it. One key element in the Tories loss was a budget measure proposing an 18 cent a gallon excise tax on gasoline. The Tories also struggled with an election promise to disband the national oil company Petro-Canada. They discovered, to their cost, that PetroCan was popular with the Canadian electorate. The lessons of these failed energy policy initiatives were not lost on the Liberals. They returned to power promising lower energy prices than the Tories, "Canadianization" of the oil business, and energy security through self-sufficiency. These promises were somewhat vague, but by the fall of 1980 they had been transformed, with the aid of a fiercely committed group of backroom policy advisors and public servants, into one of the most revolutionary policies in Canadian history.

The rationale of the energy mandarins for sweeping policy change was based on a thoroughgoing and highly critical analysis of the Liberal energy policies of the 1970s — policies forged in the heat of conflict with Peter Lougheed. The bureaucrats believed that the federal side had come off the loser from these political wars, and that the principal beneficiaries had been the province of Alberta and foreign-owned oil companies.

The very conspicuous symbol of Alberta's wealth was the Heritage Fund, set up to hold a portion of the province's energy revenues against the day when they ran out. By 1980, the fund was fast approaching $10 billion. As for the foreign-owned oil companies, said Ottawa's analysts, if the existing system was not changed, then they would wind up owning an inordinate amount of the national wealth. The Liberal politicians and their backroom advisors had returned to power considering energy policy initiatives to be a matter of political expediency. Ottawa's energy mandarins soon persuaded them that they were a matter of economic necessity. A new policy would have to make a bold grab for Alberta's petroleum revenues and provide a

147

new fiscal system that would in some way help Canadian companies and discriminate against their foreign counterparts.

Through the spring and summer of 1980, the policy was hatched in Ottawa's corridors of power with minimal industry consultation. On October 28, 1980, the National Energy Programme was unveiled. Its central thrust consisted of new revenue taxes, in effect quasi-royalties, that would take petroleum income at the wellhead, plus a new grant system that provided more generous incentives to Canadian companies and to companies drilling on federal as opposed to provincial lands. The main new revenue tax was the Petroleum and Gas Revenue Tax (PGRT). The grants were called Petroleum Incentive Payments, or PIP grants. The other main element of the NEP was a retroactive back-in for 25 per cent of federal land-holdings.

The policy created a furor both at home and abroad. However, for Canadian companies, the PIP grants appeared to offer new opportunities, and Bow Valley would move quickly to take advantage of them. However, the external turmoil caused by the NEP was matched within Bow Valley by changes at the senior management level.

The Departure of Dick Harris

Doc Seaman and Dick Harris had always been very different in their style and approach. Doc was a man of few words; Harris was loquacious. Doc liked to take the big picture; Harris liked to get involved in administration and details. Doc liked to deal with things verbally; Harris liked to put everything in writing. Nevertheless, this diversity had helped form an effective team throughout the 1970s. Harris's main task had been to organize the drilling of the exploration prospects brought from Syracuse. When he had been appointed president and chief operating officer, it seemed that Doc had clearly marked him as his successor. However, at some stage Doc had second thoughts. A number of policy differences, exacerbated by an underlying clash of personalities, eventually made Harris's departure inevitable.

Part of the problem may have arisen from Dick Harris's impatience to become chief executive. He felt he had served his apprenticeship and established his credentials. But Bow Valley was still regarded as Doc's company, and Doc showed few signs of loosening the reins of power.

From his earliest days Doc had always mulled over problems and then acted upon them. He consulted people only when he felt it would help clarify his decision. If he felt the decision was a clear one, he did not consult. Harris took a negative stance on a number of corporate decisions and strategies on which he felt he had not been consulted sufficiently. This quite naturally irked Doc and increased the gap between the two men.

The final, intractable, difference arose over financing strategy. In 1980, Doc, seeking to strengthen the company's financial controls and reduce its floating-rate bank debt, brought in Bill Tye as Bow Valley's new chief financial officer. Tye, a former senior executive at Pacific Petroleums, which had been taken over by Petro-Canada, was to report directly to Doc. Harris saw this as a diminution of his authority, and also disagreed with what he saw as the greater centralization that Tye's appointment and style implied for the company.

Perhaps out of a sense of frustration, Harris refused to lend his support to a number of financing moves. These included the sale of shares in Bow Valley Resource Services (BVRS), the wholly owned BVI subsidiary set up in 1977 to hold the company's drilling, manufacturing, service and supply activities. By the fall of 1980, the atmosphere between Harris and Doc was already creating discomfort in the executive suite on the eighteenth floor of Bow Valley's new headquarters on Sixth Avenue. The problems over the BVRS financing brought matters to a head. It became clear that the company was not big enough for both men, and it was obvious who had to go.

Harris decided that there was no way in which he was going to be asked to leave. In his mind, the conflict had developed because of a greater centralization with which he disagreed, and because of Doc's tendency to make decisions without consultation. From Doc's point of view, Harris was taking a negative attitude, in particular to what Doc saw as the pressing need to convert the company's floating-rate bank debt into equity or equity-related securities. In fact, interest rates took off very quickly in 1981, and Bill Tye helped Bow Valley made a number of financings — in particular one for U.S.$80 million and Can$20 million with a group of insurance companies — that softened the impact of 20 per cent-plus interest rates.

Harris was perhaps understandably bitter that the most important and fruitful decade of his business life was to end in such a way. Disillusioned, he wrote a letter of resignation to Doc on February 28, 1981, along with notes to board members and other senior executives. Then he simply packed up his personal files and photographs, cleared his office, and left.

The Arrival of Gerry Maier

Doc now had to find a new operating head of the company who could also take over from him as chief executive. For the time being, he told the board, he would take over the operating role himself. That role was made the tougher by the fact that Fred Wellhauser decided in June of 1981 to follow Dick Harris into a new company Harris was planning. Wellhauser had played a critical role in Bow Valley's exploration success. As ever, Doc viewed the situation calmly. He was prepared to wait for the right man. That man soon appeared on the scene. Ironically, he was made available, indirectly, by the National Energy Programme.

The NEP had virtually declared a holy war against foreign oil companies. Utilizing a "Trojan horse" theory that such companies represented a growing — if somewhat vague — threat to the national economy, the policy said that these companies had to be taken over at once. "Of the top twenty-five petroleum companies in Canada," noted the NEP, "seventeen are more than 50 per cent foreign-owned and foreign-controlled, and these seventeen account for 72 per cent of Canadian oil and gas sales. This is a degree of foreign participation that would not be accepted — indeed, simply is not tolerated — by most other oil producing nations."

The NEP stressed that, with oil and gas prices certain to continue to rocket into the stratosphere — thus increasing the value of foreign oil companies — "a further delay will put the value of companies in the industry so high as to make the cost prohibitive, leaving Canada with no choice but to accept a permanent foreign domination by these firms." Suddenly, to have more than 50 per cent of your equity owned outside Canada was virtually to have a target painted on your back.

Six months before the announcement of the NEP, Gerry Maier, a tough, former hockey-playing farm-boy from Saskatchewan, had achieved what seemed like the pinnacle of a distinguished career as an oil executive. In April, 1980, he had been the first Canadian to be appointed both chairman and chief executive of Hudson's Bay Oil & Gas. HBOG was a rock-solid corporate empire with extensive land-holdings and high-quality oil and gas production. Its complex history stretched back to its formation in 1926 as the result of an agreement between the ancient and venerable trading concern, the Hudson's Bay Company (HBC), and an American Anglophile oilman, Ernest Whitworth Marland. Marland admired HBC both for its romantic British roots and for the fact that it possessed the most essential of the oil business's raw materials — land.

Under a charter granted by King Charles II in 1670, the "Governor and Company of Adventurers of England trading into Hudson Bay" were granted possession of a huge tract of land, known as Rupert's Land, which was drained by Hudson Bay and stretched from the Rockies to the Great Lakes.

In 1869, two years after Confederation, the Hudson's Bay Company sold Rupert's Land to Canada for $1.5 million, but retained title to some 7.5 million acres spread between Winnipeg and the Rockies. At first, the Company sold this land off to settlers, complete with underlying mineral rights. However, after 1889, it began to retain these rights, not primarily for petroleum but in the hope of finding gold. Between 1909 and 1925, these rights were disputed in a case that finished up in the British House of Lords. The case eventually went against the Hudson's Bay Company, and the Lords decided that the Company held rights to all minerals except gold and precious metals.

It was these petroleum rights that led the American Marland, in 1926, to seek out the British governor of the HBC and persuade him to form an exploration company, Hudson's Bay Marland Oil Company. A couple of years later, however, Marland found himself in severe financial difficulties and was forced to sell out. His interests wound up in the hands of Continental Oil Company, Conoco, a mid-Western oil producer and marketer. Hudson's Bay Marland was now renamed Hudson's Bay Oil & Gas. The Hudson's Bay Company continued to hold one-sixth of the company, with an option to increase its holding to 25 per cent (which it exercised in 1952).

In fact, the company lay largely dormant for the following twenty years, until the Leduc find stirred interest once more in its enormous land holdings. Although it did not earn its first profit until 1956, it grew very rapidly thereafter. By 1968, the book-value of its assets, at $247 million, surpassed those of the Hudson's Bay Company itself.

When Gerry Maier left the University of Alberta with his degree in petroleum engineering, his first job had been with Sun Oil Company. However, when Sun's top exploration man, Bill Topley, went off to join a new consulting firm, Cactus Engineering, he persuaded young Maier to join him. The principals of the new company were Charles "Spud" Thompson, a former vice president with U.S. giant Sohio, and Wright Bradley, who had been one of Mobil's top production men. Maier, then in his mid-twenties, borrowed the money to take a 5 percent stake in the new company. However, Thompson and Bradley subsequently fell out and the assets of Cactus, including Maier's stake, became tied up in a lengthy litigation.

When Maier joined Hudson's Bay Oil & Gas as a drilling and consulting engineer, his primary concern was paying off his Cactus-related debts. His plan was to go then to law school at Stanford. However, he caught the eye not only of the HBOG management, but also that of Conoco, and a temporary job turned into a rapid climb up the corporate ladder. In the mid-1960s, he was invited to work in Conoco's Australian subsidiary, returning to HBOG in 1967. In 1973, Conoco once again brought him into its corporate orbit, and he moved to their headquarters in Stamford, Connecticut, as head of production for the eastern hemisphere. In 1974 he was appointed to head up Conoco's North Sea operations, which were based in London.

In 1976, he was lured back to Canada with the promise of a top management position at HBOG. Ironically, in the light of subsequent events, Maier held some misgivings about returning to Canada following the damaging dispute between the federal and Albertan governments. He also realized that he was giving up the possibility of one day heading Conoco. Nevertheless, he believed that he could make HBOG a Canadian-based, international resource company of considerable corporate clout. Just four years later, he had reached HBOG's most senior managerial position.

When Gerry Maier moved into the chairman's office in the forty-two-storey HBOG Tower on Calgary's Seventh Avenue, he inherited one of the most attractive companies in the Canadian oilpatch, one that he had played a significant part in building. HBOG was Canada's third largest producer of natural gas and its ninth largest producer of oil and natural gas liquids. It held extensive mining, pipeline, and gas-processing interests. It explored in ten countries and already had significant production in Indonesia. In 1980, HBOG's revenues were $605 million and its net earnings $145 million. The company had virtually no long-term debt. But it had one problem: it was more than 50 per cent-owned by a U.S. company. Although Conoco had permitted HBOG's management autonomy, and although its president, Dick Haskayne was, like Gerry Maier, a Canadian, HBOG suddenly found itself statistically damned by the National Energy Programme.

Despite the belligerent tones of the NEP, the policy produced no sense of panic at HBOG. The company's size and obvious value protected it from all but the very largest predators. Also, Gerry Maier didn't believe that Conoco would sell them out. But he hadn't reckoned with the company that sat next to him on Seventh Avenue, Dome Petroleum.

The Dome Whirlwind

Dome was originally the creation of "Smilin'" Jack Gallagher. In 1950, the year Doc Seaman was also starting with his seismic rig business, Gallagher had decided to leave a promising career within the Imperial-Exxon system and strike out on his own. Backed with U.S. money, Gallagher had gradually built Dome over its first twenty-five years. In the mid-1970s, the thrust of Dome's corporate development had increasingly been taken over by Gallagher's more openly aggressive corporate alter ego, Bill Richards. Richards had taken Dome on a takeover binge, convinced — like the authors of the NEP — that petroleum prices had only one way to go, and that companies would never be as cheap as they were at the moment.

The oilpatch is a small world, and the paths of Bow Valley and Dome Petroleum had crossed many times. Over the years, Bow Valley had drilled many of Dome's wells, and as avid golfers, Doc and Gallagher saw each other often on the links. Bow Valley, in its partnership with John Scrymgeour's Westburne, had drilled wells for the Panarctic consortium of which Dome was a member. Moreover, Dome's takeover binge involved several companies with which Bow Valley had business associations, or which Bow Valley had considered as potential targets. Dome took over Siebens Oil & Gas — a partner with Bow Valley in the Brae field and in its Far Eastern ventures. It acquired the Canadian interests of T. Boone Pickens' Mesa Petroleum — in which Bow Valley had been interested. And it took over Kaiser Resources — which, as Ashland Canada, Doc had almost bought a couple of years previously. But in drawing a bead on HBOG, Dome was countenancing a deal of unprecedented size.

Dome developed an ingenious plan to force Conoco to loose its grip on its Canadian associate. It would buy shares of Conoco and then offer to swap them for the American company's stake in HBOG. Part of the rationale for this form of deal was that it would be tax-free for Conoco. However, when Dome made its offer for a block of Conoco shares, more than half of Conoco's stock was tendered. The U.S. company's horrified management suddenly discovered that they were vulnerable to takeover themselves. Dome's plan opened a Pandora's box that eventually saw Conoco taken over by chemical giant Du Pont in what was — at the time — the largest takeover in U.S. history.

Conoco agreed to let Dome have its stake in HBOG in return for the 22 million Conoco shares that Dome had acquired through its U.S. tender offer plus U.S.$245. That came to just over $2 billion for slightly more than half of HBOG.

A little over a year after he had assumed HBOG's chairmanship, Gerry Maier suddenly saw his corporate world begin to crumble around him. Maier's first priority, once Dome had managed to secure the 53 per cent of HBOG held by Conoco, was to ensure that Dome did not pressure HBOG into corporate activities not in the interests of the remaining minority HBOG shareholders — the majority of whom were Canadian. Once Dome had declared its intention to buy-out the minority shareholders, Gerry Maier played a key role in ensuring that they received as good a deal as Conoco. In fact, in the end they received a better one.

It became clear to Maier that Dome's financial position meant that it would be forced to divest itself of part of HBOG's assets once the minority had been bought out. In particular, he believed that the company's widespread foreign assets might be spun off. Once he had resigned from the chief executive's position at HBOG early in 1982, he began to hold discussions with a number of foreign and Canadian companies about putting together a consortium to operate these properties. Among the Canadian companies he contacted was Bow Valley.

Doc Seaman was not only interested in the proposal, he was interested in the man. Both seemed uniquely suited to Bow Valley's needs. HBOG had interests in ten countries, and was already producing in Indonesia, where Bow Valley had now made major exploration commitments with Asamera. Gerry Maier, meanwhile, was one of the best-respected executives in the Calgary oilpatch. He had also run Conoco's U.K. operations, which had given him extensive experience in Bow Valley's main area of overseas operation, the North Sea.

When it became clear that he would not stay at HBOG — despite the attempts of Dome to keep him — Maier had received a large number of top executive job offers, including approaches from PetroCan and Conoco. From his point of view, Bow Valley was a smaller organization than he had become used to running. Nevertheless, Doc explained that he and his brothers were looking to find an appropriate way of realizing their investment in Bow Valley and leaving the company in strong management hands. Gerry Maier had little interest in merely running someone else's corporate creation, but he saw a combination of Bow Valley and the former HBOG overseas interests as a new international company presenting managerial challenge and the potential for growth. First, however, he had had to conclude his business at HBOG.

On January 13, 1982, at a tense special shareholders' meeting, the deal he had fought for from Dome was approved by the shareholders. His work at HBOG sadly done, he resigned. The takeover in the end proved to be not just the end of HBOG, but almost equally disastrous for Dome. The debts piled up for the company's takeover binge proved crippling as the NEP's booming market projections turned out to be far wide of the mark.

Now, however, Gerry Maier was officially free to join Bow Valley. The plan was that he would become chief executive at the next Bow Valley annual meeting. His appointment as president, chief operating officer, and a director was made by the board of directors at a meeting in London, England, in April, 1982. Following the meeting, Doc and Gerry Maier and the rest of the directors headed north to see progress on the Brae platform jacket being built at Ardersier in Scotland. Following the annual meeting in May, 1982, and as part of the package he had offered to entice him to the company, Doc stepped down as chief executive in favour of Maier, although he maintained his titles as chairman of the board and of its executive committee.

As things turned out, one of Gerry Maier's main reasons for joining Bow Valley — the purchase of the HBOG overseas interests — did not come to pass. Dome delayed the sale, the market turned down, and perceptions of values changed. HBOG's foreign lands wound up in other corporate hands. Nevertheless, Gerry Maier soon discovered that he was joining Bow Valley at a challenging time. By the time he had arrived on the Bow Valley scene, the company's next major thrust — and one of the boldest in its history — had already been charted. That move was designed to take advantage of the NEP, and would bring BVRS into the corporate limelight. It was a commitment to exploration equipment the likes of which had been seen in Canada only once before, when Dome, in the days when the company was better known for innovation than acquisition, had built a fleet to drill in the Beaufort Sea.

Bow Valley had hatched a similarly ambitious scheme to build and operate a drilling fleet in an area that would soon take over from the Beaufort as Canada's prime frontier exploration prospect — the East Coast.

18
East Coast Opportunities

The National Energy Programme promised a bonanza for Canadian oil companies in general and for offshore exploration in particular. Although it imposed hefty new revenue taxes that would hit the entire industry, it also introduced a new exploration grant system, PIP grants, to replace the existing tax-based incentives. Under the new system government funds would be doled out to companies on the basis of their Canadian ownership and the area in which they were drilling. For exploration on frontier lands — including Canada's East Coast — PIP grants would cover 80% of costs if a company was more than 75% Canadian owned.

More specifically, the NEP declared that although jurisdictional disputes with Newfoundland and Nova Scotia were outstanding, the federal government would "use its regulatory powers to accelerate exploration in this area." Moreover, the NEP declared its intentions were to direct the benefits of this increased activity towards Canadian companies. Offshore drilling was singled out as an area of special attention. "In Western Canada," declared the NEP, "the oil service industry is largely Canadian owned, and it is a dynamic and profitable industry. Offshore drilling, however, has thus far tended to be dominated by foreign firms. This type of drilling requires large equipment and more sophisticated technology. Also, the offshore production facilities that would be required will be at the leading edge of technology. Canadians should be in the forefront in this effort. Canadians have the ability to capture these opportunities, and the government wishes to support Canadian firms wishing to do so. ... The government will use its regulatory power, too, in support of an expanded Canadian presence across the spectrum of industrial activities related to the petroleum boom."

The program also declared the government's intention of speeding up offshore activity — with a heavy bias towards Canadian companies — through new land regulations and preferential financial terms for domestic explorers.

Bill Hopper, the chairman of Petro-Canada, Canada's state oil company, had been vociferous in his condemnation of land regulations under which major foreign companies like Mobil had been able to hang on to offshore acreage with very little obligation to carry out exploration. The NEP obviously agreed. It introduced not only stiffer work requirements, but also a provision for PetroCan "or some other designated Crown corporation" to "back into" 25 per cent of every existing or future right on Canada Lands, as opposed merely to taking 25 per cent of permit renewals, as PetroCan now could. The provision aroused a furor among domestic and foreign companies, and among foreign governments. The NEP further required that a minimum of 50 per cent Canadian ownership would be required before any production was approved from a licence on Canada Lands. Finally, it declared that applicants for exploration and production rights would have to demonstrate how their operations would "bring industrial and employment benefits to Canadians."

The underlying assumption of the NEP was that world oil prices would continue their diagonal rise as petroleum resources continued in short supply. In this it was to prove disastrously wrong. However, the immediate objection of the business community and foreign trading partners to the thrust of the program was that it was discriminatory and involved expropriation. Moreover, it indicated a much greater degree of direct government involvement in the oil business, which, as critics pointed out, opened the door to political bias and the skewing of economic objectives.

Nevertheless, it also appeared to offer opportunities that were too good to miss.

Bow Valley had never been considered a "political" oil company in the way that either Jack Gallagher's Dome or Bob Blair's Alberta Gas Trunk Line had been in the 1970s. Both Blair and Gallagher had used political influence to further their corporate ends. During the time of the financial crisis of the early Brae wells, Doc had approached federal energy minister Donald Macdonald about possible government participation — on the basis that North Sea oil would provide a valuable foreign source of oil at a time of supply uncertainty — but Bow Valley had eventually resolved its problems via the private sector and the Ashland farm-out.

Bow Valley had in fact been more political overseas, where — particularly in the North Sea — knowledge of government priorities and national objectives were essential to gaining licences. Now it appeared that the Canadian federal government was pursuing an even more nationalistic route to offshore development, and although provincial jurisdiction was a complicating factor, Doc saw clear opportunities similar to the gaining of the Brae licences and the building of the *Odin Drill*.

With its experience in the North Sea, Doc believed Bow Valley had clearly established its offshore credentials. Now, with federal grants bound to cause an upsurge in activity off the already attractive East

Coast, opportunities were obviously present for those bold enough to make the massive outlays involved in both offshore exploration and offshore exploration equipment.

Excitement at Hibernia

In 1979, the major oilfind at Hibernia 200 miles northeast of St. John's, Newfoundland caused a resurgence of interest in the potential of Canada's East Coast. The Hibernia field was soon established as an "elephant" and aroused hopes for further elephants. Nova Scotia had added to the excitement with the discovery of the Venture gas field at Sable Island on the Scotian Shelf. Visions of North Sea-sized fields and North Sea-sized development captured the minds of governments and oil companies alike.

The discovery of Hibernia followed twenty years of disappointment for explorers off Canada's East Coast. During those two decades, $850 million had been swallowed in the search for hydrocarbons. It had long been thought that a fifth or more of Canada's ultimate reserve potential lay beneath the seabed off Newfoundland and Nova Scotia. But until Hibernia, the search for the geophysical and geological keys that would unlock the area's potential had proved fruitless. The key was eventually found by Chevron Standard, the Calgary-based subsidiary of Standard Oil of California, one of the world's largest oil companies.

Chevron Standard made the Hibernia find on a farm-out from Mobil Canada, one of the first companies to demonstrate enthusiasm for Canada's East Coast. Mobil had carried out its first aerial surveys of the region in 1959. Exploration permits had been acquired on the Scotian Shelf in 1960 and on Newfoundland's Grand Banks in 1965. Mobil shared the first reported Canadian Atlantic find, in 1971, with Texas Eastern Transmission Corporation (Tetco), at Sable Island. However, seven appraisal wells failed to confirm commercial reserves and operations on Sable Island were suspended in 1973. In 1975, Mobil's East Coast exploration program had been suspended indefinitely. This suspension of activity was partly due to Mobil's lack of success, but it was also due to the company's corporate distaste for the Canadian business environment following the bitter disputes between the federal and provincial governments in the wake of the first OPEC crisis in 1973-74. Shell, another major East Coast explorer in the 1970s, had abandoned activities in the area in 1977 after sinking $125 million into forty-seven disappointing wells.

Perhaps ironically, the two key factors that would contribute to the resurgence of East Coast offshore activity and the Hibernia discovery were also fruits of that same highly political environment that had discouraged many of the oil companies. The first was Petro-Canada, the national oil company born out of fear of OPEC and the federal Liberal government's increasing preference for economic intervention. The second factor was the system of "super-depletion" introduced in the 1977 budget for wells costing more than $5 million.

From its creation at the beginning of 1976, Petro-Canada had made a firm commitment to reviving interest and activity in the frontier areas, particularly the Scotian Shelf and offshore Newfoundland and Labrador. The architect of this thrust was Don Axford, Mobil Canada's former exploration manager, who had left Mobil for PetroCan out of frustration at the slashing of his exploration budget by his New York head office. Both Axford and the man who would succeed him as PetroCan's head of exploration, Bob Meneley, had particularly strong faith in the potential of the Sable Basin off Nova Scotia, and the Crown Corporation made agreements with both Shell and Mobil to earn acreage in the area.

In 1977, its second year of operation, PetroCan was the most active player on the Scotian Shelf, and, overall, participated in thirteen of the twenty-seven wells drilled in Canada's frontiers that year. By the end of 1979, it had participated in the major gas find at Venture off Sable Island. More important, it had muscled its way into the very large find at Hibernia on Newfoundland's Grand Banks.

More than forty wells had been drilled on the Grand Banks since Amoco and Imperial had first drilled shallow tests there in 1966. Over the following thirteen years, Chevron, Elf, Mobil, and others had joined the search. Mobil had enjoyed a promising well called Adolphus, but step-out wells — to establish the real size of the discovery — had proved disappointing.

The Rocky Road to Exploration Success

The essence of exploration success is faith and ideas. Chevron had already earned considerable kudos for its Canadian exploration expertise with the discovery of the important West Pembina field in Alberta in the mid-1970s. Its belief in the oil potential of the Grand Banks followed a farm-out it had taken from Amoco. But the California-based company came up with the Hibernia prospect as a result of taking seismic work done by Mobil and "working it over" with advanced, computerized techniques. However, it is far from certain that

159

Chevron would have taken a farm-out from Mobil and drilled the well if super-depletion had not made it so cheap to do so.

Super-depletion had been thought up by the whizz-kids at Dome Petroleum when they discovered that the drilling fleet they had assembled to explore in the Beaufort Sea might turn out to be a white elephant. Dome's silver-tongued chairman, Jack Gallagher, had used his unique persuasive powers to cajole Ottawa into providing extra tax-incentives for frontier exploration on the basis that enormous potential lay in the Beaufort. Super-depletion gave large additional write-offs to wells costing more than $5 million. Since, at the time the measure was introduced, Dome was the only company drilling wells costing more than $5 million, super-depletion was soon dubbed the "Gallagher Amendment" in the "Dome Budget." Nevertheless, the measure was not restricted to wells in the Beaufort, and it was a key factor in Chevron's decision to go ahead with its expensive wildcat at Hibernia.

The land on which Hibernia was drilled had originally been held by Mobil alone. Then Gulf Canada had taken a 25 per cent interest through a farm-out and PetroCan had taken 25 per cent through exercising its rights under federal land provisions. Normally, Chevron, when seeking its farm-in, would have taken a pro-rata share from each landholder. However, PetroCan wanted to maintain its full 25 per cent, as did Gulf, so each paid a share of Chevron's drilling costs. As a result, Mobil wound up with 28.125 per cent of the well, Gulf and PetroCan had 25 per cent each, and Chevron held 21.875 per cent (part of which was taken under a previous agreement with Columbia Gas Development).

The well was spudded on May 27, 1979. By the time testing had finished late in December of the same year, it was clear that Hibernia was the most significant well drilled in Canada since the find at Leduc in 1947. Oil had flowed from the well at over 12,000 barrels a day, but it was clear to Chevron that it was capable of producing 20,000 barrels a day.

The same year saw Mobil drilling the Venture D-23 well, east of Sable Island, which promised a natural gas field of commercial proportions. These finds indicated that the East Coast had the potential to become a petroleum exploration province of worldwide significance. There were, however, complicating factors. Just as the North Sea had provided a spur to the claims of the Scottish nationalists, so the East Coast finds stirred the aspirations of the Atlantic provinces, in particular, Newfoundland and Nova Scotia, off whose coasts the key discoveries had been made.

Provincial Aspirations

Both because it had been the last province to join Confederation and also because of its unique status as the only province that could claim to having been a sovereign nation, Newfoundland was to make a particularly powerful pitch for its jurisdiction over offshore resources. Under its feisty premier, Brian Peckford, it saw the offshore oil promise of Hibernia as its chance to climb beyond federal dependency into self-sufficient wealth. The province, which had not joined Confederation until 1949, had from the first claimed its right to ownership of offshore resources. In 1964, Premier Joey Smallwood had dispatched divers to deposit a plaque on the ocean floor, 200 miles from the coast, asserting Newfoundland's claim to the riches of the ocean and the Earth beneath it.

British Columbia had waged a similar fight for ownership of its offshore resources in the mid 1960s, but had lost. However, Newfoundland said that its claim was not like that of B.C. The mineral rights of each province, it asserted, were determined by the rights it held just before it came into Confederation. Newfoundland asserted that it had joined Confederation as a self-governing British Dominion, with all the rights of a sovereign state, not — as B.C. had done in 1871 — as a 19th century colony.

In 1977, the federal Liberal government of Pierre Trudeau had attempted to establish a memorandum of agreement with the premiers of the four Atlantic provinces that purported to give these provinces three-quarters of resource revenues but would leave control of development up to Ottawa. Newfoundland's then-premier, Frank Moores, not only rejected the notion, he also refused even to meet with the federal Liberals on the issue. Peckford, who was then Newfoundland's energy minister, headed a group of young, aggressive politicians and public servants — the first generation of university-educated Newfoundlanders to have grown up within Confederation — determined to assert themselves through the resource issue against a distant and much-resented Ottawa.

In a glossy pamphlet produced by the province to support its claims, Peckford wrote: "We have begun a new phase in the fight to gain recognition of our rights to control the development of our offshore oil and gas resources and to turn them to our lasting benefit. The outcome of that fight will determine the key to our future. It will determine whether we will remain dependents of Ottawa or whether we will be able to create a viable economic and social context for our people's development.

"Moreover, even if the Supreme Court of Canada rejects our legal case, we must not give up. We must make it plain to Ottawa that we will not meekly accept the negative impacts and lost opportunities of federally controlled offshore oil and gas developments.

"Ottawa must be made to recognize the legitimate interests of the people of this Province."

In 1977, Peckford introduced legislation to ensure that as many benefits as possible, in terms of jobs and supply contracts, came to Newfoundland. Peckford and his team had examined North Sea development in particular and had concluded that they favored the Norwegian model of tight control and insistence on local content rather than the initial full-speed-ahead approach of the British government.

As for Nova Scotia, Premier John Buchanan, who had come to power in 1978, drew back from the agreement his predecessor had made with Ottawa on the basis that the fine print could whittle the province's share down to nothing.

During the brief reign of Joe Clark's Tories in 1979-80, the pendulum had appeared to swing in the provinces' favor, just as the Hibernia find was upping the stakes involved. However, the Tories had been supplanted by a Liberal government determined to assert itself in the energy field. That determination was to become abundantly clear with the introduction of the National Energy Programme.

The Liberals' return to power in Ottawa in February, 1980 coincided with unprecedented optimism about East Coast prospects. PetroCan was estimating that if the summer's delineation drilling at Sable Island was successful, then a $1 billion investment to deliver 250 million cubic feet of gas a day to the Maritimes by 1987 could be justified. Newfoundland's Department of Energy was forecasting revenues of $40 billion from Hibernia, based on recoverable reserve estimates of 750 million barrels of oil. The prospects offered not only massive economic development to a depressed part of Canada but also huge savings for the balance of payments on oil imports, and insulation from a turbulent world oil market, still reeling from the implications of the Shah's fall in Iran.

Not surprisingly, the political rhetoric grew more heated as the fruits of success appeared greater. As geophysical and drilling activity reached record heights all along the East Coast in 1980, Newfoundland officials spoke of fighting a "legal guerrilla war" against Ottawa. In June a bill was introduced in the Newfoundland legislature to create a Newfoundland and Labrador Petroleum Corp., which would not only own 40 per cent of any oil and gas discovered, but would also conduct exploration on its own account and control processing and distribution. Meanwhile, Newfoundland declared its intention of fighting PetroCan's back-in rights on permit renewals, which had been responsible for its 25 per cent stake in Hibernia.

When they had returned to power, the Liberals had offered Nova Scotia and Newfoundland the rights to 100 per cent of all "provincial-type" resource revenues up to a certain level of wealth, whereafter revenues would be shared with other provinces. They had also offered them a say in "matters of direct concern to them." However, both provinces had rejected the specifics of such a deal. The NEP's new revenue taxes were obviously of concern to both provinces since they represented an attempt to increase the federal tax take. However, the tax implications were less immediate, since there was, as yet, no oil and gas production. Ownership remained the principal bone of contention both between Ottawa and the Atlantic provinces, and between the Atlantic provinces and the oil companies.

Shortly after the NEP was introduced, Mobil shocked Newfoundland by declaring that it was planning to take the question of jurisdiction to court. The U.S. oil company declared that it would not go ahead with the development of Hibernia until the dispute had been settled. Newfoundland threatened privately to cancel the company's exploration permits. Ottawa promised to support Mobil. But while the political war of words escalated, encouragement was coming from another very political source, PetroCan.

Petrocan Heats up the Action

Despite the increasing heat of the political debate, the Hibernia and Venture finds seemed to corroborate PetroCan's enthusiasm for the East Coast in general, if not for the state oil company's exploration program in particular. Apart from its involvement off Sable Island and the Grand Banks, PetroCan also had an ambitious program in the much more demanding conditions offshore of Labrador. However, shortages of drilling equipment meant that it was still not moving as fast as it wanted with East Coast offshore development. In 15 years, only 150 wells had been drilled off the East Coast. Bill Hopper, PetroCan's chairman, another big fan of the area, liked to point out that in the North Sea, more than 800 wells had been drilled by the end of 1979 in an area only one-third as large. But of course the North Sea had seen many commercial finds. The East Coast still appeared to have only two. Nevertheless, Hopper and Meneley believed that the East Coast would continue to boom.

Internal studies at the national oil company indicated that the rig count off Newfoundland and Nova Scotia could increase from eleven in the latter half of 1980 to thirty by 1985, with PetroCan itself operating as many as a dozen. But the problem, declared Bill Hopper at a conference in St. John's in September, 1980, "is that we doubt very much whether we will be able to get twelve rigs from the international market by that time. The rigs we now have on contract will barely satisfy Petro-Canada's needs until 1983. The obvious conclusion is that like any other major offshore operator, Petro-Canada will have to gain long-term control over a fleet of offshore rigs." For Bow Valley, the opportunities seemed clear.

Petro-Canada had declared before the NEP that it wanted to construct one or more semi-submersible drilling rigs for its operations. Given the national oil company's mandate, it seemed inevitable that a Canadian drilling contractor, using Canadian ship-building facilities, would have priority over foreign-owned and -operated equipment.

However, Bow Valley had experienced frustrations in earlier attempts to become involved in East Coast offshore drilling. When Gerald Regan had been premier of Nova Scotia, he had been enormously keen to promote offshore exploration. In the early 1970s, Offshore Industries Ltd. had been formed, with ownership split between the Nova Scotia government, local businessmen, Acres Consulting, and Norwegian interests — the latter two partners being represented by Emil Dinkla, the Norwegian consultant who had been of critical importance in lining up Bow Valley with the Norwegian partners in the *Odin Drill*. The OIL group needed a driller and Bow Valley was invited in to take 35 per cent of the company. The provincial premier had declared that he would use his suasion to make sure that OIL was given offshore business, but when Mobil drilled its first wells at Sable Island, it chose Peter Bawden's drilling company to do the drilling. When East Coast activities wound down in the mid-1970s, OIL quietly broke up. But prospects appeared brighter now for gaining offshore work.

Petro-Canada obviously had a mandate to encourage Canadian expertise, but its attitude was complicated by the politically sensitive position in which it found itself. Hopper had always spoken out about the danger that Canadian companies might see the state oil company as a "soft touch" for contracts. He was also acutely aware that PetroCan's performance was always under the microscope. These twin concerns ironically made PetroCan appear to hold a bias against using Canadian companies. PetroCan was reluctant to link up with either Canadian contractors, which it felt to have insufficient experience, or Canadian shipyards, whose costs were not only higher but which were also reluctant to take on rig construction in any case.

Faced with difficulties in chartering drilling vessels, the national oil company had in 1980 already contracted four dynamically positioned drill-ships. It had also contracted a semi-submersible, the *Bredford Dolphin* — owned by a British-based subsidiary of Norway's shipping magnate, Fred Olsen. But when it announced its first semi-submersible construction joint venture, the partner turned out to be Sedco Inc. of Dallas, acknowledged as the world-leader in offshore drilling. PetroCan entered into a 50 per cent joint venture with Sedco to construct a dynamically positioned semi-submersible at a cost of about $125 million (the cost would wind being up closer to $150 million).

This arrangement caused considerable grumbling among the Canadian drilling community, various members of which, including Bow Valley, felt that they were capable of building a semi-submersible in Canada. Partly in response to political pressures, therefore, PetroCan also invited proposals from private Canadian drilling contractors for the design, construction, and operation of a semi-submersible, which it would both partially-own and also contract to drill for it.

Bow Valley, with its experience and its reputation for corporate aggressiveness, was determined to get more than just a piece of the action. Meanwhile, within little more than a month of Bill Hopper's remarks in St. John's, the introduction of the National Energy Programme had apparently increased the potential size of the action enormously. For Canadian companies, the opportunities of gaining a key position appeared unprecedented. But investment in Canada's East Coast waters was imperilled not merely by the technological difficulties of exploring and producing in the area, but also by the uncertainties of the nationalist politics that had inspired the NEP, and by the snares of the ongoing federal-provincial dispute over jurisdiction and control of development.

19
BVRS Moves Centre Stage

For many years, the service side of Bow Valley — run by B.J. and Don — had operated in the shadow of the company's oil and gas activies. Now, the opportunities of the National Energy Programme would suddenly thrust this side of the business into the limelight.

From the time Doc first started moving into exploration, there had been an uneasiness about the fit between these activities and drilling, primarily because of the perceived conflict of interest. Another problem arose once the company moved into manufacturing and other related businesses because although these were important for generating cash flow for exploration, they weren't felt to be "sexy" in terms of the company's public image.

Quite apart from the issues of potential conflict or corporate sexiness, however, there had always been an underlying tension in the company between the oil and gas group and the other parts of the business. Explorationists inevitably tend to have a more romantic aura than those in the practical business of drilling the holes to test the formers' geological theories. And if drilling did have its own rough and tough mystique, there was no way that any form of mundane manufacturing activity could share the limelight with the oracles of the oil and gas business. In Bow Valley, this sense of mystique was particularly strong because the explorers operated in the most exotic locations. The drilling and manufacturing side paid the rent, but all the glamor lay in Bow Valley's exploration.

Doc had never made any secret that his long-term strategy emphasized oil and gas. This inevitably left the resource services side of Bow Valley feeling a little like second-class citizens. Sometimes they felt they were just there to make the money, whereas the oil and gas people were there to spend it. While oil and gas was a business of spectacular successes — and sometimes even failures like Vietnam that seemed like lots of fun — the other side of Bow Valley, with its myriad divisions, could only move ahead by hard work. There was no way a furnace manufacturer was going to strike the motherlode, or a rig supply business suddenly enjoy a spectacular increase in sales.

Nevertheless, by any standards — apart from those of the oil and gas division — Bow Valley's service and manufacturing arm made tremendous strides in the 1970s. Part of this was due to the boom in drilling, particularly in the latter half of the decade, but it was also due to the exceptional management that the drilling side had kept — and acquired — over the years.

One outstanding example was Bill Hay, who joined Bow Valley in 1967 after a sparkling career as a professional hockey player — which included both captaining and winning a Stanley Cup with the Chicago Blackhawks. Hay was the son of Charlie Hay, the president of Gulf Canada. Throughout his hockey days, he had always known that he would one day move on to the oilpatch. While his colleagues played away their summers on the golf course, he took a job with Imperial Oil. However, when the time came for him to make the full-time transition, Imperial was concerned about his father's position at Gulf.

One day, Don Seaman was sitting with Hay's boss from Imperial at a hockey game. Don mentioned that he was looking for some help with the Sedco side of the business — which was being expanded into exploration and production drilling from its previous seismic and slim-hole drilling specialities. Hay's boss said that he should take a look at Hay. A meeting was arranged and Hay was quickly signed up. Hay proved to be a natural at the contracting game. His principal problems during his first couple of years at Bow Valley were in steering customers away from talking hockey to talking rig contracts, and in fighting off the lucrative offers to return to the hockey arena!

Hay gradually assumed more and more operational responsibility for the drilling side of Bow Valley, working with skilled managers like Bobby Brownridge, Dick McGhee, and Selby Porter. On the operations side, there were men like Buzz Cotter, Norm Vetters, John Gillard, Bob Engberg, John Gorsak, and "Spike" Kovaks, who between them had literally hundreds of years service with Bow Valley and its predecessors.

Between fiscal 1971 and fiscal 1980, net sales of the non-exploration side of Bow Valley — which was dominated by drilling (and which after 1978 included coal) — increased sevenfold, to $265 million, while its operating income rose 500 per cent to $50 million. However, the oil and gas division showed even more spectacular rises over the same period. Net sales increased by a factor of 40, to $97 million, while operating income rose from $1.7 million to $51 million. In addition, the really spectacular money-spinners, the North Sea and Indonesia, had not yet begun to produce (in the case of Indonesia, the fields had not even been found!)

At the time of the Syracuse acquisition, Bow Valley already had more than 20 different profit centres under its resource services side. Throughout the 1970s, the board had had many discussions about splitting off the resource side of the business. A long-range plan had been hatched to reduce the profit centres and — once the oil and gas side could stand on its own feet — split the company into two. Finally, in 1980, the decision was taken to sell some of BVRS's shares to the public, although at the time it was the financial needs of Bow Valley Industries which were the primary motivation for the deal.

Short of funds, the BVI board decided in 1980 that a sale of shares in BVRS would be one obvious means of raising cash. The original intention had been to sell a larger chunk of BVRS — with a view to possible complete separation at a later date — but the post-NEP market meant that only 3 million BVRS treasury shares were offered in a financing underwritten by Greenshields. This meant that BVI's stake in BVRS was reduced from 100 per cent to 78 per cent.

BVRS's four divisions — oilwell drilling, industrial products, diamond drilling, and environmental products — had between them generated net income of $15 million on sales of $186 million in 1980. The proceeds of the issue of convertible debentures and common shares was to be used to pay off BVRS's long-term debt of $61.4 million ($28 million of which represented an advance from BVI). The issue was successfully launched in February, 1981. However, when it was made, few people realized the impact that the NEP would have on BVRS's business. On the one hand, the program would severely damage the land drilling market. On the other, it created the opportunities for a huge expansion in offshore drilling activity. By the end of 1984, BVRS would have spent more than $400 million on buying and building a major drilling fleet that would quintuple its assets and take it into the forefront of offshore Canadian exploration.

Plotting an East Coast Strategy

Bow Valley had seen legislation at least as punitive as the NEP in other countries. It had endured the British Labour government and its overzealous bureaucrats over the issue of North Sea participation. It had coped with the hair-tearing frustrations of doing business in places like Vietnam and Indonesia. But for once Bow Valley now appeared to be on the winning side of nationally biased legislation.

As a sizable service company with offshore operating experience in the North Sea, it was in an ideal position to benefit from the Canadian government's commitment to encourage Canadian companies in East Coast offshore drilling. As an aggressive explorer, it could not afford to ignore the large PIP grants available to predominantly Canadian-owned companies drilling on the Canada Lands.

Even before the NEP, Bow Valley had been looking at offshore East Coast rig operation. Now the prospects looked much more attractive.

PIP grants meanwhile increased the attractions for the company to drill on its own account. The stage was set for Bow Valley to make another of the bold and aggressive moves that had become its hallmark.

Although PetroCan had declared that it wanted a Canadian semi-submersible built by a Canadian contractor — in addition to the rig it had contracted from Dallas-based Sedco — the state oil company still indicated its preference for a Canadian company with an experienced international partner. Although Bow Valley didn't feel that it needed a foreign partner, it contacted a number of major semi-submersible manufacturers and operators. Sedco, as the international leader, was approached to see if it would sell Bow Valley one of its exclusive rig designs, but the company said no. Bow Valley wanted to run its own offshore rig show, but the foreign companies it approached wanted it to play the role of a more or less passive investor.

In February, 1981, Bow Valley's aspirations appeared to have received a mortal blow when PetroCan announced that the contract to build a semi-submersible in Canada had gone to Peter Bawden Drilling. Bawden, another self-made Albertan millionaire, was considered an eccentric genius, and had offshore rig experience both off the East Coast and in the North Sea. The tender that PetroCan had put out to Canadian companies asked basically: what kind of rig would you build for us for East Coast operation, and where and how would you go about building it? Bawden's recommendation had been that, for purely economic reasons, PetroCan not build the rig in Canada. However, PetroCan's political mandate demanded that a rig be built here. The yard that emerged as the best candidate was that of Saint John Shipbuilding & Dry Dock Co. Ltd., which belonged to the wealthy and influential Irving family, in New Brunswick.

Although Bow Valley appeared to have been beaten out for this key contract, Doc and his brothers remained determined to gain a major role off the East Coast. It was while talking to another offshore operator, Blandford Shipping — Norwegian shipping giant Fred Olsen's British subsidiary — that Bow Valley conceived a bold strategy for forcing its way into the action. Blandford was the company that owned the *Bredford Dolphin*, the semi-submersible that Petro-Canada had acquired under long-term contract for East Coast operations. At a meeting in Oslo in January, 1981, between B.J. and Bjorn Johansen, one of Fred Olsen's directors, B.J. suddenly said: "Why not sell us the *Bredford Dolphin*?" Johansen at first laughed, but B.J. said: "I'm serious. You can't have that much money that the rig doesn't have a price. What's the price?"

To purchase the rig would be daring — and expensive — but it would pre-empt the competition and put Bow Valley into East Coast operations much more quickly than through rig construction. The problem of course would be to gain PetroCan's approval for such a deal. A price also had to be negotiated. The price was, in fact, tied up with PetroCan's approval, because the state oil company demanded that Olsen provide a guarantee of the *Dolphin's* performance under Bow Valley's operatorship. Fred Olsen, in turn, was obviously reluctant to provide a guarantee for a situation that would ultimately be outside Blandford's control. PetroCan also wanted Olsen to continue operating the rig until the national oil company was happy that Bow Valley could take over. This latter provision was less of a problem for Bow Valley since it would, in any case, take time to recruit an operating crew. After further negotiations with Olsen management in New York, a price of U.S.$112 million was reached for the rig, which had meanwhile been sub-contracted by PetroCan to British Petroleum to drill wells offshore Ireland and Spain.

In March, 1981, a month after the Bawden contract was announced, Bow Valley announced the purchase of the *Bredford Dolphin*. B.J., always the wit, had suggested they might rename the rig *Bow Derrick*! The *Dolphin* was eventually renamed *Bow Drill One*. It would be the first Canadian-owned semi-submersible contracted to a Canadian company to work in Canadian waters. Bow Valley was back in the offshore drilling business.

The *Bredford Dolphin* had been built in 1976 in Verdal, Norway, by Aker-Verdal as a construction support vessel for Olsen's British subsidiary Blandford. However, it had been decided to convert it into an offshore rig and while Bow Valley was negotiating its purchase, the conversion process — which included the addition of two support columns to increase deck capacity — was still going on in Rotterdam. One of more than 250 semi-submersibles either already in service or under construction, the *Bow Drill One* would be typical of the giant breed. It was 355 feet long, 220 feet wide and 320 feet from its lowest point to the top of the drilling derrick. Each of the 8 anchors that held it in position during drilling weighed 30,000 pounds, and each was equipped with 4,000 feet of chain. Powered by 2 huge Siemens engines, which between them generated 7,000 horsepower — the vessel could travel at 8 knots and had accommodation for almost 100 people on board. It could drill to 26,000 feet in water depths up to 1,200 feet. The vessel would not be officially renamed until it arrived in Halifax in November, 1981, but by that time, Bow Valley's commitment to East Coast offshore drilling would have taken another mighty leap. That leap would be made in concert with another of Calgary's outstanding businessmen, Nova Corporation's Bob Blair.

The Husky Partnership

Blair had leaped into national prominence in the mid-1970s with a series of bold corporate moves. First, he had won regulatory approval to construct a gas pipeline from Prudhoe Bay, Alaska, through Canada to U.S. markets. Then, he had snatched control of Husky Oil Ltd. from under the noses of both PetroCan and Los Angeles-based oil giant Occidental Petroleum in what was, at the time, the country's largest takeover struggle.

The pipeline "victory" in fact proved problematic, since the pipeline still had to be built, and there were considerable doubts over whether it ever would be. Nevertheless, Bob Blair had clearly established himself as a champion of both Albertan and Canadian business.

The company Blair headed, Nova Corporation, held a key position within the province's energy business. Formed as Alberta Gas Trunk Line (AGTL) in the early 1950s, it had been given the monopoly on collection and transportation of natural gas within the province. When Blair had ascended to the presidency of the company in 1970, however, AGTL appeared to be a company in decline. Blair had set about revitalizing the organization through a bold bid to bring the natural gas discovered at Prudhoe Bay south through the province. He had also moved to diversify AGTL's business — a corporate objective that linked closely with the broader economic goal of Alberta's iron-willed premier, Peter Lougheed. As part of this diversification process, Blair had seized the leadership of a massive petrochemical development program in the province.

Blair's devotion to economic nationalism did not always sit easily with his fellow Calgary oil executives. Nevertheless, Doc Seaman, who had known Blair for a long time, and who had sat on his board for a decade, respected the genuineness of his convictions.

The Seamans could match their credentials as good Canadians against anyone, but to be a good businessman meant obedience to the bottom line. Nevertheless, what was now happening off the East Coast, combined with the incentives introduced and promised under the National Energy Programme, created what appeared to be a unique set of opportunities to serve both Canadian nationalism and the bottom line.

BVRS was already involved in a joint venture with Nova to take over the truck operations of White Motor Corporation of Canada Ltd. White Motor assembled custom-built heavy diesel trucks at a plant in Kelowna, B.C. and had a marketing and administration centre in Mississauga, Ontario. The concept for its purchase came out of Shieldings, the venture capital arm of Greenshields, which had long been Bow Valley's main investment advisor. The strategy was that White could be used as the basis for expansion into the manufacture of trucks and truck parts, demand for which — although currently depressed — was expected to increase with the building of the northern gas pipeline and other megaprojects. Such a purchase would also fit clearly into both Canadian and western aspirations to have more of the country's manufacturing capacity held locally.

The move was highly controversial because of the depressed state of the trucking industry, but in April, 1981, BVRS and Nova acquired the White interests and renamed them Western Star Trucks Inc. An agreement with Volvo White Truck Corporation enabled Western Star Trucks to be marketed throughout the Unites States.

While the Western Star deal was being negotiated, mainly by Don Seaman, Doc and Bob Blair had been putting their heads together on a much more ambitious scheme to exploit opportunities on the East Coast.

Over the years, Bow Valley had built much of its land position by taking a piece of the action in return for drilling wells. One obvious strategy for gaining an exploration foothold off the East Coast, therefore, was to pursue this time-honoured route and gain land through increasing drilling operations in the area. Bow Valley had already taken the first step with the purchase of the *Bredford Dolphin*. Now it was decided that Bow Valley and Nova's oil exploration affiliate, Husky Oil, would build a number of semi-submersibles on their own account. Semi-submersibles were in any case in short supply while PIP grants would make the economics of offshore operation even more attractive. Meanwhile, the two companies thought they could use commitments to build parts of the new drilling fleet in Canada as a bargaining lever to obtain lands from the federal government.

Within the space of just a few months, Bow Valley and Husky would launch a scheme for the construction of two semi-submersible drilling rigs, a fleet of state-of-the-art supply boats, and extensive shore-based facilities in St. John's, Newfoundland and Halifax, Nova Scotia.

Moreover, the costs of the drilling fleet were only part of the massive commitment involved in the East Coast venture, for the new rigs, *Bow Drills* 2 and 3 would be drilling on behalf of Bow Valley and Husky. The two companies were committing themselves not only to enormous capital expenditure for equipment, but also to a major exploration program. But as yet, they lacked land, the key factor of exploration. Moreover, they still had to finance and build the rigs.

Financing and building the rigs, acquiring the land, and, finally, gaining the promised PIP grants were all to prove tremendous challenges for Bow Valley and its partner.

20
Moving into the Vanguard of East Coast Exploration

Bow Valley's decision to participate in a fleet of semi-submersibles, support ships, and shore facilities ranked among the boldest of its long list of daring corporate moves. With the commitment to expenditures of more than $400 million, Bow Valley Resource Services, BVI's 78 per cent-owned drilling and manufacturing arm, took itself into the forefront of Canadian offshore exploration. Bow Valley's exploration commitment, meanwhile, dwarfed all its previous similar endeavors in Canada.

Doc and Nova's Bob Blair were both keen to construct a semi-submersible in Canada, since they believed this would aid them in their quest for offshore lands. But they found it difficult to arouse Canadian yards' interest. Offshore rigs had been built in Canada before, but although technically sound, their builders had tended to run into financial problems.

A Canadian rig would almost certainly be more expensive than a rig built abroad. This, in turn, would be reflected in the cost at which it was charged out to customers, the day-rate, and thus affect the economics of its operation and its competitiveness with other rigs. One way of compensating for this would be via some form of government financial assistance to reduce the effective cost.

In most countries, heavy equipment built for export can usually gain some form of government assistance. In Canada, the prime instrument of helping companies finance exports at preferential rates is Ottawa's Export Development Corporation (EDC).

Bow Valley had first been involved with the EDC when that Crown Corporation had provided political risk insurance for its operations at Arzanah in Abu Dhabi. When Bow Valley and Husky started looking at the construction of a semi-submersible after the purchase of *Bow Drill One*, Trevor Legge, who had now moved over to head finance at BVRS, called contacts in the EDC and broached the question of the government helping to finance the rig. The problem, of course, was that the rig was not strictly speaking for export. This led to great soul-searching in Ottawa. One of the government's fears was that the financing might be seen as a precedent that would open the floodgates to a deluge of similar financing demands. Another was that it would be seen as an example of not playing by the sensitive rules of international trade. Although the EDC's officials were keen on providing assistance, the corporation's board turned the deal down. This meant that economic considerations inevitably forced Bow Valley to look to foreign builders.

As soon as they had hatched their East Coast strategy, Bow Valley and Husky had begun to canvass shipyards around the world. By far the best price obtainable on a semi-submersible came from the Framnaes yard in Norway, which was just completing an *Enhanced Pacesetter* design rig. By ordering such a rig, Bow Valley and Husky would obtain the benefits of the Framnaes yard's "learning curve," (that is, that the more times a production unit builds something, the more efficiently it does so because it learns from its earlier mistakes). The partners were also able to gain excellent financing on the Norwegian rig through the Norwegian government's Eksportfinans, the equivalent of the EDC. The part of the rig that Bow Valley had to finance privately was funded by a consortium led by its closest banks in Canada and Europe, the Royal and Den norske Creditbank.

Once word reached Ottawa that Bow Valley was planning to build a rig in Norway, concern began to be voiced that more effort should be made to develop rig-building capacity in Canada, in line with the firmly stated objectives of the National Energy Programme. Although the Department of External Affairs was still concerned about the EDC financing a non-export, the Department of Industry, Trade and Commerce was keen to gain such business for Canada. The EDC board was still wary of financing such a deal, so in the end approval for the financing of *Bow Drill 3* had to come from the Liberal cabinet. Concerns over whether the rig was an export were satisfied by setting up a Bermuda subsidiary to own the rig. Suddenly, Bow Valley was involved in the potential construction of a second semi-submersible.

A Deal with Saint John

The only Canadian yard prepared to undertake such a venture was the yard with which Peter Bawden had already — somewhat reluctantly — agreed to build a rig for Petro-Canada: Saint John Shipbuilding & Dry Dock. From the shipyard's point of view, the order was attractive because its management believed there were other orders in the pipeline — that of Bawden and possibly a third from Esso Resources — that could help them develop an expertise in rig construction. The shipyard also badly needed the work. Nevertheless, they realized there were problems with the construction of a semi-submersible. Apart from the fact that the yard had never built such a vessel before, its dry dock was not suited for the construction of most semi-submersible designs. Even when Bow Valley and Husky found a design, the *Aker H-3.2*, that could be built there, the rig would still have to be built in two halves, with further modifications to make it fit into the dock.

Nevertheless, on September 8, 1981, the agreement between BVI, BVRS, and Husky Oil Operations Ltd. was officially announced, along with the orders for the two new rigs, the estimated cost of which was $300 million. The original plan was that the rigs would be owned 50 per cent by BVRS and 25 per cent each by BVI and Husky. However, this was modified so that in the end they were owned 65 per cent by BVRS and 35 per cent by Husky. In addition, the fleet of six supply boats was announced, four of which would be built in Korea by Hyundai and two in Canada by West Coast shipyards. These would be owned 50/50 by the partners.

By early 1982, work was under way at both Saint John and Framnaes. The steel began to move from the holding yards into the shops where it would be cut and bent. Then it was welded together before being taken to be blasted and painted. Eventually the parts were lifted by giant cranes into the dry docks at the two yards before being welded into place.

At the Canadian yard, which sits across Courteney Bay from Saint John on the other side of the town from Saint John Harbor, the first section of steel was cut on February 12. The keel was officially laid on June 8. By February, 1983, the legs of the two sections of the rig jutted above the side of the dry dock as the rig's superstructure was being put together at its landward end. In March, the first of the deck sections was installed. By the end of that month, a section of super-structure had been added with clearly recognizable rooms and stair-ways and railings, the first real sign that this behemoth might be a thing of human design or purpose. In May, the dock was flooded, the green, murky waters bringing the debris of over a year's work to the surface. The dock gates were swung open and the little tug, the *Irving Poplar*, looked like a zoo-keeper leading an elephant as it towed the halves of the *Bow Drill 3* — with just inches to spare — out of the dock . Then, moored at pier 19, the two halves of the semi-submersible were welded together above and below the water-line. In July, a massive barge-mounted crane arrived from the U.S. to lift — with its great, mechanical swan-neck — the deck sections onto the rig plat-form. On July 18, 1983, the giant crane dipped its derrick in salute and departed. By August, the rig had clearly come to life. Its own derricks now lifted gear onto its deck. By November, the rig appeared completed. The bridge of the vessel now looked down on the dock where it had been brought to life; most of the equipment had been installed; glittering stainless steel bedecked the galley. There were tables and chairs and curtains. But the construction deadline had arrived, and the rig wasn't finished.

Problems with parts suppliers had caused part of the delay, as had the inexperience of the initial supervisory and management staff. But another significant part of the delay had also been caused by the zeal of the officials from the EDC. If they were going to finance a Canadian-built rig, they wanted to make absolutely sure that it was Canadian-built. They not only specified levels of Canadian content, they wanted proof that the parts really were Canadian. This only added to the already extensive headaches of the two men in charge of the construction — Gordon Rennie from the Bow Valley side and John Shepherd from Saint John Shipbuilding.

An additional problem also loomed. Whereas the labor force had been co-operative in the early stages of construction, it was by now apparent that no further work was coming into the yard. The Bawden contract with Petro-Canada had been suspended and the state oil company had taken another foreign-built rig, the *Vinland*, on long-term contract. The workers in the Saint John yard now realized that when the *Bow Drill 3* left, so did their jobs. Work slowed to a crawl.

It was little use trying to explain to workers or unions that delays and cost-escalations meant that the yard was unlikely ever to gain another semi-submersible job. A worker with a family has more immediate concerns than the country's broad industrial future. He has to put bread on the table.

The priority became to get the rig out of the yard, although it was not completed. On November 26, 1983, in a howling storm, B.J.'s wife Evelyn, hanging onto her hat in the face of near gale-force winds, performed the ceremonial honours at Saint John as the *Bow Drill 3* was officially launched. Then it moved to Halifax for its final fitting.

Although the experience at the Saint John Dry Dock was far short of disastrous, it suffered by comparison with the construction of the Norwegian-built *Bow Drill 2* at Framnaes, where the operation went relatively smoothly. Moreover, partly due to exchange rate movements, *Bow Drill 2* came in under cost, and markedly cheaper than *Bow Drill 3*. In order to meet the highest international safety standards, the rigs were considerably upgraded in the course of construction, but the Norwegian rig's final cost was around U.S.$30 million below its Canadian counterpart. As well, the two support boats built in Canada worked out a full 50 per cent more expensive than their Korean-built sister-vessels.

The Canadian boats, the M.V. *Bonavista Bay* and the M.V. *Placentia*

Bay, constructed at Vancouver's Bel-Aire Shipyard and Vito Steel Boat and Barge Shipyard, were officially delivered on June 4, 1983. They set sail, via the Panama Canal, to Norway to escort the *Bow Drill 2* from Framnaes. They were joined on the way by the first Korean-built boat, the M.V. *Gabarus Bay*. When the *Bow Drill 2* reached its Canadian destination, the rig wasn't even pulled into Halifax harbor. As soon as it was within helicopter range of Halifax, the full complement of its crew was flown out and it went straight to its first drill-site. The three other boats built by Hyundai, the M.V. *Chignecto Bay*, the M.V. *Mahone Bay*, and the M.V. *Trinity Bay*, were delivered October 3, October 31, and November 18 respectively. The *Bow Drill 3* went into service in March, 1984.

The successful financing and construction of the rigs represented a major achievement. However, throughout this whole period, another critical challenge of Bow Valley's East Coast commitments was also very much on the minds of the company's management: that of obtaining land.

The Fight for Offshore Land

One of the riskiest parts of the commitment to the East Coast off-shore was that Bow Valley had no land on which to drill. Jack Gallagher's Beaufort drilling fleet had been able to exploit Dome's position as the only company able to drill deep offshore wells in order to gain a land position from those who had made work commitments to Ottawa. The Bow Valley/Husky strategy had been somewhat similar. Although their semi-submersibles wouldn't be the only game in town, they counted on a shortage of rigs and on strong activity to enable them to take farm-outs on land on which they drilled wells. They also trusted that the federal government would prove as good as its word in providing lands to dedicated Canadian companies on a "direct issuance" basis. However, in the event, the shortage of rigs confidently predicted by PetroCan did not emerge. Meanwhile, the question of direct issuance was complicated both by the federal government's difficulty in getting its act together and the continuing squabbles over federal-provincial jurisdiction.

In mid-1981, Marc Lalonde declared the federal government's commitment to speed East Coast exploration by offering Crown reserve acreage more regularly, perhaps twice a year. He also asked oil companies to submit exploration proposals for seven parcels of land, six offshore Newfoundland and one offshore Nova Scotia. The Liberals asked for a typically exhaustive list of commitments and proposals.

One of the main ones, not surprisingly given the thrust of the NEP, was the degree of Canadian participation. But the problem was that ownership of the lands was still in dispute.

Newfoundland objected strongly to Ottawa's unilateral search for exploration commitments and threatened not to meet further with the Liberals on settling the jurisdictional dispute unless the deadline for the companies' proposals was delayed.

In February, tragedy marred the whole of the East Coast exploration scene when the *Ocean Ranger* semi-submersible, the largest rig of its kind in the world, foundered, and eighty-four crew members were lost while drilling for Mobil on the Grand Banks. Suggestions that the hiring of inexperienced Newfoundlanders may have contributed to the disaster hardly helped Brian Peckford's thrust for greater provincial involvement. Nevertheless, with what appeared to be a major breakdown in negotiations with Ottawa, Peckford referred the jurisdiction issue to the province's Supreme Court.

In March, while federal Tories sought to block the omnibus energy legislation of the NEP by refusing to vote on it — the great "bell-ringing" incident — a beleaguered Marc Lalonde announced agreement with Nova Scotia on energy control and revenue sharing. The agreement gave the lion's share of revenue from petroleum production to the province for the immediate future. Nevertheless, control over development rested with the federal majority on a joint board, and the federal energy minister retained the ultimate right to override the board's decisions. Although the issue of technical ownership had still not been settled, it was determined that the agreement would stand whatever the courts decided.

Shortly afterwards, Peckford called a provincial election for April. "What I need now," he told the electorate, "is a clear mandate which will show Ottawa that you support my administration and the stand we are taking." Peckford swept the election, but a couple of weeks later, the Trudeau government referred the jurisdictional issue to the Supreme Court of Canada.

In September, 1982, Jean Chrétien took over as federal energy minister. One of the key issues remaining was the contention as to who had final say on the pace of development. Under the Nova Scotia deal signed earlier that year, final say rested with Ottawa. Newfoundland was adamantly opposed to such a relationship and demanded a neutral chairman for any such management board.

Meanwhile, Peckford was reported to be running the clock on the negotiations in anticipation of a federal Tory government after the next election. From the federal side, Chrétien was eager to gain agreement with Newfoundland as a feather in his cap to be sported during any upcoming race for the federal Liberal leadership. Nevertheless, by the end of January, 1983, talks had broken down amid mutual recriminations and suggestions that Newfoundland now had no intention of doing a deal. Chrétien meanwhile was causing discomfort among his cabinet colleagues because of the lengths to which he appeared to be going to do a deal.

As the talks broke down, John Stoik, president of Gulf Canada, one of the key players in the Hibernia field, noted that even if the two levels of government solved their differences, the $8 billion job of bringing the field into production was still "fairly borderline" given the continuing weakness of world oil prices and the prospects of excessive taxation.

The scenario of the NEP and the subsequently much-flawed agreement between Ottawa and Alberta seemed to be being repeated. Governments were becoming so involved in the splitting up of revenue-in-the-sky that they were forgetting that enough had to be left with the oil companies to make it worthwhile to undertake projects in the first place.

Eventually, a single block on the Scotian Shelf, the Abenaki block, was issued to Husky/Bow Valley. However, even this relatively unattractive block wound up being the subject of further political bickering. When PetroCan heard of the federal government's plans for the block, it pulled its Ottawa strings in order to make sure that it received 50 per cent of the acreage while the interests of Bow Valley and Husky were reduced to 25 per cent each. In any event, Bow Valley's exploration staff decided not to participate in the well on Abenaki. Their judgment was shrewd; the well was dry. But the well also had a silver lining; it was drilled under Bow Valley's drilling contract with Petro-Canada by the *Bow Drill One*!

Taking the Farm-Out Route

With direct issuance proving so messy, it was left to Bow Valley and Husky to take the farm-out route. On the gas-prone Scotian Shelf, Bow Valley and Husky executed deals with Mobil, PetroCan, Scotia Energy and Durham (formerly Onaping) Resources to earn interests in a "fairway" of blocks that ran northeast-southwest beneath the Venture field and Sable Island. These blocks included Mohican, Chebucto, South Sable, Gully, Banquereau and East Banquereau. By the end of 1983, the company had earned — or was entitled to earn — varying interests in 8.9 million acres in the area.

From the point of view of all the oil companies, however, the Grand Banks was the more exciting exploration prospect, principally because of Hibernia and subsequent oil finds nearby at Hebron, Ben Nevis, and a number of other locations. The major landholder in the area remained Mobil, which, in fact, wanted to farm-out all acreage except that surrounding the Hibernia field. Bow Valley and Husky approached the New-York based giant in 1982 with a view to making commitments to drill wells on Mobil's acreage in return for a portion of it. The resulting agreement would be the largest in Canadian history. It would also be one of the hardest negotiated.

Late in 1982, Bill Clark, the former Imperial man who had joined Bow Valley shortly before the Syracuse acquisition eleven years before, and who was now in charge of land for the company, was joined by Patrick Wesley, one of a number of former HBOG employees who came to Bow Valley after Gerry Maier. For almost a year, Clark and Wesley and Bow Valley lawyer Bill Keys would devote the bulk of their time to one of the most complex farm-outs in exploration history.

For a company farming-out, the basic strategy is simple: gain as many work commitments on your land — in order to assess its potential most fully — in return for giving away as little of it as possible. For the company, or, in this case, companies farming-in, the strategy is obviously reversed. The Mobil acreage being farmed-out consisted of a bottom-heavy northwest-southeast chunk of blocks sitting to the east of the clump of oil finds around Hibernia. Mobil wanted to give away as little as possible close to the discovery, on the "inner ridge" of acreage, but to force Husky and Bow Valley to drill wells on the "outer ridge" to establish what they had there. They also wanted Bow Valley and Husky to take over their obligations on some unrelated acreage — specifically, to help drill a well at Amauligak in the Beaufort — as part of the deal.

Further complications arose because Mobil had semi-submersibles on contract which it wanted Bow Valley to take over. There were also differences in tactics between Bow Valley and Husky. Meanwhile, the whole process was made much more frustrating by the need of Mobil Canada — which was now headquartered in Toronto — to constantly check back with its New York head office for approval. At times, the Mobil Canada group would indicate their acquiescence to a negotiating point only to return from New York, after the inevitable bureaucratic delay, to announce that head office had turned it down.

It was not unusual for the farm-out to take up three full-day meetings a week. On one occasion, the men from Mobil called and said they thought they had Husky/Bow Valley's proposal ready to go to New York, but would the partners mind coming down to Toronto to clear up a few final points. The result of that trip was two weeks of consecutive daily meetings which eventually broke up without agreement. Whenever a really large sticking point arose, the heavy hitters,

Dale Beischel — another former HBOG man who now headed Bow Valley's exploration — and Bob Pogontcheff, his counterpart from Husky, would join the negotiations.

One very important additional complicating factor in the deal was that Mobil had partners — Gulf Canada and PetroCan — who were not part of the farm-out but who had already established an exploration strategy for the acreage. A well was due to be drilled on one of the blocks being farmed-out, so Bow Valley and Husky were under pressure to complete a deal since negotiations would become much more complex once drilling on the acreage had started. However, the speed of negotiation was also retarded at every stage by the need to clear farm-out proposals with government authorities such as the Ottawa's Canada Oil and Gas Lands Authority (COGLA) and the Petroleum Incentives Administration, the all-important body that would dole out the hefty PIP grants.

Finally, in November, 1983, the agreement was ready for its formal signing. This took place in a conference room in the gold-windowed Husky Tower in Calgary. For Clark, Wesley and Keys, it was — as these occasions so often are — an anticlimax. Only the participants could really appreciate how many thousands of hours of work, and how many dozens of drafts, had gone into the slim document that was now being signed.

This, the largest farm-out in Canadian history, involved 4.7 million acres on the Grand Banks. It allowed Bow Valley to earn a working interest of up to 14 per cent by paying 28 per cent of seismic and drilling costs on the six blocks. Eight wells were required to be drilled during the initial phase of the agreement, with Bow Valley retaining options to drill another six wells to earn a maximum of 25 per cent of Mobil's 56.25 per cent interest in the exploration agreements. Husky's deal with Mobil was the same.

Bow Valley had concluded during the farm-out negotiations that — due to the size of exploration commitments on the East Coast — it would be prudent to farm-out part of the acreage it was in the process of farming into. No sooner had Bill Clark and Patrick Wesley finished with the long and exhausting Mobil negotiations, than they began a new round of negotiations. A number of companies were interested in participating in Bow Valley's acreage, but the farm-out was eventually taken — after further long negotiations — by a consortium, PAREX (Partnership for Atlantic Regional Exploration) made up of Quebec provincial oil company, SOQUIP, Calgary-based Aberford Resources, and Toronto-based Denison Mines. Under this agreement, Parex would earn 50 per cent of Bow Valley's rights in 5.2 million acres on the Grand Banks and Scotian Shelf by paying approximately one-half of the company's commitments.

Now that Bow Valley and Husky had their land, they had to start drilling, and they had to start drilling quickly. For under the federal government's new land regulations, companies now had a much shorter time to evaluate their acreage. The clock was already ticking.

Since the Scotian Shelf acreage was acquired first, Bow Valley participated in its first East Coast wells there. As soon as the *Bow Drill 2* and *Bow Drill 3* came into commission, they moved to their well sites. The sites depended on the geological analysis of the partners, but the task of bringing the rigs to the sites and operating the wells fell to the Husky/Bow Valley East Coast Offshore Project, a special taskforce with operations both in Halifax and St. John's. Bow Valley, as contractor of the rigs, also had a very large East Coast staff under the aegis of Bow Valley Offshore Drilling, a specially-formed subsidiary of BVRS. Together, these groups were responsible for the mind-boggling logistics of staffing and supplying the *Bow Drills* while they undertake the demanding task of drilling wells in some of the most storm-ridden and ice-infested waters in the world. Despite some inevitable teething problems, the *Bow Drills* moved into operations relatively smoothly. However, the politically charged East Coast environment had one final curve to throw at Bow Valley's commitment to offshore drilling, and it related to PIP grants.

Ottawa's Second Thoughts on PIPs

The purchase of *Bow Drill One* and the construction of *Bow Drill 2* and *Bow Drill 3* meant a large financial drain on BVRS at a time when its other operations were being severely affected by the post-NEP turn-down in the Canadian exploration business. Between 1981 and 1982, BVRS swung from a net income of $15 million to a net loss of $6.75 million, before returning to profitability in 1983. Its debt, however, mounted rapidly due to the cost of the semi-submersibles — from $19.7 million in 1980 to $374.7 million by the end of 1983. Capital expenditures in the previous three years had totalled $446 million. B.J., BVRS's chairman and chief executive, and brother Don, its president and chief operating officer, faced a challenging time. However, they knew that once the two semi-submersibles were in commission, then their four-year fixed contracts with parent Bow Valley Industries and Husky would guarantee a return to profitability.

Because of the construction of *Bow Drill 3* and two of the supply boats in Canada, their day-rates were relatively high. But there seemed to be no problem because 80 per cent of the costs were supposed to be covered by government PIP grants. Given that one agreed with the concept of PIP grants in the first place, these higher rates for Canadian-built equipment were not unreasonable. Bow Valley and Husky had sacrificed economics to a degree in order to pursue national objectives of promoting domestic construction, employment, and technological skill. Since the resultant higher costs were incurred in pursuing the federal government's objectives, it did not seem unreasonable that the federal government should pay for its proportionate share under the PIP grant program. However, the administrators of PIP decided otherwise.

Political pressure about the overall cost of the PIP program meant that its administrators ruled that rates for equipment had to be broadly "competitive." As a result, part of the costs of the Husky/Bow Valley East Coast equipment were declared "non-pippable" to the obvious frustration of Bow Valley and Husky.

As this book goes to press, Bow Valley and its partners continue to drill in the East Coast's harsh conditions. In February, 1985, some political uncertainty was removed when the new federal government of Brian Mulroney reached agreement with Brian Peckford's Newfoundland Tories on offshore jurisdiction. The question of revenue-sharing, however, remained to be settled. Further major question marks remained over the future of the National Energy Programme and, in particular, its PIP grants, without which Bow Valley and the other relatively smaller Canadian companies would surely not have joined the foreign-controlled majors in East Coast exploration. These questions have still to be resolved, but Bow Valley's major commitment to the East Coast remains.

As yet — and by standards of similar exploration areas such as the North Sea — relatively few holes have been drilled offshore the East Coast. Nevertheless, the finds at Hibernia and Venture have established the presence of world-scale hydrocarbons. For the moment, relatively soft oil prices and an oversupply of oil on world markets have decreased enthusiasm somewhat for offshore oil and gas. However, the petroleum industry has always been cyclical. The market will eventually turn once more, issues of national security will again become paramount, and, when they do, the East Coast will likely continue to be the principal hope for a major increase in Canada's reserves. When that happens, Bow Valley's commitments will ensure that it is a major force in the area.

21
Bow Valley in Transition

Bow Valley is now a company in transition. Doc and his brothers, although still vigorous, have been thinking for some years about an appropriate way to pass on their equity in the company. Late in 1978, discussions had been held with the young Toronto financier, Conrad Black, about one of his corporate vehicles, Hollinger Mines Limited, acquiring the shares of the Seaman brothers five years down the road, in 1983. However, when it became clear that the Ontario Securities Commission would require Hollinger to make a bid for all the outstanding shares of Bow Valley, Black withdrew from the deal. So far, a means of relinquishing ownership that would at once be perceived as positive for the company and acceptable to regulatory authorities has not been found.

However, the mantle of management has already been passed to Gerry Maier. Doc remains as chairman both of the board and of its executive committee, while B.J. and Don remain as major shareholders and board members of both BVI and BVRS. B.J. is chairman and chief executive of BVRS, while Don is still its president and chief operating officer. Both are still very much involved in the management of BVRS, although Doc has deliberately stepped back from day-to-day involvement in BVI in line with Gerry Maier's status as chief executive. This passing of executive responsibility from an entrepreneur to a professional manager means a major change in the way that Bow Valley will be run.

Under an aggressive risk-taker like Doc Seaman, it is almost inevitable that the size of an organization will outstrip its structure. At some stage, therefore, some breathing space is necessary to consolidate activities. Bow Valley's management style, reflecting Doc's preference for delegation, evolved from its earliest days as loose and decentralized. Don Binney — for so long the heart of Bow Valley's drilling business — recalls being at meetings in Norway on the construction of the *Odin Drill*. He was accompanied only by a lawyer from Bill Howard's law firm, while the other partners had squadrons of executives and legal advisors. As negotiations developed, the team from Home Oil kept phoning their boss, the legendary Bobby Brown. One of them eventually looked at Binney and said:" Aren't you going to phone Doc?" Binney said: "I don't have to." He knew that when

Doc delegated responsibility, he also delegated the authority. Doc felt that managers left to make their own mistakes usually made less of them.

Doc's management style didn't follow any textbooks, but it worked. By any bottom-line standards, it was spectacularly successful. Doc, having built the company from scratch, learned all he needed to know about organization as he went along. When faced by an increasing number of large and complex corporate decisions, a leader must be able to distill the basics quickly and surely. Doc was never a great fan of lengthy discounted cash flow or sensitivity analyses — the supposed essentials of scientific management. Doc knew the numbers, "boxcar numbers," as Doc's old Greenshields advisor, Bud Willis, puts it, and he had the ability to grasp them in big chunks. Doc always believed the most important element of a decision was the ability to read people and situations. It came down to business intuition, that mysterious element — like Wayne Gretzky's sporting ability — that ultimately defies analysis.

Organization theory had never held too much appeal for Doc. In 1956, a man from the U.S.-based George S. May management consultancy firm had turned up at the steel-sided headquarters on 39th Avenue and offered to give the organization the managerial once-over. He spoke to everybody and then suggested all sorts of structural pyramids, and how important it was to write things down. B.J. thought to himself at the time: "We're engineers, we don't write stuff down, we *do* it." And Doc pointed out to the man that they seemed to be doing all right the way they were going. Since the company subsequently grew beyond recognition, Doc's view was more than justified. It would be perhaps interesting to discover where the management consultant is today!

Over the years, Bow Valley inevitably picked up many of the elements of corporate bureaucracy — organization charts, sub-committees, and written-up job descriptions — but Doc always retained an uneasiness about having too many head-office staff. He reluctantly acknowledged that accountants and lawyers were essential to a growing organization to meet both the demands of internal monitoring and external reporting requirements, but in the end they weren't "productive." "Don't hire any more accountants," he'd tell Trevor Legge, the company's chief accounting man throughout the 1970s and then senior vice-president of finance at BVRS once it split off. "They breed like rabbits!"

"Richer but More Miserable"

Among the oil business's most successful risk-takers, there are those like Angus Mackenzie and Bill Siebens who simply enjoyed the cut

185

and thrust of negotiating successful multi-million dollar deals, and who always kept organizational trappings to a minimum. As Angus Mackenzie summed it up: "We'd be richer and more miserable if we'd continued running things." Doc was different; he was a builder. But he still preferred building the organization to running it. The more time you spent in administration, he believed, the less time you had for examining new ventures and expanding the business. Nevertheless, there comes a stage in any corporation's development when its size — and the inevitable mortality of its founder — demand a more formal approach.

In a previous book, *The Blue-Eyed Sheiks*, I noted that the exceptional growth rates of companies like Bow Valley had enabled them to achieve "the unusual combination of size and flexibility. The corporate arteriosclerosis of bureaucracy has not had time to set in. Where businesses of a similar size in the East may have seen ten or twenty generations of professional management come and go, many of the West's burgeoning business giants still have their founder ... in the top spot."

I went on to say that "the important thing about having a 'founder' in control is not only that he inevitably knows the business well, but he is also usually the major shareholder. ... These individuals have no trouble in making multi-million dollar corporate decisions overnight that a whole bevy of committees in an eastern corporation would take many weeks to pore over." But perhaps that judgment was a little too harsh on "corporate bureaucracy."

Although systems and structures are often the butt of criticism, they are ultimately essential to corporate continuity. Even the healthiest of founders must one day pass on. For an entrepreneur who builds a large organization, there is inevitably frustration as he watches the "system" take over. Nevertheless, if corporations are to survive their founders, they must inevitably become more systematized. Doc realized towards the end of the 1970s that a more centralized system would be necessary.

In fact, Bow Valley was inevitably diverse in its organization for a number of reasons. A particular effort had always been made to separate the exploration from the drilling side of the business, which was just part of an extremely diverse group of companies ranging from saw-mill machinery to pollution-control equipment. Doc's emphasis on giving autonomy to local managers was also deliberately designed to encourage success at the expense of uniformity. At some stage in the late 1970s, however, Doc realized that tighter financial control was needed, which led to an unavoidable increase in centralized control of the company.

One critical move towards a more formal and tighter management structure was Doc's appointment, in 1980, of Bill Tye as chief financial officer. Tye had been born in Lacombe in central Alberta, where his father was an engineer with the CPR. He went to school in Edmonton, studying commerce and economics at the University of Alberta before going to work for Hudson's Bay Oil & Gas. After six years there, he joined Pacific Petroleums under Kelly Gibson in the production department. He worked his way up the Pacific ladder, becoming the number three executive at the company under Merrill Rasmussen and Al McIntosh. When Petro-Canada took over Pacific in 1979, Tye went over briefly to the state oil company. While there he was approached by Doc Seaman to join Bow Valley as chief financial officer.

Doc's prime motivation for appointing Tye was to strengthen the company's finances. Over the following couple of years, Bill Tye would help raise a great deal of money for Bow Valley, but he would also become the focus of organizational changes, and perhaps accompanying organizational resentments.

When Bill Tye arrived, Bow Valley was a very loose federation of parts. The exploration group — still essentially the team that had come with the Syracuse acquisition — functioned quite separately from Bow Valley's resource service arm, and both operated with considerable freedom from the Bow Valley Industries corporate staff, which theoretically should have had control over the whole operation.

Doc agreed that Tye should commission a report on the company from Price Waterhouse. The report indicated that changes in financial and administrative methods were needed. It pointed out that Bow Valley's rapid growth, diversification, and geographic dispersion had created management problems. There was, said the report, a need for improved planning, information and control systems at all levels of the company. There was also, it declared, a requirement to improve and clarify communications and reporting relationships "to minimize conflicts, misunderstandings and duplication of efforts." The plan to split off BVRS would also create the need for changes

The report recommended a new corporate structure in which the company's staff functions would report through the chief financial officer to the chairman and chief executive, Doc. This appeared to leave Dick Harris — although still president and chief operating officer — "off to one side." Harris felt that he had not been consulted sufficiently about Tye's appointment, and was thus particularly unhappy when this report's recommendations appeared.

As a man who wanted to tighten financial controls and bring the overseas subsidiaries more directly under Calgary's control, Bill Tye hardly had a popular job. Moreover, he went at it with a determination that raised the hackles of many of Bow Valley's long-serving management.

The London operations under Clive Randle, those in Denver under Rod DeLuca, and the Singapore office of Lloyd Flood had all been

187

allowed considerable autonomy. In terms of central budgeting and financial controls, declared the Price Waterhouse report, they had been allowed too much. The report recommended a considerable beefing up of head office staff. This, of course, was setting in motion trends that Doc had long sought to avoid.

Although Bow Valley's organizational looseness had produced results, it had also inevitably led to different management systems growing up in various parts of the empire. The consultant's report noted that parts of the organization used different accounting methods and computer systems. The manual preparation of accounting statements often meant delays. Employee records were incomplete, compensation was inconsistent within different parts of the company, and manpower planning was considered inadequate. Of course, these were all the criticisms based on the ideal of perfection rather than reality. It was obviously more important to have created employment than to possess "employee records." Compensation might be inconsistent, but at least compensation was there. Would you rather have an immaculately turned-out goon on your team, or Wayne Gretzky in an ill-fitting uniform?

However, it was also true that lack of systems would eventually prove a constraint on good decision making and hence corporate growth. If, for example, you didn't know quickly how much different parts of the organization were earning and spending, then overall budgeting became very difficult.

Bill Tye attempted to move on a number of these areas, but met some resistance. The resistance was not surprising. No organization or part of an organization relishes being under tighter control. Moreover, managers would point out, if things were really that bad, how had the company been so successful in the first place? Nevertheless, there was an admission that changes were needed.

Although Gerry Maier's original rationale for joining Bow Valley had been the creation of a larger company with the takeover of Hudson's Bay Oil & Gas's foreign interests, his arrival fitted well with the challenging objective of tightening financial controls and formalizing structure. Gerry Maier certainly didn't see himself as merely an "organization man," nevertheless, his experience at both HBOG and Conoco had developed his management skills to a very sophisticated level. Both companies had enjoyed powerful but flexible structures and pervasive "team spirit." To arrive at the relatively much looser Bow Valley organization was therefore initially something of a shock. Quite naturally, given that Doc had made him chief executive soon after he arrived, Maier set about putting his own stamp on the company. It was also natural that he reached for executive help from the pool of former HBOG talent that now sat unwillingly under the yoke

188

of Dome Petroleum. Bill Tye, after his first three hectic years, wanted to ease his management duties, so he agreed with Gerry Maier that HBOG's former chief financial officer, Orest Humeniuk, should be brought in as vice-president of finance, while Tye remained a senior vice-president. Other former Hudson's Bay employees who joined up included Dale Beischel as vice-president of exploration, Walter "Walt" DeBoni as vice-president of production, and Charlie Fischer as head of corporate planning. Patrick Wesley, who joined Bow Valley's land department under Bill Clark, took over as head of land following Clark's retirement.

A Change of Style

Doc's legitimacy came from the fact that he had founded and nurtured the company, and still held a large chunk of its stock. The company was — and still is, as long as he retains his shares and remains chairman — "his" in a way it could never be for a professional manager. Doc's decisions have never been hastily made, but his proprietorship has enabled him to take greater risks. Although he listened to advice and heard other opinions — and was ultimately subject to his board of directors — the final decision was usually his and his alone. Most of the time, the decisions proved to be right. Of course, not every venture met with success. Finding oil depends on willingness to face exploration failure; if a company was terrified of experiences such as Bow Valley's in Vietnam, it would certainly never become involved in successes like Brae. Several of the acquisitions of BVRS, such as diamond drilling and helicopters, proved to be more managerial trouble than they were worth. But what counted in the end was overall corporate achievements, and the figures spoke for themselves.

Nevertheless, Gerry Maier has taken over the Bow Valley empire at a trying time. He is faced with both uncertainty about political regulation — particularly as it affects the East Coast operation — and uncertainty about the course of world oil prices, which affect Bow Valley's global petroleum revenues. Quite apart from these factors, however, Gerry Maier's style must be different from Doc's. Stewardship inevitably implies less freedom — although no less responsibility — than ownership. The professional manager must be more concerned with erecting a system of expert advice, a structure in which decisions will be subject to more comprehensive examination. He must always take pains to ensure that the roots and reasons for corporate decision making are carefully catalogued. He has no mandate to "bet the company." Moreover, whereas the founder can afford to risk moves that may fail, the manager's head tends to be on the line with every decision he makes. Gerry Maier realizes better than anyone that his challenge is to strengthen the structure without losing too much flexibility and corporate originality; to make sure that the company is still able to spot the winners ahead of the pack. For that task, he has impeccable credentials. In the three years since he joined Bow Valley, he has made significant strides in formalizing Bow Valley's structure and tightening its financial controls. But equally important, he has tried to ensure that originality has been maintained and a system of "entrepreneurial management" installed. He has firmly asserted that he wants to be a "deal-maker, not a deal-taker." Some parts of his system, such as the much more comprehensive budgeting process, are far more demanding on management. Gerry Maier likes to get the heads of departments together and, in the words of one long-serving Bow Valley employee, "put the gladiators in the arena." But this aggressive, competitive approach has a purpose. It not only forces management to think through the costs and benefits of their proposed projects more carefully, it also gives them a much clearer perspective of their projects within the whole Bow Valley empire. Although "gut-feeling" remains an important factor, a sophisticated decision-making system such as that installed by Gerry Maier forces a more objective approach.

22
Reflections on a Career

Bow Valley has been the story of many people. It will be the story of many more in the future. The company has drawn on the skills of a vast range of individuals. There are the service-industry men like Bill Warnke, Doc's partner in his first seismic-rig; the fellow risk-takers like Ralph Will and Angus Mackenzie, whose creations Doc took and developed; the tough, practical men from the drilling business, like Don Binney, who helped make Bow Valley the country's leading drilling contractor; the visionary geologists, like Dick Harris, Fred Wellhauser, and Lloyd Flood, who made Doc's dream of building an international oil company a reality; the office staff, like Betty Fisher, Doc's secretary for twenty years, and Liz Adair, who have contributed so many selfless twelve-hour-days to the smooth running of the company; the long-service Bow Valley executives, like Keith Lazelle, Bob Phibbs, and Trevor Legge, who have helped Bow Valley through a good part of its remarkable growth; and the thousands of others who have wheeled and dealed and drilled and manufactured and managed in Doc's corporate orbit.

Some of these people never did became a part of Bow Valley. While many remain, many others have now retired, or moved on. Bill Warnke still operates seismic rigs out of the converted garage of his house opposite Wetaskiwin Airport, south of Edmonton. Ralph Will, who is now well over eighty, still goes to his office on 5th Avenue every morning at 7:00 A.M. when he is in Calgary. Then, at noon, he heads for the gin rummy table downstairs at the Petroleum Club. Angus Mackenzie — when he is not still circling the globe — plots his deals from a huge antique-laden suite in a building owned by his Abu Dhabi friends overlooking London's Hyde Park. Don Binney — who made the most unusual career change of all, leaving his position as a senior vice-president at Bow Valley in order to join the church — now administers the affairs of his diocese from the big old house opposite Calgary's Glencoe Club. Dick Harris and Fred Wellhauser now run a junior oil company, Corrida, out of an office whose reception area sports an arresting display from Harris's quartz collection. Betty Fisher — in retirement — busies herself with local projects from her cosy little bungalow in Okotoks, south of Calgary.

But if the old guard, including Doc and his brothers, must look to retirement sooner or later, the corporate creation lives on. The echoes of a founder's decisions reverberate down the years. The implications of a deal like that of the Brae farm-out can last for decades. Gerry Maier now holds the managerial reins at Bow Valley, but the company he directs remains for the moment the one painstakingly built by Doc over the past thirty-five years. Brae will remain a major factor in Bow Valley's cash flow for the remainder of this century at least. The experiences of Indonesian oil and U.S. coal — among many others — will be built upon to provide further corporate expansion. Reflections on this empire — built on guts, intuition, and luck — inevitably lead us back to the mysterious drive and talents of the successful risk-taker.

From talking to dozens of people who have worked with or for Doc over the years, a remarkable consensus emerges about his nature and his character: his brain works incessantly on business problems; he doesn't blow his top; he doesn't panic; he doesn't hold grudges; he doesn't shy away from tough decisions. Of course, there are exceptions to this somewhat cool picture: Betty Fisher remembers his elation once Charles Bluhdorn had given in over the price of Flying Diamond; someone remembers his anger when Vancouver wheeler-dealer Nelson Skalbania made a rival bid for the Atlanta Flames while Doc and his colleagues were attempting to bring them to Calgary.

Doc remains a low-profile, almost shy, public figure. When he was presented with an honorary doctorate by the University of Saskatchewan in recognition of both his personal achievements and his charitable contributions towards his alma mater, he was, remembers his sister Dorothy, "almost tongue-tied." Public recognition disturbs him. He has contributed a great deal towards hockey development, although he talks little about it.

But although Doc is no more of a word-waster today than he was when he started the business, he has never had any problem communicating. Indeed, as Bill Hay, who is now senior vice-president of BVRS says: "Doc gets on as well with the drillers up at Nisku (the operations office for BVRS) as he gets on with the minister of finance." But communication in this sense really means holding the respect of this broad spectrum of people. It is this ability to speak to — and bring together — such a range of people that has been one of the keys to Bow Valley's success.

The Wall Of Fame

Doc's ambitions have moved Bow Valley a long way from the drilling roots that are still planted today up at Nisku, just outside Edmonton, but his ambitions have not severed them. The drillers realize that Doc has, over the years, used the funds from their operations to finance his larger vision, but in the end, they hold no resentment. Nisku still holds pride of place as the oldest and longest-serving part of the Bow Valley empire. In its board room there is a "wall of fame," with six framed photographs in a row. Beneath the pictures, a name and two dates: the date the men in the photographs joined Hi-Tower and the date they retired. Don Binney, 47-78; Walter "Smokey" Zutz, 50-80; Elmer "Pistol" Snyder, 45-81; Norm Vetters, 43-82; Julian "Dad" Zmean, 59-83; and Buzz Cotter, 42-83. To see this row of tough, weather-beaten faces is to understand the meaning of the word "character."

Just down the hall from the wall of fame is a row of offices where the operations managers and superintendants of Hi-Tower and Sedco sit. On every wall there hangs — beside the inevitable metal pin-ups of drilling rigs — one or more long-service plaques. John Gillard and Bob Engberg, the operations managers of Sedco and Hi-Tower respectively, sometimes joke that they're just going out to have their pictures taken for the board room!

Doc has never forgotten his roots. Each year, he holds an "Old Codgers" party around Christmas, when he re-establishes contact with those he left in business terms long ago, or with whom he has dealt for many years. Among those at the 1984 party are the alumni from the company's first headquarters, the steel building on 39th Avenue, including Mac Baker, Hal Godwin, and Stan Rokosh. There are retired bankers, including John Ashburner and Jim Boyle; and there is Doc's old wartime colleague Pete Hamill. Now, as always, when any speeches have to be made, it is B.J. who takes the podium. A smiling Len Walker, who sold the Seamans their first Cardwell rig, is identified, at seventy-three, as the oldest of the codgers.

Hal Godwin has brought some pictures of the Friday night parties on 39th Avenue: of Don and B.J. hamming it up; of Pate, with his wire-rimmed spectacles and kindly expression, looking a little like Norman Rockwell; of everybody having a good time because they knew they'd worked hard enough to deserve it.

But Doc has come a very long way since 39th Avenue. Here at the 1984 Old Codgers party is also Rod McDaniel, another member of the Alberta establishment who grew up, in business terms, with Doc. McDaniel who, among other things, owns one of the most respected consulting firms in Canada and is chairman of Pacific Western Airlines, is a founding member, like Doc, of the Lougheed Club, that handful of businessmen who funded Peter Lougheed's entry into politics. Doc and McDaniel are both still very close to the premier, part of a very select group that he uses as a private-sector sounding board.

Over the years, Doc has developed many friends in the oilpatch. Some of his best friends are to be found among the members of the "Ratpack," a team of oilmen originally brought together by a love of golf. They include McDaniel; Bob Phibbs, the former Canadian Olympic basketball captain and long-time Bow Valley employee; Jack Sparks, the former head of Texaco Canada; Don Lougheed, a senior executive of Esso Resources; Dr. George Govier, a much-respected former head of the Alberta Energy Resources Conservation Board and a director of BVRS; Bruce Watson, the former head of Canadian Homestead and another BVRS director; Ron Coleman and Mauri Paulson, both former Home Oil senior executives, and Mauri's brother Stan; Louis Lebel, the former Chancellor of the University of Calgary and a former senior executive of Chevron Standard, the subsidiary of Standard Oil of California; and John Poyen, the former Imperial Oil executive and current BVI board member. All these men have established over the years their positions as charter members of Calgary's oil establishment.

Of all Doc's friends, the closest remains B.J. They still hunt and fish together, go to their condominium in Hawaii together, and play gin rummy as if they were competing for the last dollar on Earth. B.J. has always been Doc's sounding board and his greatest supporter, his right-hand-man and the guardian of his flank. Don, although he has played an important role in the development of the business, has remained socially more of his own man. Nevertheless, that three brothers should have remained in business together for thirty-five years is in itself a remarkable achievement.

Back to the Mystery

Doc's business influence and clout go far beyond the province. He was invited by former federal energy minister Donald Macdonald to sit on the Macdonald Commission on the Canadian economy, whose report will appear in 1985. The Commission was something of an eye opener for Doc; to be surrounded by so many wordy academics and bureaucrats who spoke of creating wealth when he was one of the few there who had actually *done* it. It was, perhaps, in that gathering that the full mystery of the risk-taker may have hit him for the first time: a realization that not even *he* could explain how, or exactly why, he had done it.

With nothing but his intelligence, his vision, and his persuasive powers, Doc has created a an international business empire where there was none before. To say that he did all this for money would be akin to suggesting that Michaelangelo had painted the roof of the Sistine Chapel "to show off." Looking for seminal sparks, it is tempting to suggest that Doc's hard-driving youth — working heavy equipment at night in the middle of the prairie; hiding from Messerschmitts in the clouds as a bomber pilot — must have been a determining factor. Certainly they must have enhanced his belief in his own powers, but the contribution of these experiences to his ultimate achievements can never be known.

It is also tempting to suggest that Doc was lucky to be in the right place at the right time. His entry into the business came with the Leduc find that sparked a long-term boom in the oil business. The quarter of a century after the end of the Second World War was a period of unprecedented prosperity and growth. The OPEC crises of the 1970s created enormous opportunities in the oil business. But if being in the right business at the right time were enough for success, then there would be a great many Docs. There are not.

A key element in Doc's success is undoubtedly his competitiveness. What Doc has always derived most fun from is winning. There has grown almost a mythology around Doc's sporting ability. Pete Hamill, his old air force colleague, whom Doc helped set up his flourishing insurance business in Calgary, remembers Doc bagging several doubles on ducks in succession and being genuinely disappointed when he finally missed one. The story of Doc's playing an entire golf season with one ball is another part of the mythology. Once, he was challenged by Harry Van Rensselaer to a game of table tennis in the basement of Van Rensselaer's Connecticutt home. Van Rensselaer had been a nationally ranked tennis champion, but he played until 3:00 A.M. trying to get the ball past Doc! In the end, perhaps all we can say is that Doc's secret lies somewhere between that table tennis ball and a multi-million dollar empire with over 3,000 employees.

In April, 1984, at a sparkling array of events featuring banquets in London and dedication ceremonies in Scotland that were televised around the world, the Brae platform was officially dedicated. The men from Bow Valley and its advisors who had put in the effort, made most of the crucial decisions, and slogged through the legal complexities relating to that jewel in Bow Valley's crown — Doc, Dick Harris, Fred Wellhauser, Edd McRory — were not there. In a way, it was a little sad, but it also said something about corporations in general and the nature, size, and scope of the international oil business in particular: companies and projects have lives of their own.

In the end, that complex combination of factors that has made Doc

195

a successful risk-taker — nerve, judgment, charisma, and the ability to make people work for him — are locked in his cranium. Just as Wayne Gretzky's skills are only apparent when he dons skates, so Doc's skills are only apparent through his corporate actions. But whereas Gretzky can, in the end, only hope to leave behind fond memories and record statistics from his hockey career, Doc's corporate stick-handling has created a living, breathing empire that will survive him. Whatever his motivations, it is an achievement — if one has any regard for wealth and employment creation — for which more people than Bow Valley's employees and long-term shareholders should be thankful.

Index

201